# *Onward Christian Soldiers?*

# Dilemmas in American Politics

Series Editor: **Craig A. Rimmerman**, Hobart and William Smith Colleges

If the answers to the problems facing U.S. democracy were easy, politicians would solve them, accept credit, and move on. But certain dilemmas have confronted the American political system continuously. They defy solution; they are endemic to the system. Some can best be described as institutional dilemmas: How can Congress be both a representative body and a national decisionmaker? How can the president communicate with more than 250 million citizens effectively? Why do we have a two-party system when many voters are disappointed with the choices presented to them? Others are policy dilemmas: How do we find compromises on issues that defy compromise, such as abortion policy? How do we incorporate racial and ethnic minorities or immigrant groups into American society, allowing them to reap the benefits of this land without losing their identity? How do we fund health care for our poorest or oldest citizens?

Dilemmas such as these are what propel students toward an interest in the study of U.S. government. Each book in the Dilemmas in American Politics series addresses a "real world" problem, raising the issues that are of most concern to students. Each is structured to cover the historical and theoretical aspects of the dilemma but also to explore the dilemma from a practical point of view and to speculate about the future. The books are designed as supplements to introductory courses in American politics or as case studies to be used in upper-level courses. The link among them is the desire to make the real issues confronting the political world come alive in students' eyes.

---

## BOOKS IN THIS SERIES

# Onward Christian Soldiers?

## *The Religious Right in American Politics*

FOURTH EDITION

**Clyde Wilcox**
*Georgetown University*

**Carin Robinson**
*Hood College*

WESTVIEW
PRESS

A Member of the Perseus Books Group

*Cover photo:* Pastor Rick Warren (center) gives the invocation as President-elect Barack Obama and President George W. Bush bow their heads during the 56th presidential inauguration ceremony for Barack Obama, January 20, 2009.

Published by Westview Press,
A Member of the Perseus Books Group

Find us on the World Wide Web at www.westviewpress.com.

Every effort has been made to secure required permissions to use all images, maps, and other art included in this volume.

Westview Press books are available at special discounts for bulk purchases in the United States by corporations, institutions, and other organizations. For more information, please contact the Special Markets Department at the Perseus Books Group, 2300 Chestnut Street, Suite 200, Philadelphia, PA 19103, or call (800) 810-4145, ext. 5000, or e-mail special.markets@perseusbooks.com.

Library of Congress Cataloging-in-Publication Data
Wilcox, Clyde, 1953–
    Onward Christian soldiers? : the religious right in American politics / Clyde Wilcox and Carin Robinson. — 4th ed.
        p.    cm. — (Dilemmas in American politics)
    Includes bibliographical references (p.) and index.
    ISBN 978-0-8133-4453-9 (alk. paper)
    1. Christianity and politics—United States—History—20th century.    2. Christianity and politics—United States—History—21st century.    3. Religious right—United States.    4. United States—Politics and government—1989-    5. United States—Church history—20th century.    6. United States—Church history—21st century.    I. Robinson, Carin.    II. Title.
    BR526.W53 2011
    320.5'50973—dc22
                                                                                                                2010013113

10 9 8 7 6 5 4 3 2 1

# Contents

# 4 Assessing the Christian Right          139

# 5 The Future of the Christian Right          177

# Illustrations

## Tables

## Figures

## Boxes

## Map

# *Preface*

Writing about the Christian Right always brings out the schizophrenic elements in me, as my roots war with my politics. I grew up in rural West Virginia, and many of my family and friends who still live in that area are supporters of the Christian Right. My father was a fundamentalist Sunday school teacher who taught me the Bible and was a fan of Jerry Falwell. My mother was a charismatic who regularly watched Pat Robertson's *700 Club* and greatly enjoyed a Spirit-filled religious retreat every spring. My great-aunts, to whom this book is dedicated, seldom missed a televised sermon by Charles Stanley.

As a child I attended the Walnut Grove United Methodist Church, a church in the revivalist tradition of Spirit-filled fundamentalism. I was often drafted to play the piano in revival services in small churches in the surrounding area, where I spent a few hectic minutes trying to determine in which key to play each song so as to minimize the number of dead keys on the very old, poorly maintained pianos. The people in those churches are fair-minded, warm, and compassionate. I could fill a book with tales of their extraordinary kindness and generosity. Most of them are also very conservative; they oppose abortion, gay rights, government welfare programs, and most other liberal policies. Although I am no longer part of that culture, I respect, admire, and love the people there.

Yet I also came of age politically in the late 1960s and was shaped by the civil rights, antiwar, feminist, and environmental movements. I strongly oppose most of the policy agenda of the Christian Right. I want my daughter and son to grow up in a world in which they have equal access to a wider range of roles than society now provides. I want my gay and lesbian friends to live free of discrimination based on whom they love. I want the public schools to teach my children to think for themselves, be tolerant of diverse lifestyles, and know about the latest scientific thinking. Thus my political values are in conflict with my roots, and I engage in much internal debate when I write about the Christian Right.

I hope this internal dialogue has produced a fair assessment of the role of the Christian Right in American politics and the dilemmas it creates for the polity. If I have succeeded, it is due in no small part to the suggestions of colleagues over the years: Mary Bendyna, John Green, Ted Jelen, Matt Moen, Ken Wald, Rachel Goldberg, my wife Elizabeth Cook, and many others. In this edition as well as the third, I benefited from the collaboration of Carin Robinson, who has graduated from student to equal collaborator. It has been a pleasure working with her on the book, and I have enjoyed our e-mail dialogues over various issues. We would like to thank the staff of Westview Press, specifically Toby Wahl, Sharon DeJohn, Erica Lawrence, and Michelle Welsh-Horst, for their kind assistance on this project.

I wrote the first edition of this book while teaching a small seminar on the Christian Right at Georgetown University in the fall of 1995. The thirteen students in that class were a lively group who inspired me to rethink many questions, assisted me in locating important information, and helped remind me why I enjoy teaching. Over the next ten years I taught the class several other times, and in many cases had wonderful students whose papers have been influential in my understanding various issues. In 2009 I had another stellar group of students, some of whose papers are cited in this edition.

This book is dedicated to my grandmother, Zoe Wilcox, and her two sisters, Beulah Musgrove and Grace Ice. Although these women lived quite different lives, they shared a lifelong interest in learning and teaching. Their strength, compassion, decency, and love of life inspire me daily.

*Clyde Wilcox*

I grew up in an evangelical church. My family attended church every Sunday, and I went to Bible camp each summer. My first exposure to American politics came from Focus on the Family and Christian news magazines. At an early age, I learned about the culture wars. Though my parents gave me the freedom to choose my own path, the evangelical subculture of my youth left me little room for exploration. By early adulthood, I had grown disillusioned with a tradition that was more about behavior than beliefs, more about feelings than facts. Around the same time, I encountered evangelicals who believed in evolution, voted for Democrats, and supported gay rights. The experiences did not negate my religious beliefs but did refine them.

Therefore, today I approach the study of the Christian Right with great ambivalence. My ambivalence is a function of my sympathies for portions of the movement's platform mixed with my understanding of scripture that leads me to forsake all political warfare for the simple message of salvation through Jesus Christ. Although I can agree with certain sentiments of the Christian Right, I do not readily endorse the movement as a reflection of biblical Christianity. I fear Christians in this country have Americanized the Bible and limited our scope of influence by equating the Gospel with public law and in some cases a political party. Although my political attitudes have no doubt been shaped by my religious upbringing and professed faith, I refrain from making claims about God's will for America, for He has the *whole* world in his hands.

Revising this book has been a great exercise for me as I sort through both my support and my opposition to the social movement as it stands in 2010. I hope the perspective I bring to this edition contributes to the balance my coauthor achieved in earlier versions. I am incredibly grateful to him for the opportunities he has given me to participate in this scholarly discussion as well as the challenges he poses that refine my own faith. I also thank the many students who have dialogued with me about my research and have kept me curious and humble along the way.

My contribution to this book is dedicated to my church family in Bethesda, Maryland. I am thankful for their support as I press on.

*Carin Robinson*

# 1

·····································································

# Introduction
## The Christian Right in Context

The America I know and love is not one in which my parents or my baby with Down Syndrome will have to stand in front of Obama's "death panel" so his bureaucrats can decide, based on a subjective judgment of their "level of productivity in society," whether they are worthy of health care. Such a system is downright evil.

**Sarah Palin,** in a message posted on Facebook about President Obama's health care plan, August 7, 2009

O N  S E P T E M B E R  4 ,  2 0 0 8 , Alaska governor Sarah Palin addressed a wildly cheering crowd at the Republican National Convention in Minneapolis, accepting her party's nomination as vice president. Christian Right activists who had lamented Sen. John McCain's victories in GOP primaries were delighted with Palin's speech. As television cameras lingered over her young daughter Piper slicking back the hair of Palin's baby son Trig, pro-life activists cheered Palin's decision to give birth to a child with Down syndrome.

Her selection by John McCain was testimony to the power of the Christian Right in the Republican Party. McCain's first choice, Connecticut senator Joe Lieberman (D), and his second choice, former Pennsylvania governor Tom Ridge (R), were both pro-choice. McCain had calculated that any votes he lost by their selection would be offset by gains among moderate voters, and that the selection of a former Democratic vice presidential candidate would signal to voters that McCain was a change agent. But Christian Right leaders threatened to stage a walkout at the Republican National Convention if either man were chosen, and their veto stuck.

Palin's choice helped McCain win support from many Christian Right activists, who had strongly opposed him ever since he had referred to movement leaders Pat Robertson and Jerry Falwell as "agents of intolerance" during the 2000 presidential campaign. Although McCain had tried to mend fences, including meeting privately with Falwell and giving the commencement speech at Falwell's Liberty University in 2006, most activists were not appeased. McCain received the fewest number of votes of the ten Republican presidential candidates in a straw poll taken in 2007 at the Values Voters Summit, a gathering of Christian Right activists. **Focus on the Family** founder James Dobson said at the time that he would not support McCain's candidacy "under any circumstances."[1] But one month after Palin became McCain's running mate, Dobson changed his mind. He told his radio listeners he was as happy on the day Palin became the prospective vice presidential nominee as he had been on the day Ronald Reagan was inaugurated president. *Newsweek* declared her nomination the start of a "religious right revival" (Miller, 2008).

Yet Palin exemplified many of the contradictions of the contemporary Christian Right. Though celebrated by movement leaders, Palin also reflected the traditional weakness of Christian Right candidates by alienating moderate Republicans and independent voters, many of whom saw her as an ideologue who lacked the knowledge and experience required of someone a heartbeat away from the presidency. YouTube videos circulated showing Palin at the Assembly of God church in Wasilla referring to her oil pipeline project as "God's will" and of a Kenyan pastor in a different service praying for protection against witchcraft in the Alaska legislature.

The days preceding Palin's speech were marred by controversy when it was revealed that her seventeen-year-old, unmarried daughter was five months pregnant. Palin quickly announced that her daughter had plans to marry the father; Christian Right activists rallied behind Palin and cheered her daughter and her boyfriend onstage. In 1992 Christian Right activists had similarly cheered when Republican vice presidential nominee Dan Quayle attacked a fictional television character named Murphy Brown, who found herself pregnant after sleeping once with her ex-husband and chose to become a single mother. Bristol Palin was praised for her pro-life decision, but Quayle had charged that the *Murphy Brown* show contributed to the "poverty of values."

Palin's opposition to same-sex marriage, abortion, and stem cell research, and her support for abstinence education and the discussion of **creationism** in public schools, excited Christian Right activists. But during her vice presidential debate, Palin defended her state's partnership benefits for same-sex couples and declared her personal tolerance for same-sex couples.

Perhaps most strikingly, Sarah Palin has made decisions that sharply contrast with Christian Right ideals. Whereas Christian Right groups argue that women should stay home with young children, Palin took a transcontinental flight while in labor, gave birth to a child with special needs, and was at work in the governor's mansion the next morning. The mother of five children, including a pregnant teen and two children under the age of five, Palin eagerly accepted the opportunity to take on one of the most demanding jobs in the world. After her defeat in 2008 Palin resigned her job as governor, not to spend more time with her family, but to campaign more actively for president. Her new position as commentator on Fox News gives her an impressive opportunity, but also an imposing schedule.

In 2010 the Christian Right is not dead, but neither is it thriving. In 2008 movement leaders were unable to agree on a favorite Republican presidential candidate, and their least favorite candidate won the nomination. Barack Obama's victory in the 2008 election was a major defeat for the movement, made even more bitter by the defection of a number of young **evangelical** voters to the Democratic ticket. In 2005 the movement had easy access to Republican leadership in the White House, the U.S. House of Representatives, and the Senate, but in 2010 the Democrats control all of these institutions.

Over the past few years former **Christian Coalition** leader Ralph Reed and former president of the **National Association of Evangelicals**, Rev. Ted Haggard, have been embroiled in scandals. Movement leaders Rev. Jerry Falwell and Rev. D. James Kennedy died in 2007. Beverly LaHaye stepped down as president of **Concerned Women for America** (CWA) in 2006, and James Dobson retired as chairman of Focus on the Family in early 2009. The new generation of leaders is not as well known and thus is far less able to mobilize their constituency.

Moreover, in the wake of Christian Right activism there has been a growing unease over the mixing of religion and politics. A national survey in 2008 revealed that the majority of Americans (52 percent) believe that churches and religious institutions should "keep out" of politics, the highest level of opposition since the question was first asked in 1996. Even among white evangelicals—the base of the Christian Right—concern with religion's effects on politics rose from 16 percent in 2004 to 36 percent in 2008.[2]

Today a more moderate brand of evangelical political activism has gained visibility through people like Rick Warren and Joel Hunter, pastors of theologically conservative megachurches who have expressed concern for the environment and AIDS in Africa from the pulpit. Both men are pro-life and opposed to same-sex marriage, and this allows them to maintain credence with the evangelical community while at the same time broadening its political agenda and nudging it outside Republican Party politics.

Young evangelicals appear particularly open to this new style of politics, as numerous studies find young evangelicals to be less conservative than their older counterparts. In 2008 only 40 percent of evangelicals under age thirty called themselves Republicans, compared to 55 percent in 2006.[3] In addition, younger evangelicals express more concern than their parents for the environment, health care, poverty, and even same-sex unions. Today large portions of the Christian Right's agenda and its partisan style are unappealing to the next generation of evangelicals, suggesting that the movement will struggle to attract support in the coming generation.

There are also signs that the movement is even losing some of its original stalwarts. One of the founders of the contemporary religious right, Cal Thomas, who has repeatedly expressed concern over the direction the Christian Right has taken since the 1990s, had this to say at the end of 2008:

> Thirty years of trying to use government to stop abortion, preserve opposite-sex marriage, improve television and movie content and transform culture into the conservative Evangelical image has failed. The question now becomes: should conservative Christians redouble their efforts, contributing more millions to radio and TV preachers and activists, or would they be wise to try something else? I opt for trying something else.[4]

Just a few years after many analysts credited white evangelical voters with returning George W. Bush to the White House and swelling the GOP margin in Congress in 2004, the same analysts were saying that the Christian Right was finished and evangelical politics were floundering. But media accounts of the influence of the Christian Right have gyrated wildly, from underestimating the movement's considerable resources to overstating its numbers and impact. In 1995 most accounts supported claims by Ralph Reed (then director of the Christian Coalition) and others that the Christian Right helped the Republicans gain control of the House of Representatives for the first time in a generation and win control of the U.S. Senate (Wilcox, 1995). Just three years earlier, many commentators had blamed Christian conservatives for damaging President George H. W. Bush's chances for reelection by using divisive and often extreme rhetoric at the Republican National Convention.

In 1980, after Ronald Reagan won the White House with a margin that surprised pollsters, the media credited Jerry Falwell and the **Moral Majority** with the Republican victory. Journalists "discovered" the strength of the Christian Right, and some painted the Moral Majority as a juggernaut that represented a substantial portion of the American citizenry. But public opinion polls soon revealed that Jerry Falwell was one of the most unpopular men in America, and journalists then "discovered" the weakness of the Christian Right. They painted the movement as small, extreme, and so deeply fragmented that further growth was impossible. By 1983 the media had pronounced the Christian Right moribund. In 1984, when Jerry Falwell, Pat Robertson, and their followers were a visible presence at the Republican nominating convention, the media rediscovered the assets of the Christian Right, only to rediscover its weaknesses by 1986. Early in the 1988 presidential campaign, when Pat Robertson did surprisingly well in the very early Michigan balloting and placed second in the Iowa caucuses, the media again discovered a hidden army of Christian Right activists. At the end of the campaign, when Robertson had spent more money than any other candidate but won only a handful of delegates, the weakness of the Christian Right was again the story. In late 1988, with a moderate Republican in the White House, Robertson back on television, and the Moral Majority essentially bankrupt, the media wrote the movement's obituary. Journalists were not alone; some scholars saw the movement as moribund at various points in its history and depicted its downfall as inevitable (Bruce, 1988).

In fact, throughout much of this period public support for the Christian Right and its issue agenda changed little. What did change is the sophistication of movement leaders and the presence of grassroots organizations. Between 10 and 15 percent of whites support the Christian Right and have done so since the formation of the Moral Majority in 1979 (Wilcox, 1992; Wilcox, DeBell, and Sigelman, 1999). Yet the organizations of the Christian Right became more effective in mobilizing some of those supporters into activism and providing informational cues for voting. The power and visibility of the movement varied over time as organizations were formed or disbanded, and as Republican strategists focused on evangelical votes as a core of the party coalition.

The movement has important strengths and weaknesses. It is likely that the fiery speeches by Christian Right leaders at the Republican National Convention in 1992 hurt the GOP in that election, and that the quiet mobilization of Christian conservatives in the 1994 elections helped the Republicans win a number of closely contested House and Senate races.[5] Christian Right support helped George W. Bush win the White House in 2000 and 2004, but it did little to make John McCain competitive in 2008. The movement has great assets. It has dedicated, savvy activists who have worked for many years on issues they care about and a broader base of members and supporters. Most of these supporters attend church once a week or more, which means that they regularly meet face to face, giving the movement an infrastructural advantage that liberal groups envy.

But many of the movement's leaders are prone to publicly voicing extreme statements, which often results in ridicule of the movement. For example, the late Jerry Falwell, speaking soon after the terrorist attacks in September

2001, proclaimed on national television: "I really believe that the pagans, and the abortionists, and the feminists, and the gays and the lesbians who are actively trying to make that an alternative lifestyle, the ACLU, **People for the American Way**, all of them who have tried to secularize America. I point the finger in their face and say, 'You helped this happen.'"[6] Falwell later apologized, but he became the target of angry blogs and television and radio talk show jokes for months. In August 2005 Pat Robertson called for the assassination of Venezuelan president Hugo Chavez. Robertson later insisted that he had been misunderstood, but because he had spoken on national television, a video record of his remarks remained, and his denial did little to quell the international uproar. After powerful earthquakes devastated Haiti in January 2010, as the world rushed to provide aid, Robertson claimed that Haitians had long ago pledged to serve the devil if he would help them win independence from France. Religious leaders across the spectrum condemned Robertson's bizarre response to this disaster.

## What Is the Christian Right?

The Christian Right is a social movement that attempts to mobilize evangelical Protestants and other orthodox Christians into conservative political action. Many of its leaders object to the term "Christian Right," which they believe depicts a narrow movement. Some prefer the term "religious right," which would encompass all "people of faith," including conservative Jews and possibly Muslims. Yet despite the visible presence of a few orthodox Jews at Christian Coalition conventions in the 1990s, the movement remains concentrated primarily among white evangelical Christians, and especially among the **fundamentalist** and **pentecostal** wings of evangelicalism (Green, 1995). Others object to both "Christian Right" and "religious right" on the grounds that labeling the movement as part of the "Right" implies that it is outside the political mainstream. Ralph Reed, formerly of the Christian Coalition, prefers the term "Christian conservative," but many conservative Christians opposed the Christian Coalition and similar organizations. Other Christian Right leaders insist that theirs is truly a "**pro-family**" movement, although the agenda of the Christian Right includes many issues unrelated to the health of American families. Moreover, many liberals believe that Christian Right policies would harm families. We use the term "Christian Right" in this book without any necessary implication that the movement lies outside the American mainstream.

Like all social movements, the Christian Right is composed of social movement organizations, leaders, activists, and members, and it seeks to attract support from a broad potential constituency. Robert Zwier argued that

the primary audience, or constituency, for these groups was the approximately 50 million evangelicals in the country, and in particular the fundamentalist wing of that community. The aim from the beginning was to mobilize a group of people who had traditionally avoided politics because they saw it as dirty, corrupt business . . . by convincing people that political involvement was a God-given responsibility. (1984, 9–10)

Movement leaders have been and remain more ambitious, seeking an even larger constituency. Jerry Falwell spoke of appealing to "Catholics, Jews, Protestants, Mormons, and fundamentalists." Ralph Reed and the Christian Coalition made major efforts to expand its appeal to mainline Protestants, Catholics, African Americans, and Jews. In their efforts to ban gay marriage, the **Family Research Council** and Focus on the Family have reached out to African American, Hispanic, and Korean churches, and even to **social conservatives** in other faiths, including Muslims and Jews (Campbell and Robinson, 2007).

It is important to distinguish among movement leaders, movement activists, movement supporters, and the potential constituency of the Christian Right. Media accounts frequently equate the Christian Right with all born-again Christians. Such reports greatly exaggerate the movement's strength, for there are many born-again evangelical Christians in the United States. Many born-again Christians are African American, and their faith leads them to a somewhat different policy agenda than that of the Christian Right. Among white evangelicals, some oppose the Christian Right, many are neutral toward the movement, a sizable minority are supportive, and a much smaller number are active members. White evangelicals are considered to be the core of the potential constituency of the Christian Right.

The organizations of the Christian Right are national groups, such as Focus on the Family, the Family Research Council, and Concerned Women for America, as well as countless state and local organizations. The movement's leaders include James Dobson, Tony Perkins, Wendy Wright, and Gary Bauer, among others. Its activists are those who volunteer their time and money to work for these groups, and its members are those who have joined an organization but do not actively participate. The strength of the Christian Right lies in its activist base. For example, activists have distributed **voter guides** in churches throughout America, and the information in those voter guides may have influenced people who have never considered joining the Christian Right. Activists lobby state legislatures and local school boards and try to influence the nominations of Republican candidates in their districts.

Social movements are decentralized, differentiated, and sometimes disorganized. John Green, a political scientist, observed, "There are many modes of mobilization, many pools of resources, many sources of complaint, differential goals and beliefs, and a wide variety of activities, all occurring more or less simultaneously and more or less spontaneously."[7] Thus, no one organization or spokesperson represents the movement. Although Focus on the Family and leaders such as Dobson, Perkins, and Wright receive the lion's share of media exposure, there are many Christian Right activists who are not supporters of these groups or figures and would support only part of their policy agenda.

Moreover, the Christian Right has no single agenda, but rather a collection of overlapping agendas. Some Christian Right activists focus almost entirely on ending abortions in America; others are concerned primarily with issues surrounding homeschooling. Some are motivated to fight what they call the "radical homosexual agenda," whereas others focus on banning same-sex marriage. Others seek to reduce the amount of sexually explicit material in television, movies, and popular music. Some seek to promote a role for religion in public life: prayer in public schools, nativity scenes on city property, and a public acknowledgment that the United States is a Christian (or sometimes Judeo-Christian) nation.[8] Some activists care about all of these issues and more, whereas others focus on one issue.

As has been the case with other social movements, some elements of the Christian Right have become institutionalized. Focus on the Family began as a Christian ministry seeking to strengthen the traditional family. Initially the organization stood apart from the political arena, but in 1983 it launched its political involvement by helping to found the Family Research Council, an educational organization in Washington, D.C., that advocates for socially conservative public policy. Later Focus on the Family partnered with the Family Research Council to oversee the creation of more than thirty state affiliates, and then created its own political arm in 2004. Its state-level affiliates played an important role in legislative battles in many states.

Part of the institutionalization process involves training leaders, and even members, in the rules and norms of political action. Leading up to the 2008 election, affiliates of Focus on the Family distributed information to churches and pastors explaining how they could politically mobilize their congregants. The material included information on "political lingo" and a "resource arsenal" that explained how they could have "maximum patriotic impact" while working within the constraints of the political system. At other times the institutionalized social movement has used its infrastructure to challenge the norms of political action. In 2008 one Christian Right group, the **Alliance Defense Fund**, organized a concerted effort to overturn a long-standing rule prohibiting endorsements from the pulpit, claiming that the rule violates freedom of speech. More than thirty pastors agreed to endorse Sen. John McCain, hoping to trigger an investigation by the Internal Revenue Service, which the Alliance Defense Fund could then challenge in court, potentially leading to the rule being found unconstitutional by the U.S. Supreme Court.[9]

In general, however, organizational leaders have sought to distance the group from activists who make extremist statements in public and to discipline the organization to behave well in political activity. When newly mobilized homeschool advocates threw ice at speakers at the Virginia Republican nominating convention in 1993, Ralph Reed quickly pointed out that the hecklers were not members of the Christian Coalition, but rather backers of homeschool advocate Michael Farris (Rozell and Wilcox, 1996). State and local Christian Right activists were often dismayed at the public statements made by Pat Robertson and Jerry Falwell, and many are happy to have less flamboyant movement leaders in 2010.

Whereas some movement activists have worked to institutionalize interest groups of the Christian Right, others have been involved primarily within the Republican Party and now constitute a major faction of the GOP. Although movement leaders sometimes insist for tax purposes that theirs is a nonpartisan movement, it is clear that the Christian Right is active almost exclusively in the GOP. This was not always the case. The most visible spokesman for an earlier manifestation of the Christian Right in the 1920s was William Jennings Bryan, a perennial Democratic presidential candidate. Moreover, when Pat Robertson first entered politics, he backed a candidate who sought to win the Democratic nomination. In addition, Robertson's father was a Democratic senator.

Yet as the turn of the twenty-first century approached, the movement was so closely identified with the Republican Party that when a Christian activist told a Christian Coalition gathering that his brother was a strong

Christian and a Democratic officeholder, he was greeted by stunned silence (Hertzke, 1993). Jerry Falwell left little room for Christians to vote for Democratic presidential candidate John Kerry in 2004 when he spoke to those attending the Christian Coalition's Road to Victory Conference: "Vote Christian. This means pro-life, pro-family, and pro-national defense. These are second nature to God's people. . . . You cannot be a born-again Christian who takes the Bible seriously and vote for a pro-choice or anti-family candidate."[10] After Democrats won the White House and took control of Congress in 2008, one organization announced to its members, "the assault on family values has begun in Washington."[11]

Christian Right activists flocked to the Republican Party in 1980 as the Moral Majority mobilized for Ronald Reagan, and they participated in even greater numbers in 1988, when Robertson sought the GOP presidential nomination. Some of these early activists retired from politics over the next decade, but others remained active in the Republican Party. By the 2000s the Christian Right was a clearly identifiable faction in the Republican Party at the national and state levels. In some states, such as Colorado, the movement divided the party, contributing to a Democratic victory in the state's U.S. Senate race in 2004. In other states the movement was part of a larger conservative coalition that worked together to oppose Republican party moderates and Democrats alike.[12]

As a **party faction**, the Christian Right contends with moderates for control of nominations; control in turn leads to access to campaign resources and the party platform. The Christian Right provides the Republican Party with a pool of potential voters and volunteers and a ready communications network and infrastructure. But these resources come with a price. The Christian Right refuses to be taken for granted and uses its leverage as an established voting bloc to move the party's platform to the right on social policy. At a meeting for conservative leaders in 1998, James Dobson threatened to break ties with the Republican Party if it did not back the Christian Right agenda on moral issues: "Does the Republican Party want our votes, no strings attached—to court us every two years, and then to say, 'Don't call me; I'll call you'—and to not care about the moral law of the universe? . . . Is that what they want? Is that the way the system works? Is this the way it's going to be? If it is, I'm gone, and if I go, I will do everything I can to take as many people with me as possible."[13] Dobson echoed his threat in 2008 when he indicated that he would support a third-party candidate if former New York mayor Rudy Giuliani was the Republican nominee.

Catering to Dobson's supporters, and the Christian Right more generally, however, does not guarantee success for the Republican Party or Republican candidates. The 2008 presidential election is a case in point.

## The Controversy

Is the Christian Right good or bad for America? This question inspires answers from Christian conservatives and their opponents that differ radically in substance but are similar in their passion. Among those familiar with the Christian Right, the movement is a source of great controversy.

The Christian Right is controversial for several reasons. First, its central social agenda includes issues that are among the most heated in American politics. Christian Right activists generally seek to sharply limit and eventually ban access to legal abortions; eliminate all laws that protect gays and lesbians from job and housing discrimination; and alter the curriculum in public schools in a variety of areas, ranging from sex education to history and sociology to biology and geology. The agenda of most Christian Right groups includes many other issues as well, but abortion, gay rights, and education fuel the greatest enthusiasm. These are issues about which many Americans care passionately and upon which the public is deeply divided. Each issue has spawned well-organized, well-funded interest groups that represent many Americans who oppose the Christian Right agenda.

Second, some citizens object to the general effort to mobilize conservative Christians into political action. They do so for various reasons. Some believe that America is officially a secular society and that religious arguments should not play a role in the public debate. For others, religious values have a place in politics, but religious leaders should not become political leaders, and churches should not be the locus of political mobilization. Still others believe that religious values and leaders should play an active role in politics but are offended by claims by the Christian Coalition and others that they speak for all Christians.[14] They argue that the Bible does not contain passages calling for a flat tax or opposing government health care for the poor, positions advocated by Christian Right organizations.

Although Christian Right groups take conservative positions on economic issues, many other Christians take opposing positions, asserting that their views are derived from their religious beliefs. Catholics follow the teachings of their church on the necessity of caring for the poor, and liberal Protestants may point to biblical passages that uphold the virtues of the poor and criticize the behavior of the rich. These Christians object to an organization called the Christian Coalition that presumes to speak for them in politics and to take positions that some Christian Right activists assert are the "true Christian" stands.

Finally, the Christian Right is controversial because of the heated rhetoric that its leaders, and especially its most ardent activists, sometimes produce. On a variety of issues, Christian Right activists have taken quite extreme positions, and many Americans find their rhetoric threatening. Feminist mothers and wives recoiled when newspapers published a quotation from one of Pat Robertson's fund-raising letters in which he claimed: "The feminist agenda is not about equal rights for women. It is about a socialist, anti-family political movement that encourages women to leave their husbands, kill their children, practice witchcraft, destroy capitalism, and become lesbians."[15] Robertson's rhetoric on gays and lesbians has been similarly vitriolic, and some local and state movement leaders have advocated very harsh punishment of homosexuals.

Many fear that these activists will come to exert undue influence on American politics, through subtle and stealthy political action. Pat Robertson struck fear in the hearts of moderate Republicans when he promised to take over all fifty state party committees and when he wrote that "a small, well-organized minority can influence the selection of candidates to an astonishing degree" (Robertson, 1992). Ralph Reed, in explaining the success of the "stealth" candidates who won election to San Diego's school boards, claimed: "I do guerrilla warfare. I paint my face and travel at night. You don't know it's over until election night" (Blumenthal, 1994, 114). One Christian Right activist used a war metaphor to describe efforts to ban same-sex marriage in 2004, saying a "strategic insurgence" is more effective than a "nuke."[16] And during a "Protect Marriage" rally in California in 2008, support for the right of same-sex couples to marry was described as "the devil's strategy to destroy the church, a confrontation between light and darkness."[17]

Christian Right activists argue, quite correctly, that all organizations that raise money through direct mail seek to demonize their political opponents because such appeals result in more effective fund-raising. Indeed, liberal groups such as People for the American Way and the **American Civil Liberties Union** (ACLU) make fund-raising appeals that caricature Christian conservatives and seek to heighten fear of the Christian Right. And Christian conservatives argue, again correctly, that political leaders frequently fire up their supporters with bold rhetoric that promises coming victories. Christian

Right rhetorical appeals may be no more extreme than those of their political opponents, but they nevertheless make many citizens uneasy.[18]

Of course controversy is not necessarily a bad thing. If debate over the Christian Right stimulates Americans to deal with their core values and inspires the nation to consider its policies in light of those values, then something worthwhile will be achieved. But critics charge that the Christian Right stirs up intolerance, sexism, and homophobia, and that its involvement in politics is therefore a net detriment to the public discourse.

In the introduction to his thoughtful and balanced book about a legal struggle between Christian conservatives and educators over textbooks used in the Hawkins County, Tennessee, schools, Stephen Bates posed one variant of the dilemma of the Christian Right: "How should a secular, tolerant state cope with devout but intolerant citizens, both in the public schools and in the public square?" (Bates, 1993, 12). The answer to this question depends critically on how we characterize the Christian Right—as a defensive movement seeking to protect the religious liberties of conservative Christians, or as an offensive movement seeking to impose a narrow morality on all Americans.

Although Christian Right leaders use different rhetorical appeals with different audiences, they frequently argue that theirs is a defensive movement—one designed to protect their moral values and especially their ability to impart those values to their children. Many see their beliefs and values ridiculed in mainstream media, undermined in schools, and ignored by a consumer culture that promotes a multiculturalism that appears to have no room for evangelical culture. In October 2005 **Vision America** hosted a "Countering the War on Faith" conference for Christians who were "disgusted by Hollywood's attacks on Judeo-Christian ethics, outraged by media slander of Christians, incensed by judicial assaults on Americans' right to publicly acknowledge God, [and] sick and tired of seeing our children indoctrinated in the homosexual lifestyle."[19]

For its supporters, the Christian Right is an attempt to restore Judeo-Christian values to a country that is in deep moral decline. They quote William Bennett, former secretary of education in the Reagan administration: "We are in a race between civilization and catastrophe. . . . We have record murder and violent crime rates, huge increases in births to unwed mothers, educational decline, broken families. . . . All of this, and we are told that the very religious are those we must fear. Religion is on the side of civilization; more people ought to begin to realize it."[20] Christian Right supporters believe that society suffers from the lack of a firm basis of Judeo-Christian values, and they seek to write laws that embody those values. Ralph Reed maintained that "people of faith are not . . . asking people to subscribe to their theology; they are asking them to subscribe to their public policy views, and to respect their right to participate without their religion being impugned" (Reed, 1994a, 41). He argued that the Christian Coalition merely sought to have "a seat at the table," not to dominate discussion around that table. He characterized the agenda of the Christian Right as a mainstream agenda and argued that Christian conservatives want what most Americans want: stronger families, safety from crime, successful schools, and democracy.

Although many movement activists describe a defensive movement seeking to protect religious liberties, other Christian Right activists concede that they seek to apply their moral views to all Americans. Gary Bauer, former head of the Family Research Council and presidential candidate in 1999, noted: "So the question is not whether you legislate morality. The question is whose morality you're going to legislate. Somebody's values are going to win. We just have to have the confidence to get in the public square and say that our values will be best for the country" (1999, A12).

Critics of the movement take a different view, charging that the Christian Right is an intolerant movement seeking to impose a narrow, sectarian morality on America. Some describe the Christian Right as a reactionary movement that would censor books, throw gays and lesbians into jail, and confine women to the kitchen.[21] Soon after the 1994 elections, the Reverend Jesse Jackson charged that conservative white Christians who had used the Bible to justify slavery were "the Christian Coalition of the time" and that "the Christian Coalition was a strong force in Germany. . . . it laid down a suitable scientific, theological rationale for the tragedy in Germany."[22] Since the terrorist attacks on September 11, 2001, liberal bloggers have compared the fundamentalism associated with the Christian Right to that of Islamic extremists. One author argues that James Dobson has the "ability to manipulate unsuspecting Americans." She quotes Dobson as saying that those who control the education of the country's youth will control the future. She argues that this "is a revelation into the evangelical and fundamentalist mentality. It displays a hunger for mind control of youth, scarcely different from Pakistan and Afghanistan's Islamic Fundamentalists" (Blaker, 2003, 7). Former U.S. senator Ken Salazar (D-CO) called Focus on the Family the "antichrist of the world" after Focus questioned his faith because he opposed President Bush's nominees to the federal courts. He later apologized and retracted his comment, saying that he only meant to say that Focus on the Family's actions were "self-serving" (Sprengelmeyer, 2005).

Of course what some people see as defensive reaction to societal attacks will appear quite differently to others. For example, in response to a gay screenwriter's acceptance speech at the 2009 Academy Awards, in which the screenwriter told gay and lesbian children watching the program at home that God loves them, the Christian Anti-Defamation Commission said on its Web site, "[To] say that God loves everyone regardless of their willful, sinful rebellion is blasphemous." The group characterized the entire broadcast as an "unrelenting attack on God and common decency."[23] Christian conservatives may see this statement as a defensive reaction to an attack by the "radical gay movement," but other Americans might read this as an effort to stigmatize and isolate gay and lesbian children.

If the Christian Right is a defensive movement that seeks to protect religious liberties of conservative Christians, then there can be no question that it has an obvious place at the bargaining table of American politics. If, on the other hand, the movement seeks to deprive gays and lesbians of their civil rights, dramatically limit the public and private roles of women in society, and impose a prescientific worldview on public education, then some would argue that its policy demands are illegitimate and outside the mainstream of American politics and therefore should not be part of serious policy discussion.

Ultimately, many Americans fear the Christian Right because they see some movement activists issuing harsh condemnations of Americans whose lifestyles differ from those espoused by conservative Christians. They see local organizations working to remove books from public libraries and prohibit the reading of *The Wizard of Oz* in public schools because it contains a character who is a "good witch," as well as activists similarly condemning the Harry Potter books and movies for showing witches and wizards as moral heroes. They see an elected official in Alabama fighting to ban all works by homosexual authors from school libraries. They hear some of the more extreme movement activists suggesting that known homosexuals be imprisoned, and they watch television accounts of the assassination of abortion providers by those on the fringe of the pro-life movement. To at least some observers, these extremists do indeed echo Nazi persecution of gays and public book burnings.

In the 1980s Margaret Atwood, in *The Handmaid's Tale*, wrote about a future in which the Christian Right has triumphed and women are subservient to men. Doctors who provide abortions are executed, and women are taught that rape victims deserve their fate because they entice men. Atwood's nightmare world is a far cry from Reed's description of the Christian Right agenda. This disjuncture between the soothing reassurances of Reed and the overheated fears of the Left has made the Christian Right one of the most controversial actors in American politics.

Debates between religious conservatives and other citizens occur in many countries and regions of the world. Catholic conservatives debate moderates and liberals about abortion policy in Ireland and Italy; Islamic fundamentalists debate modernists in Iran and Saudi Arabia; orthodox Jews debate secular Jews in Israel; and Sikh fundamentalists debate Hindu fundamentalists and Muslims in India. Yet to understand the debate about the role of the American Christian Right, it is helpful to consider the American context. This includes America's unique policies on church and state, the religious diversity of the United States, and its tradition of **civil religion**.

## The First Amendment and Church and State

In 2002 the 9th U.S. Circuit Court of Appeals ruled that teacher-led recitations of the Pledge of Allegiance in public schools were unconstitutional because the phrase "under God" impermissibly coerces a religious act by students. In Alabama, Chief Justice Roy Moore was removed from the bench in 2003 after defying a federal judge's order to remove a Ten Commandments monument from the state Supreme Court building. In 2008 a district judge ruled that the state of South Carolina could not issue a special "Christian" license plate featuring a cross. In 2010 the Supreme Court will hear a case about a University of California law school's refusal to give official recognition to a Christian student group on campus because it denies membership to anyone practicing sex outside of traditional marriage. These events evoked a firestorm of protest from the Christian Right and moderate Christians as well.

The debate about the role of the Christian Right in America takes place within a larger debate about the role of religion in American politics. The debate is ongoing; it took place in the American colonies before the drafting of the Constitution and the Bill of Rights and has been reignited at various points in U.S. history. At stake are two competing visions for American democracy. One holds that the United States is a Christian nation specially blessed by God; the other maintains that the country should be officially secular, with a strong separation between church and state.

The First Amendment to the U.S. Constitution reads in part: "Congress shall make no law respecting an establishment of religion, or prohibiting the free exercise thereof." The first phrase is generally referred to as the **establishment clause** and the second as the **free exercise clause**. These sixteen words, written more than 200 years ago, have inspired millions of words in a sometimes heated debate over what they should mean. Scholars have emphasized the precise wording of the amendment—sometimes focusing on a single word, such as respecting "an" establishment of religion, or highlighting the contrast between "prohibiting" the free exercise of religion and the stricter prohibition against "abridging" freedom of speech (Malbin, 1978; Levy, 1986). They have debated the original intent of the founders and whether those intentions should bind a country that is far more religiously pluralistic it was two centuries ago.

In general, we can distinguish between two positions on each of the clauses. Those who debate the meaning of the establishment clause generally hold either **accommodationist** or **separationist** positions. Accommodationists believe that the Constitution merely prohibits the establishment of a national religion. They point out that many colonies had established churches at the time of the founding and indeed for many years afterward. They argue that the First Amendment merely prohibits the government from leaning toward one religious group over another but does not mean that the government may not prefer religion generally to nonreligion. In other words, government may endorse religion, but it may not endorse the Baptist Bible Fellowship.

Although accommodationists claim the government must merely be neutral among religions, the specifics of their arguments usually imply that the government need remain neutral only among religions in the Judeo-Christian tradition and sometimes only among Christian faiths.[24] They quote with approval Alexis de Tocqueville, who wrote in 1835, "Christian morality is everywhere the same. . . . Christianity, therefore, reigns without obstacle, by universal consent; the consequence is . . . that every principle of the moral world is fixed and determinate" (Tocqueville, 1945, 314–315). Thus the Judeo-Christian tradition is seen as giving moral coherence to the nation.

Separationists, in contrast, emphasize the potential of religion to lead to violent conflict. They note that James Madison, an early Federalist leader and later president, whose essays on the Constitution are still studied by political scientists and constitutional scholars, listed religion as a potential source of divisive factions in Federalist No. 10. In addition, separationists argue that the First Amendment prescribes what Thomas Jefferson later called a "high wall of separation" between church and state. They quote with approval Justice Hugo Black's opinion in *Everson v. Board of Education* (1947): "Neither a state nor the federal government can set up a church. Neither can pass laws which aid one religion, aid all religions, or prefer one religion over another."

Although conservatives frequently portray separationists as hostile to religion, Jefferson believed that religion would benefit from separation. He argued that "true" religion would thrive in direct competition with other religious creeds, whereas "false" religion needed protection by the state (Wills, 1990). Others have argued that religion can better play its prophetic role as critic of the state when there is little entanglement between the two (Jelen, 1991a).

Accommodationists and separationists differ in their views of the proper public role for religion. Most accommodationists think that prayers are acceptable in public schools at graduation ceremonies and sporting events. They favor public displays of nativity scenes at Christmas and other open public support for religion. They argue that as long as these prayers are nonsectarian and a Jewish candelabrum called a **menorah** is displayed along with the nativity scene, the government has not endorsed any particular religion. Few would go so far as to allow Hindu or Buddhist prayers in public schools, however, and this stance suggests there are limits to just how neutral they believe government should be (Jelen and Wilcox, 1995). Separationists would oppose all of these public displays of religion, arguing that any endorsement of religion by government is a violation of constitutional guarantees.

There are also two basic positions on the free exercise clause. One would allow all kinds of religious activity so long as no one is harmed; the other would limit such activities to those within some broadly defined community consensus. Libertarians hold that all kinds of religious practices are protected, including those of non-Christian groups. They would support the right of Sikh schoolchildren to wear special religious headgear to school, of Muslim girls to cover their heads in gym class, and of Santerians to sacrifice animals to their gods. Communitarians would argue that religious freedom for minority religious groups should be limited by community norms. If state law prohibits the use of peyote in an effort to control drug use, then Native Americans should not use it in their age-old ceremonies, and if the U.S. Army denies recruits the right to any special attire, then orthodox Jews should not wear special religious headgear.

Of course many issues fall between these two clauses, evoking both establishment and free exercise claims. For example, when student religious groups ask to use school property to hold their meetings after school, is this a question of establishment (using taxpayer funds to keep the building open) or of free exercise (allowing students to practice their religion)? Over the past several years, Christian Right groups have increasingly framed their concerns around free exercise issues rather than establishment ones. For example, instead of arguing that all schoolchildren would benefit from a public prayer to begin their school day (an establishment issue), Christian conservatives now argue that children should be permitted to offer up audible prayers (a free exercise issue).

Most Christian Right activists take accommodationist positions on the establishment clause and **communitarian** stands on the free exercise clause, making them what some scholars have called **Christian preferentialists** (Jelen and Wilcox, 1995). These activists want a public role for Christian symbols and practices, but resist the notion of non-Christian groups having equal access to public support. Christian Right leaders, however, frequently endorse a position of **religious nonpreferentialism**, which holds that all religious groups have a place in the public square. Ralph Reed wrote: "America is not solely a Christian nation, but a pluralistic society of Protestants, Catholics, Jews, Muslims, and other people of faith whose broader culture once honored religion, but which today increasingly reflects a hostility toward faith in the public square" (Reed, 1994a, 135).

It is important to understand that those who oppose the Christian Right are not universally opposed to religion or even to a role for religion in public life. However, many oppose the Christian Right because they believe the policies it promotes violate the separation between church and state and might infringe on the free exercise rights of religious minorities. Indeed, some who oppose the Christian Right are themselves devoted evangelical Christians who believe that the movement is mistaken in important ways.

To summarize, those who support the Christian Right see contemporary society as aggressively secular and generally hostile to religious values and expression. Those who oppose the Christian Right believe that the movement seeks an unconstitutional establishment of one set of religious views.

## Religion and Politics in America

America is unique among Western democracies in the intensity of its moral politics. Compared with other industrialized democracies, America is remarkable for both its religious diversity and the strength of its religious institutions. Many European countries have established churches, and in those countries the majority of religious citizens—and a sizable number of less religious citizens—are members. Large majorities of churchgoers in the nations of southern Europe are Catholic, and large majorities of those in Scandinavia are Lutheran. Germany is nearly evenly divided between Lutherans in the north and Catholics in the south. In no country are there more than three or four dominant religious groups.

In contrast, Americans belong to an almost bewildering array of churches. Many states and regions have clear religious majorities—Baptists in the South, Catholics in New England, Mormons in Utah—but every state has churches representing dozens of Protestant denominations. Moreover, in urban areas on the East and West Coasts, there are growing numbers of Muslims, Hindus, Sikhs, Buddhists, and others from outside the Judeo-Christian tradition.

Not only is America a religiously diverse country, but it is also one in which religious belief and practice are unusually common. International surveys show that more than half of Americans indicate that God is extremely important to their lives, compared with fewer than 30 percent of citizens in France, Italy, Germany, Russia, and Japan.[25] Americans attend church more often than citizens in most other industrialized democracies, pray more often, and read their Bibles more frequently.

Some have argued that it is America's religious diversity that sustains its rich religious life. In nations where one church enjoys monopoly status, that church may grow "lazy" and make little effort to seek new converts. In the United States, in contrast, Baptist, Methodist, Presbyterian, and Assembly of God pastors may compete in a small community for the same potential flock of congregants and therefore try much harder to attract and keep new members (Finke and Stark, 1992; but see Jelen 2004 for an elaboration of the debate). The combination of this religious diversity and intensity creates an atmosphere in which moral issues are hotly contested because there are competing moral visions, each with devoted adherents.

Yet underlying the diversity of American religion is a more general support for its basic civil religion. Religious imagery, language, and concepts pervade public discourse, appear on currency, and are present in the pledge to the flag. Many Christians see America as somehow chosen by God to fulfill his will. The Puritans frequently likened their new covenant with God to that of God with Abraham and sought to create "God's New Israel." This infusion of religious belief and national purpose persists today.

Researchers have found that many children and adults alike agree with statements such as "America is God's chosen people today," "I consider holidays like the Fourth of July religious as well as patriotic," and "We should respect the president's authority since his authority is from God" (Wimberly, 1976; Smidt, 1980). In many Christian churches, American flags hang behind the pulpit beside the Christian flag, and children in Sunday school classes pledge allegiance to both.

Those who support this civil religion generally believe that the president has a moral, prophetic role as well as a political one. Perhaps for this reason, surveys have shown that only a minority of Americans would vote for a candidate with no religious affiliation.[26] Presidential candidates are known to go to great lengths to persuade the public that they are not only religious, but are committed Christians within the mainstream of that faith. The 2008 presidential campaign of former Massachusetts governor Mitt Romney showcased Americans' unease with having a Mormon president, and then senator Barack Obama's campaign team had to prove he was a Christian even though his mother was an atheist and his father a Muslim.

President Reagan often used religious language in his speeches, although he seldom attended church, and President Bill Clinton called for a return to religious values in the public debate. Such public proclamations of the religious character of the nation are very much in keeping with its civil religion, and many Christian Right activists believe that the president has a unique role to play as moral as well as political leader of the nation. This view helps explain the vehemence with which Christian Right activists pressured Congress to impeach and remove President Clinton from office after it became clear that he had engaged in extramarital sexual contact with a White House intern and then lied about it on national television.

President George W. Bush frequently referred to his Christian faith in television interviews and even in candidate debates. He spoke consistently of his faith as a source of strength and comfort (Larson and Wilcox, 2006). Although Bush was himself a divisive figure in American politics, a majority of Americans were content with his religious talk. In July 2003, 62 percent of Americans believed Bush mentioned his faith "the right amount." Only 14 percent of those polled believed he mentioned it too much.[27] But in the latter years of the Bush presidency, as his job approval ratings reached new lows, this sentiment began to change.

Barack Obama has spoken of his faith openly and frequently, sometimes to the dismay of secular Democrats. At the 2004 Democratic convention he proclaimed that "we worship an awesome God in the Blue states." In his first year as president, Obama referred to Jesus more often than had George Bush. Ironically, some Christian Right activists have criticized Obama for his use of religious language, which they argue is insincere.

These tenets of civil religion are held by nearly all Christian Right activists and leaders and by many opponents of the movement as well. Civil religion provides an undercurrent of unity beneath the choppy waters of religious diversity. Yet the precise meaning of this civil religion is contested in America, with moderates focusing on the melting pot of religious diversity, and the Christian Right centering instead on the idea that Americans are God's chosen people.

The belief that there is a religious character to the American polity has important consequences for Christian conservatives. If America is God's new chosen nation, then Christian Right leaders may be likened to the prophets of the Old Testament, who repeatedly called on Israel to repent. When their warnings were ignored, God inflicted various punishments described in the Old Testament.

Jerry Falwell sounded this theme:

> The rise and fall of nations conform to the Scripture. . . . Psalm 9:17 admonishes, "The wicked shall be turned into hell, and all the nations that forget God." America will be no exception. If she forgets God, she too will face His wrath and judgment like every other nation in the history of humanity. But we have the promise of Psalm 33:12, which declares, "Blessed is the nation whose name is the Lord." When a nation's ways please the Lord, that nation is blessed with supernatural help. (1981, 24–25)

Many activists see their role as that of "redeeming America" (Lienesch, 1994), calling it to repent for its many sins and directing it to the path of salvation. Thus, Christian conservatives interpret elements of America's civil religion as mandating their political activity. Many are reluctant political warriors who feel the need to protect America from policies that might result in a loss of God's favor.

Although most Americans expect their political leaders to express religious sentiments, the public is more deeply divided about whether preachers and churches should be involved in politics. In 2004 the Bush campaign sought to identify liaisons in individual churches who would share membership lists with the campaign for use in political mobilization. This resulted in widespread criticism—even from Bush's supporters.

Nearly one in four Americans would not vote for a minister even if the person were from their party and shared their political views, and a somewhat larger number oppose the involvement of preachers in a variety of specific political activities. Liberals and conservatives alike are more likely to disapprove of political action by religious leaders if they disagree with the substance of the policies. One survey revealed that conservative evangelicals are very supportive of ministers being active in pro-life or antipornography demonstrations, but far less likely to approve of involvement to end apartheid in South Africa, whereas liberals are more supportive of antiapartheid activity and less so of pro-life activism (Jelen and Wilcox, 1995).

Both liberal and conservative Christians have been quite critical of the political involvement of churches on the other side of the aisle. Conservative clerics decried the involvement of liberal churches in the civil rights and antiwar movements of the 1960s and argued that preachers should never be involved in politics. When preachers became involved with the Christian Right in the 1980s, it was the liberal pastors who denounced such action as violating the primary mission of the church. In fact, American churches have long been involved in crusades for moral reform, including fights over slavery, racial segregation, abortion, and Prohibition (Wilcox, 2005).

However, some churches have defended slavery, alcohol consumption, segregation, and abortion rights, and it is this division among religious institutions that troubles many religious professionals. For every position of the Christian Right, there is a Christian religious body in America that takes a very different view. For this reason, many liberals resent the term "Christian" Coalition, for they believe that the Christian Right movement claims to speak for all Christians but in fact represents the views of only one segment of the Christian community. In light of this, it is not surprising that the Houses of Worship Freedom of Speech Restoration Act—a bill that would allow church leaders to speak on political matters while maintaining their churches' tax-exempt status—has never made it out of committee in the House of Representatives.

The debate over the role of the Christian Right takes place within the context of this uniquely American religious pluralism and civil religion. Christian Right activists proclaim their worldview loudly because it competes with so many different worldviews, many derived from different religious traditions. The activists seek to redeem an America that they view as the new chosen land. Opponents point to the many diverse religious views in America and argue that it is best for the state to leave many moral questions to individual choice and remain neutral as the many diverse traditions compete for adherents.

## A Culture War?

Many Christian Right activists and some social scientists see America engaged in a culture war between highly religious citizens and secular citizens. Slightly less than a quarter of Americans say they attend church at least weekly, and more than a third report that religion influences their daily lives "a great deal." These numbers are far higher than in most other Western democracies and validate claims that America is a highly religious nation. Yet many other Americans have no attachment to religious institutions, never attend church except for weddings and other ceremonies, and report that religion is not important in their lives. Others have only marginal involvement in religion. More than four in ten Americans report that religion provides at best "some" guidance in their lives and that they attend church rarely. This relatively secular set of Americans is seen as being in conflict with those with deep religious convictions.[28]

A noted sociologist, James Davison Hunter, described these two groups as being engaged in a culture war that affects public policy and individual lives (Hunter, 1991). He argued that the conflict is rooted in different worldviews—in the differing beliefs about moral authority of orthodox and progressive Americans. Although Hunter included many deeply religious Americans in his progressive category, many Christian Right leaders and some scholars have recast his argument as a battle between religious and nonreligious Americans.

Over time these differences have come to be reflected in voting behavior. According to national election exit polls in 2004, those voters who attended church every week supported Bush over Kerry by 61 to 39 percent, and those who never attended church supported Kerry over Bush by 62 to 36 percent. Despite losing the election in 2008 and rarely speaking about his religious beliefs during the campaign, Sen. John McCain beat Obama among regular churchgoers, 55 to 43 percent. In 2008 many religious leaders delivered sermons and speeches on the topic "How Would Jesus Vote?," and in white evangelical churches, Jesus would vote for Mc-

Cain. Clearly some political and religious leaders are cultural warriors, eager to have the national debate center on issues such as abortion, religion in public schools, and same-sex marriage.

Yet the idea of a culture war oversimplifies the dimensions of conflict over social and moral issues. It is clear that secular and highly religious Americans do differ in their views on political issues such as abortion, gay rights, and school prayer, but it is also true that many deeply religious Americans differ on these issues as well. Deeply religious Catholics disagree on abortion, providing birth control information to teenagers, the death penalty, physician-assisted suicide, and same-sex marriage, despite clear church teachings on these issues.

Moreover, it is not the case that secular Americans are uniformly hostile to religion. One study of attitudes on church-state issues reported that most secular citizens were generally supportive of the rights of religious expression and were actually more supportive of the rights of fundamentalist preachers to speak on college campuses than were white evangelicals (Jelen and Wilcox, 1995). Although there clearly is cultural conflict in America, there are many sides to that conflict, and the Christian Right represents only one of them.

In addition, many Americans are what some have called "noncombatants" in the culture war. A sizable number of Americans would like to restore religious values to public life but resist efforts by Christian Right groups to dictate the nature and meaning of those values. They are not moved by claims of the Left that the Christian Right is a "radical, extreme" movement that constitutes a clear and present danger to America, but they are also unconvinced that American culture discriminates against Christians and that "radical liberals" are seeking to take away religious freedom.

## Conclusion and Overview of the Book

These broader contexts help us understand the nuances of the dilemma of the Christian Right. Proponents see the Christian Right as a defensive movement that seeks to represent the interests of evangelicals and other orthodox Christians in American politics. They believe that secular Americans are waging a culture war on religious conservatives, undermining traditional values and religious practices. They see the Christian Right as a movement that merely seeks to blunt this secular assault and protect America's Christian heritage.

Critics of the movement argue that the Christian Right seeks to deny America's pluralism by establishing or restoring an orthodox Christian cultural hegemony. To these critics, the Christian Right represents one narrow segment of Christianity in a nation that also includes Jews, Muslims, Hindus, Buddhists, Sikhs, and secular citizens. They argue that the Christian Right seeks not to bargain at the table but to impose its narrow morality on all Americans. They charge that Christian conservatives would establish a sectarian religion in America, and that its adherents are the aggressors in any culture war because they seek to deny reproductive rights to women, civil rights protection to gays and lesbians, and opportunities to women.

This chapter has defined the Christian Right and discussed the various constituents of the movement. It has also defined the basic controversy over the role of the Christian Right in American politics and described the context in which that debate takes place. The contemporary Christian Right is in fact the fourth wave of conservative Christian activity during the twentieth century. The next chapter places the Christian Right in historical context, compares and contrasts the movement with its earlier incarnations, and discusses the target constituency of the Christian Right. Chapter 3 introduces the organizations of the Christian Right and their leaders. It also examines the activities of Christian Right groups, both in elections and in influencing government policy. The chapter concludes with an assessment of the movement's impact on public policy in America. The dilemma of the Christian Right is explored in greater detail in Chapter 4, which examines claims that the Christian Right has expanded American democracy by politically activating a previously apolitical group of citizens and counterclaims that Christian Right adherents do not share the democratic norms that form the foundation of American politics. In addition, Chapter 4 examines the issue agenda of the Christian Right and analyzes the potential policy ramifications should movement leaders come to dominate American politics. The final chapter considers the future of the Christian Right and its issue agenda.

# 2

# Revivals and Revolution
## The Christian Right in Twentieth-Century America

If evolution wins, Christianity goes—not suddenly, of course, but gradually, for the two cannot stand together.

**William Jennings Bryan**

This is the climactic moment in the battle to preserve the family, and future generations hang in the balance.

**Dr. James Dobson**

THE FAMILY RESEARCH COUNCIL, Focus on the Family, and Concerned Women for America are only the most recent of many conservative political organizations that have been formed from the religious enthusiasms of white evangelical Protestantism. Throughout the twentieth century, the energy and influence of the Christian Right ebbed and flowed. Many organizations claiming to represent the political views of white evangelicals have come and gone, and the latest incarnation of the Christian Right has some important similarities to and differences from these earlier movements. To fully understand the Christian Right today, it is important to know more about the earlier movements.

The principal constituency for the Christian Right in the twentieth century was white evangelical Christians, but within this broad category are many different theological groups, whose members have not always gotten along with one another or supported the same political causes or candidates. It is therefore useful to understand the history of the religious movements that created these divisions among white evangelicals, whose enthusiasms have frequently led to the formation of Christian Right groups.

## The Fundamentalist Religious Revolt

Early in the twentieth century two religious movements—fundamentalism and pentecostalism—emerged that would later provide the major constituencies for the Christian Right. Pentecostals did not become involved in politics until later in the century, but the fundamentalist movement quickly emerged as the vanguard of resistance to theological modernists. At the heart of the debate between fundamentalists and modernists was the way the church should respond to new scientific theories and discoveries, especially Darwin's articulation of the theory of evolution.

During the last decades of the nineteenth century, many of the clergy in the largest Protestant denominations began to embrace modern scientific and social ideas. Leading intellectuals in Protestant seminaries sought to make interpretation of scripture consonant with the new understandings of science. These modernists also emphasized the web of social obligations that the church could fulfill. When some social thinkers transformed Darwin's descriptive theory of natural selection into a prescriptive theory that government should leave those who were less "fit" to their natural fate, many Protestant churches instead preached a **social gospel** of responsibility to the poor and disadvantaged. In this view, Darwin's theory implied that humans were perfectible, and the best way to pursue that perfection was to ameliorate the conditions of poverty and ignorance that helped create imperfection.

This emphasis on the social gospel was controversial, for religious conservatives resisted both the policy implications of these teachings and the shift of focus away from saving souls. The conservatives, who were initially a loose coalition of pietistic revivalists, conservative Calvinists, and other evangelicals, joined forces to publish *The Fundamentals* in 1910, a collection of essays in defense of orthodoxy. Although this collection went largely unnoticed in the media and among academics, it provided the intellectual underpinnings (and the name) of a new religious movement called fundamentalism. Over the next decade, the split between the conservatives and liberals widened, and in 1919 the conservatives formed the **World's Christian Fundamentals Association** (WCFA). This marked the beginning of a bitter religious battle between the fundamentalists and modernists.

The fundamentalist leadership, including William Riley, Clarence Dixon, and John Straton, instituted a series of more than 100 conferences in the United States and Canada to preach the fundamentals. The Baptist and Presbyterian churches were deeply divided, and eventually each of these denominations split. The fundamentalists emphasized the need to remain pure and separate from the world—even separate from other nonfundamentalist Protestants.

At the core of fundamentalist doctrine were three ideas (Sandeen, 1970; Marsden, 1980; Jorstad, 1970). First, fundamentalists embraced **premillennialism**, a doctrine about the timing of the second coming of Christ. Premillennialists believed that the world must first worsen, and then an Antichrist would arise who would win power. Eventually Christ would return and summon the faithful in the Rapture. At that time all true Christians, living or dead, would go immediately to heaven, leaving the "unsaved" to endure an unsavory time of tribulation on earth under the rule of the Antichrist. Soon Christ would return to lead the faithful in a successful battle with the Antichrist. Premillennialist eschatology is dramatized in a series of novels by Timothy LaHaye and Jerry Jenkins—*Left Behind* and its sequels—which appeared on the *New York Times* best-seller lists in the 1990s and sparked a series of movies.

In contrast, social gospel theologians primarily espoused the doctrine of **postmillennialism**—that Christ would come again after the millennium, a thousand-year period of perfect peace. The debate between the premillennialists and postmillennialists had been heated in theological circles for some time, but fundamentalist leaders staked a clear position on behalf of the premillennialists.

This seemingly technical doctrinal difference has had important political consequences. If Christians must establish the millennium on earth before Christ comes again, then politics becomes an essential Christian duty. Only by improving the state of the world can prophecy be fulfilled and the kingdom of heaven be brought into existence. Christians should work for peace and justice in this world in order to hasten the transition into the kingdom. Since human history has never contained anything remotely close to 1,000 years of peace, Christians have their work cut out for them.

If, on the other hand, the world must inevitably worsen until Christ rescues his followers, then politics is a futile endeavor. Moreover, if Christ might come again at any moment and summon the pure to him, then the top priority for Christians must be to remain distinct from the sinful world to avoid temptation.[1] Political involvement might lead to compromise with sin, which would leave the Christian unready for the trumpet call that would signal the second coming. The fundamentalist acceptance of premillennialism therefore created a strong resistance to political involvement that the Christian Right leaders have worked hard at various times to overcome.

The second component of fundamentalist doctrine was **dispensationalism,** the belief that God has dealt with humans under different covenants in different eras. Most fundamentalists believed there were to be seven dispensations, and the world was in its sixth dispensation, the final days before Christ's return. Dispensationalism is an important source of fundamentalist disputes with pentecostals (discussed later in this section) and thereby undermined the potential unity of the Christian Right in the 1980s (Wills, 1990).

Third, fundamentalists believed that the way to know God's will was to study the Bible, which was the inerrant word of God. Most accepted an even stronger position—that every word of the Bible was literally true. The most politically charged issue at the turn of the century that arose out of the literal interpretation of the Bible was creationism—the teaching that the biblical creation story in Genesis is literally true. In the biblical account, the world was created in six days, and Adam was made directly by God out of the dust of the ground, with Eve constructed from one of Adam's ribs. Many fundamentalists believed that the earth was created on October 25, 4004 B.C., a date established in 1654 by Bishop Usher based on life spans of Old Testament figures.

Although the literal interpretation of Genesis was once widely accepted among American elites, in the late nineteenth and early twentieth centuries scientific theories that contradicted this reading gained prominence. Darwin's theory of evolution gained acceptance among biologists; geologists began to read the earth's history in strata of rocks, and most came to believe that the earth was far older than fundamentalist doctrine would suggest; and astrophysicists read the history of the universe from the light of distant stars and argued that the universe is billions of years old.

The heads of seminaries in the modernist denominations attempted to make peace with Darwin by arguing that although God had surely made the world, he did it over billions of years, not six days. They argued that the biblical account was a metaphor, not meant to be taken literally. Fundamentalists rejected the scientific theories, accepting by faith that the heavens and earth were created in six twenty-four-hour days. If the biblical account must be true, then scientific discoveries must be made consonant with biblical truth. In response to scientific evidence that the rocks of the earth were older than 6,000 years, for example, some fundamentalists countered that when God created the earth he pre-aged the rocks, or that the great flood of Noah disrupted the underlying geology of the earth (Brin, 1994; Numbers, 1992).

The fundamentalist movement generated enormous religious energy. Pietistic clergy preached the fundamentals in tent revivals throughout the South and Midwest, and individual congregations sometimes split apart as had their parent denominations. Some of these new churches affiliated with newly formed fundamentalist denominations; others remained as independent fundamentalist churches.

From these doctrinal elements and religious schisms, fundamentalists fashioned their most distinctive characteristic—fervent **separatism**. Fundamentalists emphasized the importance of keeping themselves apart from the impure world and from doctrinally impure Christians as well. They stressed the importance of avoiding extensive contact with "unsaved" Americans; kept to their own churches and social networks; and began to fashion their own communication channels through publications, seminaries, and other means.

Although the fundamentalist movement attracted the most attention, the turn of the century was also the occasion for the birth of pentecostalism. Whereas the fundamentalists stressed the literal truth of scripture, the pentecostals focused on the immanent power of God and especially of the Holy Spirit in their lives. The movement took its name from the biblical account of the day of Pentecost, the day the Holy Spirit was poured onto the disciples, who then spoke in tongues that people from all nations could understand.[2] Pentecostals believe the Holy Spirit imparts to many an additional blessing of special religious gifts.[3] The most common of these gifts is **glossolalia**, or the speaking in tongues; others include faith healing, prophecy, and being "slain in the Spirit."[4]

Pentecostalism began as a racially inclusive, nondenominational movement, but it spread and resulted in both the creation of new denominations and splits within existing ones (Cox, 1995). Pentecostals shared with fundamentalists an opposition to modernism and a belief in the inerrancy of scriptures, and many pentecostals at the turn of the twentieth century considered themselves to be fundamentalists. Indeed, a variety of religious movements at the time endorsed the doctrinal orthodoxy of *The Fundamentals* and shared the fundamentalists' strong rejection of modernism.

Nevertheless, fundamentalist clergy emphatically rejected the pentecostal movement. At the core of the doctrinal dispute was dispensationalism—or rather a dispute about precisely which dispensation was in effect at the time. Many pentecostals believed that the "age of the Spirit" began in the early 1900s and marked a time when Christians should expect to receive spiritual gifts. In contrast, the fundamentalists believed that these gifts were part of an earlier dispensation at the time of the apostles and that speaking in tongues and faith healing were no longer legitimate spiritual practices.[5]

Although fundamentalists and pentecostals shared a large core of doctrine, the differences between them created great hostility. Ruben Archer Torrey, dean of the Los Angeles Bible Institute and one of the most prominent fundamentalists of the period, referred to the pentecostals as the "last vomit of Satan" (Quebedeaux, 1983). Torrey's rhetoric was extreme, but most fundamentalists violently rejected pentecostal practice. The hostility has continued into the present: The fundamentalist leader Jerry Falwell once stated that those who spoke in tongues had eaten too much pizza the night before, and Nancy Ammerman reported that in a fundamentalist congregation she studied, the pastor warned his parishioners that pentecostals "are allowing Satan to work in their lives" (1987, 81).

Why should seemingly minor differences in doctrine between two similar religious movements create such hostility? There are several reasons. Most important, the doctrinal differences that may seem minor to those outside of the evangelical tradition are quite important to those within it. The fundamentalists insisted on an extreme, pure doctrine and rejected any deviations from those beliefs. For fundamentalists, salvation came through the saving grace of the **born-again experience**. Pentecostals believed in additional levels of grace, including a sanctifying grace of the baptism of the Holy Spirit. Issues such as salvation, grace, and the purity of doctrine are extremely important to evangelicals, and substantive disputes on these issues ignite a great deal of debate.

Second, both movements arose at approximately the same time and competed for roughly the same set of potential members. Fundamentalist pastors worried that they would lose their congregants to a pentecostal church and thus chose to demonize the competition to help fill their pews. Like competitors of all kinds, movement leaders chose to focus on the differences between fundamentalism and related religious movements rather than on their similarities, partly in an effort to differentiate their product and demonstrate its superiority.

Finally, there are differences in style that accompany these doctrinal distinctions that persist today. Fundamentalists are a serious lot and believe that knowing God's will requires concentrated study of "the Book." Fundamentalist sermons are laced with scripture; pastors cite the text to support their themes and frequently tie together passages from several books and chapters of the Bible. Congregants read these passages along with the minister from their well-worn Bibles. In contrast, pentecostals worship through ecstatic outpourings of spiritual joy, and in their services people shout, jump, and occasionally fall onto the floor in religious ecstasy. One pentecostal outpouring in the United States entailed uncontrolled laughter, which swept the congregation and lasted for some time. Fundamentalists are uncomfortable with such exuberant worship.

It is small wonder, then, that the serious fundamentalist clergy worried that church members might be tempted to go down the street to the local pentecostal church. Yet the fundamentalists were initially far better situated to mobilize their congregations into politics, for their sermons linked the inspired word of God to events of the day. A pastor could preach a series of sermons on a political issue, weaving together divergent scriptural references to support his position, and could finally advocate political action with some accepted evidence that it was the will of God. In contrast, the immanent religious experience in pentecostal services had no obvious political meaning and thus was more difficult to mobilize. Early pentecostal churches focused on spiritual experience, not politics.

Thus, fundamentalists formed the backbone of Christian Right activity from the turn of the century through the mid-1980s. Only in recent years have pentecostals and **charismatics** moved into political action.

## The Fundamentalist Political Revolt

The fundamentalist movement generated enormous energy and spawned the creation of many organizations. In the 1920s this energy spilled over into politics, as fundamentalist ministers began to challenge modernism head-on by defending the literal interpretation of the Genesis creation story against scientific theories. They objected to the teaching of evolution in high school classes and sought to remove evolution from the curriculum and replace it with the teaching of biblical creationism. Organizations such as the **Bible League of North America**, the **Bible Crusaders of America**, the **Defenders of the Christian Faith**, and an offshoot, the **Flying Fundamentalists**, which sent squadrons of speakers throughout the Midwest, all fought the teaching of evolution in public schools. State-level organizations formed as well and were active in many states.[6]

The antievolution groups used a variety of tactics in their efforts to pass state laws banning the teaching of evolution. Their leaders sought to meet with state legislators to persuade them of the validity of their positions, and other activists addressed large rallies in an effort to mobilize public opinion. This mixing of quiet persuasion and public pressure marked the antievolution crusades as one of the most sophisticated of the various waves of Christian Right activity.[7] Perhaps the movement's greatest asset was William Jennings Bryan, a frequent Democratic presidential candidate who held leftist-populist economic views but had ties to the fundamentalist leadership.[8] Bryan became convinced that German militarism was linked to the teachings of Darwin, and he invested much of his personal energies and reputation on behalf of the antievolution crusades. In leading the campaign, Bryan was fighting social Darwinism and, more important, the teachings of the German philosopher Nietzsche, which he believed had been the impetus for German expansion in World War I (Wills, 1990).

In all, thirty-seven antievolution bills were introduced in twenty state legislatures, but most failed to pass. One bill died in a committee on fish, game, and oysters—apparently referred there because the bill proscribed teaching that humans had evolved from lower organisms.[9] The climax of the antievolution crusades was the famous **Scopes trial**, in which William Jennings Bryan took the stand to defend the fundamentalist view of evolution, only to be humiliated by Clarence Darrow's questioning (see Box 2.1). Bryan died soon afterward, and the antievolution crusade lacked a prominent national leader (Lienesch, 1995).

Although the Scopes trial was widely interpreted as a defeat for the fundamentalist leadership, its outcome was ambiguous. John Thomas Scopes was convicted of teaching evolution, but because of Darrow's efforts to attract great media attention to the trial, the conviction was quickly overturned by the state supreme court—a move that denied Darrow an opportunity to appeal to the U.S. Supreme Court and set a national precedent. Moreover, many textbook publishers, fearing further controversy, removed references to evolution from biology texts soon after the Scopes case. Not until the Soviet Union launched the Sputnik satellite into space in 1957 did evolution again become a major component of high school biology classes, as Americans sought to catch up to the perceived Soviet lead in science and technology.

Many fundamentalists objected to the politicization of their movement, and eventually the crusade became limited to the most extreme fundamentalists and struggled financially (Cole, 1931). As enthusiasm for antievolution activities waned, some fundamentalist leaders began to focus on a different message—anticommunism. Anticommunism was a natural rallying issue for fundamentalists, for many believed the Bible predicted that the ultimate battle between the forces of Christ and the Antichrist would be fought in Israel, with the latter's forces coming from the land then occupied by the Soviet Union. Communism was a new force in the world in the 1920s, and its militant atheism resonated with this interpretation of scripture.

During the Great Depression of the 1930s and into World War II, many fundamentalist organizations remained active, but their financial base eroded substantially. Some of their leaders drifted into fascism, anti-Semitism, and bigotry (Ribuffo, 1983). The fundamentalist Christian Right continued to

**BOX 2.1  The Great Monkey Trial**

Journalists called it the "trial of the century," for it involved a clash of two strong men and, more important, of two strong ideas. In Dayton, Tennessee, John Thomas Scopes stood accused in 1925 of teaching evolution in the public schools. A state law banned the teaching of any doctrine that contradicted creationism, and modernists had encouraged Scopes to teach evolution to provide a test case of the constitutionality of the Tennessee law.

In the sweltering July heat in a time before air conditioning, more than 100 newspaper reporters crammed into the courtroom, leaving only for quick gulps of lemonade from the stands outside. By July 21 more than 3,000 onlookers crowded the aisles and stood huddled outside, listening to accounts carried back from those who stood just inside. A jury of twelve farmers listened carefully to the testimony and to the arguments of two of the era's biggest personalities.

Scopes was defended by Clarance Darrow, the premier trial lawyer of his day. Darrow was a longtime critic of creationism and a proponent of the philosophy of Nietzsche. William Jennings Bryan was a perennial Democratic presidential candidate who opposed the banks and monopolies and advocated inflating the currency to enable farmers and other debtors to pay off their loans with devalued money. Although Bryan's economic views were more leftist than those of any major party candidate in history, he became one of the leading opponents of the teaching of evolution, perhaps because he thought Darwinism and Nietzsche's philosophy had inspired German militarism that led to World War I.

Bryan and Darrow had disliked each other for years, and Darrow had published in the *Chicago Tribune* a long list of questions to Bryan about the Bible designed to undermine the position of biblical literalism. Bryan agreed to prosecute the Scopes case in part because it gave him a chance to take on Darrow. It proved to be a disastrous decision.

Bryan was in poor health, whereas Darrow was fit and energetic. The trial climaxed when Darrow called Bryan to the stand and questioned him about his belief in the literal interpretation of the Bible. Under Darrow's sharp questioning, it became clear that Bryan had not thought carefully about many of the issues of biblical literalism, and in one portion of his testimony he angered fundamentalists by admitting that the earth may have been created over a period longer than six days.

Darrow scored points in other portions of the questioning as well. At two points, he focused on apparent inconsistencies in the Bible. The fol-

*(continues)*

(*continued*)

lowing transcript omits some repetitive questioning but shows Bryan's difficulty.

| | |
|---|---|
| Darrow: | Did you ever discover where Cain got his wife? |
| Bryan: | No, sir; I leave the agnostics to hunt for her. |
| Darrow: | You have never found out? |
| Bryan: | I have never tried to find out. |
| Darrow: | The Bible says he got one, doesn't it? Were there other people on the earth at that time? |
| Bryan: | I cannot say. |
| Darrow: | There were no others recorded, but Cain got a wife. |
| Bryan: | That is what the Bible says. |
| Darrow: | Where she came from, you do not know? |
| Darrow: | Do you think the sun was made on the fourth day? |
| Bryan: | Yes. |
| Darrow: | And they had evening and morning without the sun? |
| Bryan: | I believe it was creation as there told, and if I am not able to explain it I will accept it. Then you can explain it to suit yourself. |

*Source*: *Washington Post*, May 18, 1995, p. A6.

preach anticommunism, but this theme lacked strong appeal in the depths of the Great Depression, and the organizations faded into obscurity.

In the aftermath of the Scopes trial and the failure of Prohibition, fundamentalists and other evangelicals retreated from politics in what has been called the "great reversal." Politics was seen as an ultimately futile endeavor. Yet during this period fundamentalists built Bible colleges, churches, and new organizations, including the **American Council of Christian Churches** (ACCC). The ACCC was vehemently anticommunist, and it even attacked leaders of mainline Protestant denominations for their alleged ties to communists. Its extremism alienated many moderate fundamentalists, who in 1942 formed the National Association of Evangelicals (NAE) and launched a movement that has been referred to as **neoevangelicalism**. The neoevangelicals took orthodox doctrinal positions, but were more moderate than the fundamentalists, both in religion and politics. Their religious moderation was evident in their rejection of separatism, their political moderation in their unwillingness to label their political opponents as communists.

## The Anticommunist Crusades

After World War II the Soviet Union emerged as the only serious international rival to the United States. A number of political figures began to stir up fears of domestic communist influence. The most notable was Senator Joseph McCarthy of Wisconsin, who charged that much of America's government was infiltrated by communist agents. McCarthy's campaign helped establish a political market for anticommunist groups, and fundamentalist entrepreneurs formed a set of new political organizations to take part in the anticommunist movement. The **Christian Crusade**, the **Christian Anti-Communism Crusade**, and the **Church League of America** were all formed by leaders of the ACCC and emphasized primarily the threat of domestic communists.

Using radio broadcasts and traveling "schools of anticommunism," these groups focused narrowly on the "Red Menace." They did not always emphasize the fundamentalist roots of the organizations and thus attracted not only highly religious fundamentalists who were recruited in churches, but also secular anticommunists (Wolfinger et al., 1969; Wilcox, 1992). Regardless of their religious ties, those who attended the anticommunist schools were convinced that communists had infiltrated important national political institutions (Koeppen, 1969; Wolfinger et al., 1969).

The issue agenda was slightly broader than the one pursued by the antievolution groups of the 1920s. The Christian Anti-Communism Crusade officially opposed Medicare (labeling it socialized medicine) and sex education (arguing that it would weaken the nation's moral fiber and make America ripe for communist takeover). These issues were secondary to combating domestic communist infiltration, however, and were always linked directly to the communist conspiracy.

The fundamentalist anticommunist crusades never attracted a wide audience and were not well known even among those conservative fundamentalists most sympathetic to their message. McCarthy's crusade ended in disarray after he attacked the military, but the fundamentalist groups survived McCarthy's demise and signed on with enthusiasm to Barry Goldwater's 1964 presidential bid. After Goldwater's landslide defeat, the fundamentalist anticommunist groups slid into obscurity.[10]

Yet even as the Christian Right of the 1950s faded away, the religious conservatives who were its target constituency continued to build infrastructure—Bible colleges, Christian bookstores, and specialized magazines and newspapers (Ammerman, 1987). One of the best-selling books of the 1970s was Hal Lindsey's *The Late Great Planet Earth*, which mixed pre-millennialism with far-right, often paranoid, politics. Christian radio and television programs and stations began to proliferate, providing leading fundamentalist, pentecostal, and evangelical preachers with a wider audience.

The late 1960s and early 1970s also brought rapid growth of the charismatic movement in mainline Protestant and Catholic churches. Like the pentecostals at the turn of the century, charismatics emphasized the importance of the "gifts of the Spirit," and many spoke in tongues or were slain in the Spirit. Unlike the pentecostals, however, the charismatics did not form their own churches, but instead built an ecumenical movement across denominational lines and established charismatic caucuses within their home denominations. Charismatic businessmen's groups sprang up, and in many communities charismatic Catholics, Episcopalians, Methodists, Lutherans, and others met together in churches and other public places to worship. Some individual churches within mainline Protestant denominations adopted charismatic worship styles. The charismatics became an important source of support for Pat Robertson's 1988 presidential campaign.

## The Fundamentalist Right of the 1980s

In the late 1970s, after a period of relative quiescence, a new fundamentalist Christian Right organized. Two sets of events seem to have precipitated this third wave of activity. First, a series of local political movements across the country demonstrated the potential political energy of fundamentalists and evangelicals in politics. Evangelicals rallied to protest textbooks used in the Kanawha County, West Virginia, public schools; to help repeal gay rights legislation in Dade County, Florida; and to oppose the Equal Rights Amendment (ERA) in many states and cities—in each case showing that evangelicals can be enthusiastic and effective political actors (Wald, 1992).

In 1976 the presidential candidacy of Jimmy Carter, a born-again Southern Baptist, provided more proof that evangelicals might be politicized. Carter, Democratic governor of Georgia, was a deeply religious man who had taught Sunday school for many years, and his sister was an evangelist. Carter publicly called on evangelicals to abandon their historical distrust of politics, and his campaign mobilized white evangelicals to vote in greater numbers than in past elections. When conservative leaders realized that fundamentalists and other evangelicals might be mobilized to political action on behalf of conservative Republican candidates, they provided resources to help form groups such as the Moral Majority, the **Christian Voice**, and the **Religious Roundtable** in 1978 and 1979 (Guth, 1983; Wilcox, 1992; Moen, 1989; Martin, 1996).

Of all the fundamentalist groups of the 1970s and 1980s, the Moral Majority attracted the most attention. Its leader was Jerry Falwell, a Baptist Bible Fellowship pastor who had built the Thomas Road Baptist Church in Lynchburg, Virginia, from an initial gathering of thirty-five adults into a megachurch with more than 15,000 members.[11] Falwell's televised sermons were broadcast as the *Old Time Gospel Hour* and were carried on more than 300 stations. Falwell was an eager advocate for the Christian Right, appearing on television programs soon after the 1980 election to claim that evangelicals had provided Ronald Reagan's victory margin.

The Moral Majority built its organization primarily through pastors in the Baptist Bible Fellowship (BBF). Falwell recruited most of the organization's state and county leaders through the BBF, and this enabled him to quickly establish organizations in most states and in many counties (Liebman, 1983). When the media "discovered" the Christian Right in early 1981, the Moral Majority appeared on the surface to have a thriving organization.

These ready resources came with a price, however. The BBF pastors were religious entrepreneurs, and a pastor often built a church from scratch from a small circle of friends who first met in the pastor's living room. Many pastors hoped eventually to establish a megachurch, as Falwell and some others had done. Most sought to build auxiliary organizations such as church schools. These men were frequently too busy with their religious construction to build a political organization.

Moreover, the BBF pastors were a generally intolerant lot. They were hostile to Catholics, pentecostals, charismatics, evangelicals, and mainline Protestants and not especially warm toward other Baptist churches. Their state Moral Majority organizations seldom had leaders outside of their faith, and those who did serve often felt uncomfortable and unwelcome. Not surprisingly, surveys of state Moral Majority membership generally found that a majority were Baptist, and few, if any, were Catholic (Wilcox, 1992; Georgianna, 1989).

Thus, although the Moral Majority organization looked impressive on paper, in practice most state organizations were moribund (Hadden et al., 1987). The few state and local groups that were active went their very divergent ways, often to the embarrassment of the national organization. In Maryland, for example, the state organization made its stand on the issue of a beachfront bakery's sale of "anatomically correct" cookies, which the organization labeled pornographic. The incident attracted national media attention and ultimately succeeded in boosting cookie sales.

Robert Grant formed Christian Voice at about the same time, initially from state-level antigay and antipornography groups in California. Pat Robertson provided some early funding for the group, which specialized in producing scorecards that rated the "moral votes" of members of Congress. Christian Voice established a few state chapters, but remained primarily a national organization.

The Moral Majority, Christian Voice, and other groups of the 1970s and 1980s had a far broader issue agenda than had their predecessors. The core agenda involved opposition to abortion, civil rights protection for gays and lesbians, and the ERA, and support for school prayer and tuition tax credits for religious schools. But the organizations staked positions on a variety of other issues. Falwell made a highly publicized defense of South Africa and consistently supported increases in defense spending. The *Moral Majority Report*, the organization's newsletter, attempted to build support for conservative economic issues as well, including a subminimum wage, a return to the gold standard, and cuts in social welfare spending.

Although studies showed that the Moral Majority and other groups had the steady support of 10 to 15 percent of the public, their fortunes were more directly tied to the direct-mail revenues that funded the organizations. By the mid-1980s it had become increasingly difficult for these groups to induce the primarily elderly women who constituted their financial base to part with their money.

This was true for two reasons. First, Reagan's reelection campaign in 1984 told these conservative Christians that it was already "morning in America," and the fuzzy Norman Rockwell images that were the core of Reagan's television advertising sent the message that his presidency had succeeded in restoring America to its historical values. Reagan's campaign and subsequent reelection made it appear less necessary to send money to "save" America.

Second, scandals involving televangelists in the latter part of the 1980s made many more people skeptical about the increasingly frequent appeals for money. Although these evangelists had not been political activists, their widely publicized problems hurt fund-raising by the Moral Majority and damaged the presidential campaign of Pat Robertson. Jim Bakker was accused of various sexual and financial improprieties, and he eventually served time in prison for fraud. The investigations into Bakker's financial dealings revealed that he and his wife had provided their dog with an air-conditioned doghouse and had gold fixtures in their bathrooms. Oral Roberts's claim that God had threatened to "call him home" if his viewers did not contribute several million dollars to his ministry drew widespread ridicule. A *Doonesbury* cartoon noted that Roberts's claim, if true, would mean that God was a common terrorist using Roberts as a hostage to extort ransom.

All of this made it difficult for the Moral Majority to raise money through direct mail, and by 1988 it was strapped for cash. The organization was disbanded in 1989. Falwell claimed that he quit because he had accomplished his goal, but the key issue agenda of the Moral Majority remained unrealized. Like the other fundamentalist crusades before it, the Moral Majority eventually folded its tent and went home. After its demise, Falwell created other, smaller organizations, which have never managed to gather enough resources to be active in politics.

## The Robertson Campaign

In 1987 Marion "Pat" Robertson announced that he would seek the Republican presidential nomination. Robertson was an ordained Baptist minister whose father had served as a Democratic senator from Virginia. Although Robertson had never held elected office, he had been active in Virginia politics for a decade and had built a highly successful business empire.

Robertson's **700 Club** television show was very different from Falwell's fundamentalist sermons. The program was a religious talk show, with a variety of guests sharing their music or testimony with Robertson and Ben Kenslow, his African American cohost. Robertson also regularly provided a conservative analysis of political events in the news.

Robertson was a charismatic, and in the earliest shows he spoke in tongues and healed by faith. Although his later programs did not feature these religious gifts, his audience continued to include large numbers of pentecostals and charismatics. Robertson welcomed guests from many religious traditions, including Catholics, mainline Protestants, evangelicals, fundamentalists, pentecostals, charismatics, and black Protestants. Robertson himself noted his eclectic approach: "In terms of the succession of the church, I'm a Roman Catholic. As far as the majesty of worship, I'm an Episcopalian; as far as the belief in the sovereignty of God, I'm Presbyterian; in terms of holiness, I'm a Methodist; in terms of the priesthood of believers and baptism, I'm a Baptist; in terms of the baptism of the Holy Spirit, I'm a Pentecostal. So I'm a little bit of all of them."[12]

Robertson launched his campaign by gathering some 3 million signatures on petitions asking him to run, and these individuals served as the financial base of his campaign. Most of these contributors were regular viewers of his *700 Club* program, and many made regular gifts of $19.88 as part of the "1988 Club" (Brown, Powell, and Wilcox, 1995). Robertson's first campaign finance report to the Federal Election Commission contained the names of 70,000 donors and had to be delivered on a sixteen-foot truck.

Allen Hertzke (1993) described Robertson's campaign as a populist crusade to return America to a sound moral footing. Robertson decried the failures of the American educational system, focusing not only on the teaching of **secular humanism** and the absence of school prayer but also on the failure of modern educational methods to teach "the basics" effectively. He opposed abortion, which he argued was harmful because it reduced the number of babies born, thereby also reducing the number of potential taxpayers that could eventually pay for the retirements of the baby boomers. He touched briefly on the historical Christian Right theme of anticommunism, claiming that missiles were hidden in caves in Cuba, but he focused most of his campaign on domestic politics.

His economic positions were complex and did not fit neatly into the mainstream Republican debates between fiscal conservatives and supply-side economists. He strongly criticized large corporations that put profits ahead of morals, and the world banking cartel, which he blamed for maintaining tight money that hurt working families. His most controversial stand was his call for a "Year of Jubilee," a year in which debt would be forgiven. Basing his proposal on an Old Testament account of a similar policy in ancient Israel, Robertson argued that the growing mountains of debt (both domestic and foreign) threatened to overwhelm the international economy. By calling for debt relief and looser money, Robertson echoed the earlier populist campaign of William Jennings Bryan but drew the ridicule of the *Wall Street Journal.*

Robertson's campaign got off to a good start. He probably won the first round of balloting in the early multistage Michigan caucus-convention, and he beat George Bush for second place in the Iowa caucuses.[13] But a disastrous series of events undermined his campaign. He was forced to drop a suit in which he charged that an account of how his father kept him out of combat in the Korean War was libelous; journalists reported that his wife was already pregnant when they married; Robertson claimed that he knew where the hostages were in Lebanon (though he had not shared that information with the government); and he claimed that there were secret missile bases in the caves of Cuba.

About the same time, televangelist Jimmy Swaggert was caught in a motel room with a prostitute, and television accounts reminded viewers of Jim Bakker's sex scandal and Oral Roberts's financial demands. Swaggert had supported Robertson, and Robertson initially blamed the scandal on a dirty trick of the Bush campaign, but it was soon revealed that a fellow televangelist had alerted the newspapers to Swaggert's escapades in revenge for an earlier episode in which Swaggert had accused him of sexual impropriety. Taken together, these stories took a heavy toll.

Robertson's campaign also suffered from some of the religious prejudices that limited the appeal of the Moral Majority. Fundamentalists were actually less likely than mainline Protestants to support Robertson, presumably because of disapproval of his pentecostal leanings. Studies revealed that Robertson's support was limited largely to charismatic and pentecostal Christians (Green and Guth, 1988; Wilcox, 1992; Brown, Powell, and Wilcox, 1995). Robertson made a strong pitch to Catholics and African Americans, but neither vote often in GOP primaries.

Robertson lost badly in the Super Tuesday primaries, including in Texas, where he outspent Bush by almost three to one. Ultimately Robertson spent more money than any presidential candidate in history to that point, to garner only thirty-five pledged delegates. Robertson failed to win a single primary and lost badly even in his home state of Virginia.

Yet the Robertson campaign was a vital part of the birth of a new, more sophisticated Christian Right. In many states where Bush won the Republican primary, Robertson's forces continued to work to select delegates to the convention. Ultimately there were many delegates at the national convention who were pledged by state law to vote for Bush but who supported Robertson. More important, Robertson's Republicans worked to gain influence in and even control of state and local party committees.[14] These activists provided a core of skilled political workers ready to enlist in the next Christian Right crusade.

After Robertson's defeat and the disbanding of the Moral Majority, many observers proclaimed the Christian Right to be defeated, argued that its defeat had always been inevitable, and wrote its obituary.[15] In fact, research showed that support for the movement and its agenda had not declined, any more than it had surged in the early 1980s (Wilcox, 1992).

In 1989 Robertson launched the Christian Coalition. In June 1990 the Coalition took out a full-page ad in the *Washington Post* and other national newspapers warning members of Congress to vote against funding for the National Endowment for the Arts. The Christian Coalition threatened to pass out 100,000 reproductions of controversial art by Robert Mapplethorpe and Andres Serrano in districts where members voted for funding. The text of the advertisement described the kind of organization Robertson was trying to build:

> There may be more homosexuals and pedophiles in your district than there are Roman Catholics and Baptists. You may find that the working folks in your district want you to use their tax money to teach their sons how to sodomize each other. You may find that the Roman Catholics in your district want their money spent on pictures of the Pope soaked in urine. BUT MAYBE NOT.

Robertson's clear appeal to Catholics and Baptists—two constituencies that did not rally to his presidential bid—signaled a conscious effort to build a broader, ecumenical Christian Right.

## The Christian Right, 1920–1990: Continuity and Change

The waves of Christian Right activity between 1920 and 1990 had several things in common. Each was mobilized through infrastructure and communication channels already in place—the WCFA, the ACCC, the Baptist Bible Fellowship and Falwell's *Old Time Gospel Hour* and its contributor list, and the *700 Club* and its list of donors. In each movement, anticommunism and education were important elements of the agenda, although they varied in importance.[16] Each was built around one or more preachers who used the technology of the time (mass meetings, radio, television, direct mail) to reach an increasingly broader mass audience.

The first three waves of activity were based in the fundamentalist segment of the evangelical community, and each suffered because of the religious intolerance of fundamentalist leaders. None of the three fundamentalist movements succeeded in building an enduring or even significant grassroots presence, and all faded away when the initial enthusiasm died down. The Robertson campaign, however, made conscious appeals to a wide variety of Christians and even to conservative Jews.

## A Second Coming? The Christian Right, 1990–2004

At the end of the 1980s the Christian Right seemed defeated. Most of the major organizations that had been active in that decade were disbanded or moribund, and the conservative direct-mail industry was crowded and in disarray (Moen, 1994). Yet even as the large national organizations died, movement activists planned a grassroots mobilization of immense scope. The goal was to have activists in place in every precinct in America by the millennium and to influence and perhaps control the Republican candidate-selection process. By the end of the decade, it was clear that this goal would not be achieved, and some observers were again proclaiming the end of the movement.

The most visible organization in the early 1990s was the Christian Coalition. Its executive director, Ralph Reed, wrote of the need for a new ecumenism in the movement and appealed directly for conservative Catholics, Jews, and African Americans to join the coalition (Reed, 1994b). The Coalition made a conscious effort to build its state and county chapters around political activists, not preachers, to attract members from many religious traditions. The organization distributed materials and held training sessions on how different religious groups can work well together. The organization began to decline after the 1996 election, accelerated by the departure of Reed.

In the late 1990s Focus on the Family and the Family Research Council assumed the movement's leadership role. Focus has active affiliates in many states and some counties and has a well-established network of activists who respond to e-mail alerts and other forms of communication. The Family Research Council has been especially active in coordinating opposition to same-sex marriage. However, the same-sex marriage issue has led to the creation of a number of coalitions that extend beyond the Christian Right to include more moderate Catholics, African American pastors, mainline protestants, and others (Campbell and Robinson, 2007).

This incarnation of the Christian Right has had considerable success in forging ecumenical ties. In Virginia the state Christian Coalition leader for a time was a Catholic (Bendyna, 1995), and in many other states Catholics and mainline Protestants have served as county chairs. Concerned Women for America had strong support among conservative Catholics in the northern part of Virginia, and Focus on the Family has solid support among many conservative Catholics as well.

Whereas the Christian Right of the 1980s practiced confrontation, the new organizations often used different tactics. Originally some Christian Coalition candidates ran as stealth candidates, hiding their ties with the organization. This brought complaints not only from liberals, who labeled the practice deceptive, but also from some conservative Christians, who charged that the tactic made it appear that Christians were afraid to profess their faith publicly. A Pennsylvania Christian Coalition manual that encouraged stealth candidacies was widely distributed and reprinted in the media, much to the discomfort of the organization's leaders, who argued that the manual was only a draft prepared by an overzealous volunteer.

By the mid-1990s, the Christian Right began to encourage its activists and candidates to couch their arguments differently for religious and non-religious audiences. Activists were told to "mainstream the message" by avoiding explicitly religious language in public speeches and emphasizing positions on taxes, crime, abortion, and gay rights. Although many liberals complained that this tactic is just another form of a stealth candidacy, Christian Right activists responded that all candidates tailor their message to different audiences. Michael Farris, longtime movement activist and director of a group that provides legal protection to homeschool parents, noted:

> Evangelical Christians need to find ways to communicate effectively with different people. They can't just interact among themselves. Many are learning that as they interact in the Republican Party, not everyone understands or accepts the lingo that evangelicals use when talking to each other. . . . I've got to understand the other person if I want to be persuasive. Understanding that person means respecting that other person. I've got to get around other people's mental roadblocks. That means respecting where that person is coming from. That's the way that evangelical Christians can be more effective. It's a growing up thing. That is, being able to disagree with others but still be respectful of their values. That's the trick. Not all of our spokesmen have been very effective at that.[17]

As part of their efforts to adopt the secular language of politics, Christian Right candidates and activists have couched their political arguments in the "rights" language of liberalism (Moen, 1992). Instead of arguing that America is a Christian nation and therefore public schools should begin with a Christian prayer, activists now argue that Christian children have a right to exercise their religious beliefs freely in prayer. Instead of arguing that certain textbooks endorse evil lifestyles, activists now talk of "parental rights" in molding their children's education. Opposition to abortion is framed as protecting the rights of the unborn. The substantive solution to these infringements of the asserted rights is identical to those policies advocated by earlier incarnations of the Christian Right, but the justification for those policies is markedly different.

Moreover, many Christian Right activists and candidates have adopted the language of victimization. Although conservatives have long decried efforts by African Americans, women, and gays and lesbians to portray themselves as victims of discrimination, Christian conservatives now purposely use this language. Candidates and groups that attack the Christian Right are now routinely accused of religious bigotry, and Christian Right leaders charge that opposition to their policies comes from those who discriminate against people of faith.

Like the Moral Majority, the new Christian Right has a wide policy agenda that includes domestic policy positions on health care reform, taxes, and crime, but the issues of primary concern to most activists are abortion, education, and a constellation of issues relating to families and sexuality. Yet contemporary Christian Right groups are more clearly political organizations than their predecessors were, and they attract a more eclectic set of activists with varying sets of policy concerns.

Many of these activists are also members of local organizations that stress a somewhat different set of issues. The large national organizations frequently provide resources to local activists to form small local groups and help coordinate the efforts of this network of local organizations. Because these groups usually emphasize local issues, they serve as a valuable recruiting mechanism for the Christian Right.

Speaking of Christian Right activists in the 2004 campaign, John Green, Kimberly Conger, and James Guth said of this transformation:

> These Christian Rightists appear to be somewhat more pragmatic than their counterparts in the past. Many are adherents of a new civic gospel that justifies political action in defense of traditional morality. And they certainly see politics as a positive and efficacious, probably more so than in the past. This shift in political style may well be the product of the slow and steady

integration of the movement into regular politics. (Green, Conger, and Guth, 2006)

Near the end of the 1990s two developments undermined some of the progress that the movement had made early in the decade. First, the largest national organization faltered. The Christian Coalition lost momentum when Ralph Reed, a savvy political operative with a Ph.D. in history, resigned as executive director and hung out his shingle as a political consultant. His departure destabilized the organization, which had depended on his keen ear for politics to offset Robertson's tendency to engage in extreme rhetoric and spout unexpected proclamations. After Reed's departure, Robertson played a far more active role in the organization.

Ironically, it was Robertson's moderation that led to a series of key resignations by national, state, and local leaders. In late 1998 and again in early 1999, Robertson proclaimed that a ban on abortions was not achievable and that the Coalition should work to limit abortions through additional restrictions and bans on certain late-term procedures. More important, in February 1999 Robertson called for an end to efforts to remove Bill Clinton from the presidency. Although Robertson was primarily acknowledging political reality, many activists believed that they had been betrayed—that the Coalition had asked them to commit their resources to removing the president, only to abandon that effort with no warning. The Coalition's demise was accelerated by Roberta Combs, who fired many of the most experienced personnel and discarded many of the organization's carefully prepared training documents (Vaughan, 2009).

A second, and potentially more important, development is the emergence of a debate among some long-standing movement activists over whether political action is effective. In 1999, as the impeachment effort stalled, Paul Weyrich, a longtime conservative activist who helped form the Moral Majority, announced that the culture war was lost and advised conservative Christians to begin to create alternative cultural institutions and withdraw from the culture. Two former Moral Majority activists, Cal Thomas and Ed Dobson, argued in a highly publicized book, *Blinded by Might*, that the evangelicals had been seduced by the lure of political power and should return to their primary mission of saving souls.

In 2000 the debate over the efficacy of political action was halted when George W. Bush emerged as a leading candidate for the Republican presidential nomination. Bush carefully cultivated Christian Right leaders during the 1990s, after first working to help coordinate evangelical support for his father's reelection campaign in 1992. He stressed his own personal conversion and changed life, and the importance of faith to his life, without making explicit promises on policy. During his campaign Bush avoided extreme rhetoric on issues such as abortion and gay rights, but he spoke openly of his faith, of how prayer strengthened him, and on his regular Bible study. To Christian Right activists, the contrast between the sex scandals of the Clinton presidency and Bush's open profession of faith could not have been clearer.

Christian Right leaders put aside differences to work for Bush in the primaries, helping him win crucial victories in South Carolina and elsewhere (Rozell, 2002; Wilcox, 2002). During the general election the movement worked to help his campaign, but the earlier collapse of the Christian Coalition left the movement without the ability to distribute large quantities of voter guides. Bush narrowly lost the popular vote but narrowly won the electoral vote. Karl Rove, Bush's top political strategist, attributed the narrow margin of Bush's victory to low voter turnout among evangelicals.

In 2003 the Massachusetts state supreme court ruled that the state's constitution required that same-sex couples be allowed to marry. The same-sex marriage issue came as no surprise to Christian Right activists, who had been working on it since it first emerged in Hawaii in the early 1990s. But it caught most Americans by surprise, and the Christian Right moved aggressively to define the issue in the public debate and the election. In a number of states, Christian Right groups gathered signatures to place referenda on state ballots in support of constitutional amendments to ban same-sex marriage, all of which passed handily.

The same-sex marriage issue became a central focus of the Christian Right in 2004 and figured prominently in the fund-raising appeals of the movement (Wilcox, Merola, and Beer, 2006). The issue also generated new energy among activists and helped to revitalize state organizations, including affiliates of Focus on the Family and even a few state Christian Coalition chapters. In addition, the same-sex marriage issue spurred the formation of new state and local groups and prompted a number of church leaders to enter the electoral arena for the first time. (The longer-term implications of the same-sex marriage issue for the movement are discussed in Chapter 5.) When Bush won reelection in 2004, it seemed a high-water mark for the Christian Right.

## The Passing of the Guard: The Christian Right After 2004

Since the 2004 election there has been considerable change in the Christian Right. Many of its leaders became disenchanted with the Bush presidency. In the months after Bush's reelection he made hundreds of speeches on behalf of a proposal to partially privatize the Social Security program, but did not promote a national constitutional amendment to ban same-sex marriage. Bush's nomination of Harriet Miers for a vacant Supreme Court position brought strong criticism from pro-life and some Christian Right groups, who doubted her commitment to overturning *Roe v. Wade.*

Nearly all of the original founders of Christian Right groups have died or retired since 2004. Falwell died in 2007; Robertson resigned as president of the Christian Coalition in 2000 and curtailed his involvement even more after 2004 due to declining health. Beverley LaHaye stepped down as president of Concerned Women for America in 2006, and James Dobson resigned as president of Focus on the Family in early 2003 and as chairman in 2009.

Meanwhile other evangelical organizations experienced leadership flux. Reverend Ted Haggard resigned as president of the National Association of Evangelicals soon after it was disclosed that he had engaged in a sexual relationship with a man he said had supplied him with drugs. NAE's vice president, Richard Cizik, resigned under pressure in late 2008 after he voiced support for civil unions for gays and lesbians.

Today Christian Right groups face major financial shortfalls. Focus on the Family reduced its staff from 1,400 employees in 2002 to 860 in late 2009. Concerned Women for America experienced a sharp drop in direct-mail contributions. Some of these difficulties stem from a weak economy, which has lowered levels of political and charitable giving. But some of it also stems from an aging membership.

There is some evidence that younger evangelicals are less supportive of the Christian Right. Scholars have written that younger evangelicals have a wider issue agenda, which includes "liberal" positions such as protecting the environment, helping the poor in other countries, and dealing with the worldwide AIDS epidemic. They are also more moderate on gay rights, although somewhat more conservative on abortion, as we will see later in this chapter.[18]

Christian Right group leaders say that they are experiencing difficulties in gaining members in this coming generation, leaving them with an aging membership that is not replenishing itself. Reverend Joel Hunter accepted the presidency of the Christian Coalition in 2006 and sought to appeal to younger evangelicals with a broader agenda, but left the organization before assuming the position because of disagreements with Robertson and Combs.

But other evangelical leaders, such as Rick Warren and Richard Cizik, have had some success in mobilizing younger evangelicals behind an agenda that remains pro-life but is far broader and often more moderate than those of the Christian Right organizations. Warren, a Southern Baptist pastor at one of the largest megachurches in the nation, delivered a prayer at Obama's inauguration, shown on the front cover of this book. Although he preaches that the Bible is literally true, he has focused attention on climate change, AIDS in Africa, poverty, and other issues.

Finally, in his impressive study of evangelical elites in America, sociologist D. Michael Lindsay (2007) finds that many evangelicals in positions of power do not support the Christian Right's approach to politics. Rather than pursue change through public policy, these "cosmopolitan" evangelicals take a more nuanced approach to cultural engagement and choose to live out their faith in a position of influence in a secular setting, be it media, academia, or business.

The Christian Right today faces a critical juncture. It must find a way to appeal to new members and donors, without losing the intense support of its most ardent members.

## The Target Constituency of the Christian Right

The Family Research Council, The American Family Association, Citizens for Community Values, and **Citizens for Excellence in Education** are all social movement organizations seeking to mobilize members of their potential constituency. Like all social movements, they seek to build a common identity, a common set of complaints, a shared belief that the constituency has been unfairly treated by society, and support for collective action. Two important factors that determine whether the organizations fail or succeed are how effectively they mobilize their base and whether they can expand beyond that core constituency. These two factors are sometimes in conflict, for the intensity that activates the core supporters may alienate more moderate potential supporters.

Most analysts agree that the principal target audience of the Christian Right remains the white evangelical community, especially its fundamentalist and pentecostal wings. But the contemporary Christian Right is also targeting conservative Catholics, mainline Protestants, and African Americans.

## White Evangelicals

White evangelicals are united by a common core theology: they share a belief in the importance of a personal conversion experience that involves repenting of sin and accepting Jesus Christ as personal savior. Most, though not all, evangelical churches refer to this experience as being "born again."[19] They also agree that the Bible is the inerrant word of God, and that Christians should spread their witness and seek to convert others to the faith. Yet evangelicals are also divided by their doctrine, especially on how to interpret the Bible and on how the Holy Spirit operates in their lives.

As noted above, pentecostal and charismatic Christians believe that the Holy Spirit gives gifts such as speaking in tongues, prophecy, and healing, and often practice worship styles such as being "slain in the Spirit," whereby members of the audience fall to the floor. Fundamentalists do not believe that these gifts are genuine, because we are living in a latter dispensation. Both pentecostals and fundamentalists believe the Bible is literally true, but pentecostals believe that there is additional evidence of God's will through direct experience of the Holy Spirit, whereas fundamentalists believe that the Bible alone is the source of truth. Often the label "evangelical" is used broadly to incorporate fundamentalists, pentecostals, and charismatics. But some evangelicals do not fit into any of these categories and believe that the Bible is the inspired word of God with no errors, but that not all is meant to be read literally. This latter group of evangelicals are sometimes referred to as neoevangelicals, and in some studies are simply labeled "other evangelicals."

Fundamentalists, pentecostals, charismatics, and other evangelicals can be identified in survey data in different ways, and these variations often account for the sometimes conflicting claims made about evangelicals (Hackett and Lindsay, 2008). All groups except charismatics can be identified by the denominations they attend. Those who attend Assembly of God churches are pentecostals, and those who go to Baptist Bible Fellowship churches can be classified as fundamentalists. A denominational definition of evangelicalism helps us focus on the historical and social basis for the movement and on how different denominations have splintered and merged around various interpretations of doctrine.

A denominational definition is useful in that many national and regional surveys include a question about church affiliation, and thus we can use the data from these various surveys to compare evangelicals with other citizens. Moreover, because these types of questions have been asked for many years, we can trace the political behavior of evangelicals. However, a denominational definition is less useful for identifying the theological subgroups among evangelicals. Many fundamentalists attend nondenominational churches, and charismatics are found in all mainline Protestant denominations and among Catholics as well. Some denominations, such as the Southern Baptists, are difficult to classify, because they continue to experience an internal struggle for control between fundamentalists and neoevangelicals.

Moreover, many liberal denominations contain theologically conservative congregations. One of us grew up in the Walnut Grove United Methodist Church in West Virginia. Any denominational coding would place the liberal Methodists with mainline Protestants, but Walnut Grove was and remains an evangelical church, and many of its members would call themselves fundamentalists. Finally, a growing portion of the public attends nondenominational megachurches, which usually preach evangelical doctrine.

It is also possible to identify evangelicals by their doctrine, as noted by Lyman Kellstedt: "The predominant emphasis of evangelicalism is doctrine. It is 'right' doctrine that self-defined evangelicals look for when they 'check out' a person's Christian credentials" (1989, 29). The most frequent questions used to identify evangelicals ask whether the respondents have been born again and assess their views of the Bible. These questions cannot differentiate between fundamentalists and pentecostals, because both groups teach that the Bible is literally true.

Finally, some surveys identify evangelicals by inviting them to identify themselves. They ask respondents whether they consider themselves to be evangelicals, fundamentalists, charismatics, and/or pentecostals, in some cases allowing only one positive response, in others allowing respondents to select multiple identities. Such direct questions have the advantage of helping us understand what people mean by these terms, but they also reveal considerable confusion among Americans about which terms might apply to their beliefs.[20]

In this book we separate evangelicals from mainline Protestants based on doctrine—specifically, a high view of scripture and a born-again experience. It is through doctrine that the Christian Right has sought to build social movement identity, and today the movement uses micro-targeting techniques to reach doctrinal evangelicals, rather than building through denominations (Monson and Oliphant, 2007). The tables in this chapter distinguish between literalist evangelicals (here labeled as "fundamentalist," although most pentecostals are included) and other evangelicals, who do not believe that all parts of the Bible are meant to be read literally.[21]

There are two narratives in American culture about evangelicals: that they are less educated, less affluent, older, and predominantly Southern, and that these generalizations are no longer true because evangelical churches attract a more affluent and better educated population than in the past. Table 2.1 presents the demographic characteristics and religious behaviors of white fundamentalists and other evangelicals, along with white mainline Protestants, Catholics, and those with no religious affiliation, using data from the 2008 National Election Study. The data show why these two narratives exist, for both contain elements of truth.

Fundamentalists are indeed less educated and less affluent than other white religious groups. More than half of fundamentalists have a high school education or less, compared with 36 percent of white mainline Protestants. They are also less affluent: 57 percent have incomes below $60,000, compared with 45 percent of the white mainline. Note that this does not mean that all fundamentalists have low levels of education, for nearly a quarter have at least a bachelor's degree, and more than half have attended some college. But other evangelicals are somewhat better educated than the mainline and are considerably more affluent. Both evangelical constituencies are concentrated in the South, but fundamentalists are older and more heavily female than other evangelicals.

Fundamentalists have a far higher level of religiosity than other white religious groups, and other evangelicals are both significantly less observant than fundamentalists and significantly more observant than mainline Protestants or Catholics. More than 60 percent of fundamentalists say that religion provides a great deal of guidance in their lives, and a similar number pray several times a day. A third attend church services more often than once a week, and another 20 percent attend weekly. For many fundamentalists, their church is their primary social network, and most of their friends attend the same church (Ammerman, 1987). Some fundamentalist churches may even discourage their members from developing close friendships among nonbelievers.

White fundamentalists hold more traditional values and conservative social issue attitudes than other evangelicals, mainline Protestants, Catholics,

**TABLE 2.1  Social Characteristics of White Religious Groups**

|  | Fundamentalist | Other Evangelical | Mainline Protestant | Catholic | No Affiliation |
|---|---|---|---|---|---|
| **Education** | | | | | |
| Less than high school | 14% | 9% | 8% | 10% | 10% |
| High school | 38% | 24% | 28% | 27% | 31% |
| Some college | 26% | 29% | 34% | 27% | 25% |
| College degree | 14% | 23% | 14% | 20% | 19% |
| Postgraduate | 9% | 15% | 16% | 16% | 14% |
| **Family income** | | | | | |
| Less than $24,999 | 19% | 11% | 14% | 11% | 16% |
| $25,000–$59,999 | 38% | 23% | 31% | 30% | 39% |
| $60,000–$99,999 | 22% | 29% | 28% | 30% | 29% |
| $100,000 and up | 21% | 37% | 26% | 30% | 16% |
| **Region** | | | | | |
| Northeast | 7% | 7% | 15% | 29% | 10% |
| Midwest | 26% | 11% | 28% | 21% | 28% |
| South | 57% | 67% | 40% | 27% | 31% |
| West | 10% | 15% | 17% | 23% | 31% |
| Female | 65% | 51% | 56% | 54% | 48% |
| **Age** | | | | | |
| 18–30 | 12% | 26% | 20% | 22% | 28% |
| 31–45 | 20% | 27% | 31% | 18% | 27% |
| 46–60 | 33% | 24% | 28% | 29% | 32% |
| 61 and up | 35% | 24% | 22% | 31% | 14% |
| **Religion** | | | | | |
| Religion provides a great deal of guidance in life | 62% | 40% | 21% | 33% | 12% |
| Prays several times a day | 63% | 35% | 20% | 27% | 12% |
| Attends church more than weekly | 34% | 10% | 4% | 10% | 0% |
| Attends church weekly | 20% | 14% | 10% | 17% | 0% |
| Never attends | 10% | 22% | 34% | 35% | 100% |

*Source*: 2008 National Election Study, whites only

and the unaffiliated. Table 2.2 shows the values and social issue positions of the same four white religious groups. Fundamentalists are far more likely than other white religious groups to believe that newer lifestyles cause societal breakdown, and that we should not be more tolerant of those who live by different moral standards. They are significantly more likely to value

TABLE 2.2 Political Values and Social-Issue Positions of White Religious Groups

| | Fundamentalist | Other Evangelical | Mainline Protestant | Catholic | No Affiliation |
|---|---|---|---|---|---|
| **Values** | | | | | |
| Newer lifestyles cause societal breakdown | 83% | 69% | 62% | 62% | 46% |
| Do not tolerate those with different values | 42% | 28% | 18% | 24% | 10% |
| **Traits for children** | | | | | |
| good manners > curiosity | 89% | 67% | 70% | 68% | 58% |
| obedience > self reliance | 85% | 56% | 50% | 47% | 39% |
| Not a problem if people have unequal chance in life | 41% | 34% | 27% | 31% | 20% |
| The less government the better | 58% | 49% | 49% | 49% | 40% |
| **Social/Moral Issues** | | | | | |
| Abortion | | | | | |
| Never allowed | 25% | 15% | 8% | 20% | 2% |
| Always allowed | 16% | 33% | 43% | 34% | 63% |
| Strongly favor death penalty | 63% | 61% | 64% | 46% | 52% |
| No same-sex marriage; civil unions | 68% | 34% | 28% | 29% | 15% |
| Allow civil unions only | 22% | 35% | 31% | 33% | 21% |
| No gay adoption | 79% | 49% | 46% | 48% | 28% |
| No gay antidiscrimination laws | 40% | 30% | 23% | 21% | 19% |
| No gays in military | 36% | 27% | 14% | 22% | 15% |
| Rate gays at 0 degrees | 25% | 17% | 10% | 10% | 8% |
| Friend or family member gay | 40% | 62% | 53% | 53% | 57% |
| Women should not have equal role | 18% | 8% | 1% | 5% | 4% |
| Working mothers can't have as warm relationship | 34% | 21% | 25% | 17% | 19% |
| Better if woman tends home and man achieves | 52% | 20% | 22% | 24% | 22% |

*Source*: 2008 National Election Study, whites only

good manners over curiosity, and obedience over self-reliance, in children. They are also less likely to think that unequal life chances are a problem, and more likely to think that a smaller government is preferable.

They are more conservative on abortion than other white constituencies, and less supportive of gay rights. Fully a quarter of fundamentalists rate gays and lesbians at 0 degrees on a feeling thermometer ranging from 0 to 100. Although fundamentalist leaders urge their members to "hate the sin but love the sinner," this message is not always getting through. Fundamentalists are significantly less likely than other white religious constituencies to report that a friend or family member is gay or lesbian.

White fundamentalists are less supportive of gender equality, with nearly one in five saying that women should not have an equal role in politics and society, and a majority stating that it is better if the woman tends the home while the man is the achiever outside the home. They are more likely to think that working mothers cannot have as warm a relationship with their children as stay-at-home moms do.

Although fundamentalists stand out as conservative on social issues, it is worth noting that they do not all think alike. Fully three-quarters would allow abortion under some circumstances, 32 percent support civil unions or marriage for same-sex couples, and a majority now favor antidiscrimination laws protecting gays and lesbians. A large majority favor equal roles for men and women, and nearly half do not think that it is best for a woman to tend the home while the man achieves.

The other white evangelicals are markedly more moderate, and in most cases are not statistically distinguishable from at least one other religious group. They are more conservative than mainline Protestants and Catholics on gay and lesbian rights, and this is most evident in attitudes toward antidiscrimination laws and military service. They are also more likely than these two other religious groups to rate gays and lesbians at 0 degrees, but they are more likely than other groups to report that they have a gay or lesbian friend or family member. Evangelicals who do not know GLBT (gay, lesbian, bisexual, or transgender) friends or family members have attitudes very much like fundamentalists, but they are more likely to know someone who is gay or lesbian.[22]

Fundamentalists and evangelicals are far more liberal about gay rights now than they were just eight years ago. More important, younger fundamentalists and evangelicals are far more liberal than their parents and grandparents (Wilcox and Iida, 2010). Among those under age thirty-five, fully a quarter of fundamentalists and a narrow majority of other evangelicals favor same-sex marriage. More than 80 percent of the young favor antidiscrimination laws; in 2000 this figure was 40 percent.

White fundamentalists are more conservative on many other issues as well, reflecting their Southern roots and Republican partisanship (see Table 2.3). Nearly three in four fundamentalists identify themselves as conservative, a far larger number than other whites, and more than 60 percent of both fundamentalists and evangelicals are Republicans; again, a figure far larger than white mainline Protestants, Catholics, and especially the nonaffiliated.

Fundamentalists and evangelicals are more likely to believe the war in Iraq decreased the risk of domestic terror attacks and was worth the cost, and fundamentalists are more likely to support increased defense spending. In each case, this attitude is entirely explained by partisanship: the Iraq war was George Bush's war, and Republicans were more likely to approve of it. Interestingly, fundamentalists and evangelicals are *not* more likely to support the use of torture in interrogation of suspected terrorists. Compared with other Republicans, fundamentalists and evangelicals were somewhat less likely to support the use of torture. The National Association of Evangelicals issued a strong condemnation of torture in 2007, and evangelicals appear to respond very strongly to arguments against torture based on the golden rule.

Evangelicals and fundamentalists are less distinctive on economic issues. They are not markedly more likely to favor cuts in spending on services or to oppose government guarantees of a job. Fundamentalists, however, are significantly more likely to oppose national health insurance, a longtime partisan issue that the Christian Right has strongly opposed. Although there are now evangelical interest groups promoting environmental protection, fundamentalists are distinctively less supportive of new emission standards than other white religious groups, and both fundamentalists and evangelicals are more likely than are other white religious groups to say that jobs are more important than environmental protection.

Their spending priorities are not distinctive from other whites, although they are slightly more likely to favor cuts in spending on childcare and aid to the poor. Their attitudes on immigration are only slightly more conservative than those of white mainline Protestants. On race and crime issues, white evangelicals are more likely to oppose aid to blacks, a finding that is fully explained by their partisanship and Southern residence. They are also more likely to oppose federal gun control laws.

**TABLE 2.3** Other Issue Positions of White Religious Groups

|  | Fundamentalist | Other Evangelical | Mainline Protestant | Catholic | No Affiliation |
|---|---|---|---|---|---|
| Conservative ID | 74% | 55% | 45% | 45% | 31% |
| Republican partisanship | 62% | 68% | 46% | 50% | 30% |
| **Foreign/Defense Issues** | | | | | |
| More defense spending | 42% | 33% | 31% | 33% | 34% |
| Iraq decreased terrorist threat | 36% | 43% | 27% | 26% | 22% |
| Iraq war worth cost | 45% | 38% | 24% | 27% | 20% |
| Approve torture for terror suspects | 26% | 26% | 27% | 28% | 22% |
| **Economic Issues** | | | | | |
| Spend less on services | 35% | 39% | 30% | 28% | 25% |
| Government not guarantee job | 58% | 59% | 62% | 58% | 51% |
| Oppose national health plan | 51% | 39% | 43% | 44% | 29% |
| Spend less on childcare | 22% | 25% | 16% | 15% | 16% |
| Spend less on science | 11% | 20% | 13% | 16% | 23% |
| Spend less on aid to poor | 17% | 15% | 14% | 13% | 14% |
| No new emission standards | 27% | 16% | 9% | 19% | 18% |
| Jobs more important than environment | 57% | 48% | 31% | 26% | 28% |
| Decrease immigration | 54% | 46% | 52% | 46% | 43% |
| **Race/Crime Issues** | | | | | |
| Government should not help blacks | 74% | 68% | 59% | 65% | 61% |
| Oppose more federal gun control | 64% | 70% | 56% | 57% | 58% |

*Source*: 2008 National Election Study, whites only

Overall, the data in Tables 2.2 and 2.3 show that white fundamentalists and evangelicals are not uniformly conservative and that abortion, gay rights, women's roles, and other issues divide the evangelical community as they do the rest of the nation. Fundamentalist evangelicals (including pentecostals) are distinctive in their values and social issue positions and constitute the core constituency of the Christian Right. Other white evangelicals are less distinctive in values and social issue positions.

The data from these surveys suggest that the Christian Right can attract its broadest support among white evangelicals by taking positions that are moderately conservative—allowing abortions under a few circumstances and avoiding any endorsement of gender inequality or discrimination against gays and lesbians in hiring or military service. However, these positions may also fail to motivate the most ardent activists, who generally take more conservative positions on these issues. Fundamentalists and evangelicals who attend church weekly are more conservative on nearly all of these issues than those who attend less often, so the core of the target constituency is less moderate than the data in Tables 2.2 and 2.3 suggest.

### Conservative White Catholics

Although conservative Catholics did not feel welcome in the Moral Majority, the contemporary Christian Right has made special appeals to them (Bendyna, Green, Rozell, and Wilcox, 2000). There has long been a Catholic Right in America, and some Catholics rallied to the antievolution crusades and Joseph McCarthy's anticommunism. Catholics were the principal audience for Father Charles Coughlin's ultraconservative radio broadcasts in the 1930s and later were a core element in the John Birch Society.

It is clear that many Catholics support some of the key issues of the Christian Right, but the data in Table 2.2 show that a significant minority of white Catholics support Christian Right positions on social issues. The principal issue the Christian Right relies on to win Catholic members is abortion. Catholics are also attracted to the movement's support of Christian schools and its general position that family values and Christian faith should be more prominent in public life, and to a lesser extent, to their opposition to gay rights and their support for homeschooling.

Yet despite clear teachings by the Roman Catholic Church, only a minority of white Catholics are strictly pro-life. Indeed, the data in Table 2.2 show that pro-choice white Catholics outnumber pro-life white Catholics by more than three to two, and that white Catholics are far more supportive of gay rights than are fundamentalists, and in some cases even mainline Protestants. They are also more supportive of gender equality. They were far less supportive of the Iraq war than were fundamentalists and are somewhat more likely to support spending on social programs to aid the poor, reflecting the church's long emphasis on ameliorating poverty. It seems unlikely that a majority of Catholics would support the Christian Right.

Yet the Christian Right need not attract a majority of white Catholics to be a formidable political force. If it were to attract a majority of white evangelicals, a sizable minority of white Catholics and mainline Protestants, and a significant number of black evangelicals, the Christian Right would be a vital force in American politics. In the past few years there have been signs that white evangelicals have been more welcoming of Catholics than they once were. Millions of evangelicals flocked to Mel Gibson's film *The Passion*, which depicted a very Catholic version of Christ's death and resurrection. Catholics and evangelicals worked together to ban same-sex marriage and try to keep a feeding tube connected to Terry Schiavo, a Florida woman doctors had declared to be in a persistent vegetative state. This suggests that some of the most conservative Catholics may join the Christian Right in a broader coalition in the future. Studies have shown that evangelicals have been influenced by this dialogue and now see Catholics as a positive reference group (Robinson, 2008).

### White Mainline Protestants

Although movement leaders seldom mention mainline Protestants as a target for future mobilization, there are morally conservative Christians in Presbyterian, Methodist, Lutheran, and Episcopal churches across America, and some have already joined the Christian Right. Many hold orthodox doctrinal views, and some regularly watch televangelists, who provide some of their political cues.

Overall, however, white mainline Protestants are quite moderate on social and moral issues. The data in Table 2.2 show that pro-choice white mainline Protestants outnumber their pro-life counterparts by more than four to one. Nearly 40 percent support same-sex marriage, with two-thirds supporting either marriage or civil unions. Only one in four believes that it is best if a man achieves while the woman tends the home.

Mainline Protestants were less supportive of the Iraq war and increased defense spending. When it comes to economic issues, white mainline Protestants are as conservative as white evangelicals, principally because of their relative affluence. But they are more supportive of environmental protections, government aid to African Americans, and national gun control than are fundamentalists. Given their moderate stances on these issues, it is unlikely that a majority of white mainline Protestants would enlist in a conservative moral crusade.

Nevertheless, the data in Table 2.2 show that there is support for some Christian Right positions among white mainline Protestants, and in the South a substantial minority of white mainline Protestants who regularly attend church support much of the Christian Right agenda. This suggests that there may be room for some mobilization by Christian Right groups that take relatively moderate positions on key issues and stress abstract family values.

### Ethnic and Racial Minority Christian Groups

Although it is primarily among white evangelicals that the Christian Right has recruited its activists, exit polls in recent years show that African Americans and Latinos have also voted to ban same-sex marriage in states that have conducted referenda. A higher portion of African Americans than whites are evangelicals, measured by either denomination or doctrine. A clear majority attend Baptist churches, believe that the Bible is the inerrant word of God, and report a born-again experience. Substantial numbers of blacks have had the spiritual experiences that are the core of pentecostal and charismatic Christianity. Moreover, blacks practice their religion: they attend church, read their Bibles, and pray more often than do whites.

Yet these doctrinal beliefs and religious experiences do not translate into the same political attitudes as for their white counterparts. Although African Americans and whites read from the same Bible, the meaning of the text is socially constructed in different ways in the two traditions. Most black churches interpret the Bible as a book of liberation, equality, and social compassion. Thus black evangelicals are more likely than are their white counterparts to oppose all forms of discrimination and favor social programs to help the poor.

Yet many African American evangelicals are quite conservative on moral issues, including gay rights, abortion, and school prayer, and this group would seem to constitute a potential constituency for the Christian Right. African American pastors have worked together with white evangelicals in states with marriage referenda (Campbell and Robinson, 2007). Some Christian Right leaders have clearly perceived the potential; Ralph Reed laced his speeches with quotations from Martin Luther King Jr. and often compared the Christian Right to the civil rights movement of the 1960s.

The growing Latino population includes a minority who are Protestant, most of whom practice a pentecostal-style evangelicalism. Surveys have shown that Latino Protestants are conservative on social, economic, and some foreign policy issues. Moreover, Latino Catholics are generally seen as more socially conservative than whites, and Republican strategists have sought to mobilize conservative Latinos on social issues. But like African Americans, Latinos experience discrimination and have lower average incomes, making them more liberal on economic issues.

It may be that the Christian Right could find some support among non-white groups. The 2008 National Election Study contained an oversample of Latinos, allowing us to explore their positions on the political issues listed in Tables 2.2 and 2.3. We distinguish between African American mainline Protestants and evangelicals using the same doctrinal measures we used for whites. There are not enough Latino Protestants in the survey to divide into evangelical–mainline, but the overwhelming majority are evangelical. Because there are fewer African American and Latino respondents than white ones, we are unable to show results for some survey questions that were asked of only half of the respondents.

Table 2.4 shows that African American evangelicals and Latino Protestants share with white evangelicals a belief that newer lifestyles cause societal breakdown. But large majorities of all four minority religious traditions believe that citizens should tolerate those with different views, an attitude that is likely linked to experiences of racial and ethnic intolerance.

Among all four groups there is strong preference for good manners over curiosity, and for obedience over self-reliance, among children. This latter is highest among African American evangelicals, especially in the South, perhaps linked to fears that disobedient children might face severe sanctions from the white establishment. Both African Americans and Latinos believe that it is a problem if people have an unequal chance in life and see government as a positive force. These attitudes are sharply different from those of white fundamentalists.

African American mainline Protestants are even more pro-choice than their white counterparts, and African American evangelicals and Latino Protestants are about as pro-choice as are other white evangelicals, but far less than white fundamentalists. Latino Catholics are more pro-life than white Catholics are, however. All four groups are less supportive of the death penalty than white evangelicals are, a finding that may be due to perceptions of unequal application of the ultimate sanction.

A large majority of African American evangelicals oppose same-sex marriage and also civil unions, but a majority of other religious traditions would allow either marriage or civil unions. African American evangelicals are as likely to oppose antidiscrimination laws as are white fundamentalists, and

**TABLE 2.4 Selected Values and Issues: Ethnic Minority Faith Communities**

| | Black Mainline | Black Evangelical | Latino Protestant | Latino Catholic |
|---|---|---|---|---|
| **Values** | | | | |
| Newer lifestyles cause societal breakdown | 62% | 70% | 71% | 62% |
| Don't tolerate those with different values | 15% | 21% | 15% | 14% |
| Traits for children good manners > curiosity | 87% | 91% | 92% | 91% |
| obedience> self reliance | 76% | 94% | 78% | 72% |
| Not a problem if people have unequal chance in life | 21% | 29% | 28% | 31% |
| The less government the better | 14% | 12% | 31% | 13% |
| **Social/Moral Issues** | | | | |
| Abortion | | | | |
|    Never allowed | 10% | 17% | 14% | 29% |
|    Always allowed | 53% | 35% | 36% | 33% |
| Strongly favor death penalty | 35% | 34% | 37% | 47% |
| No same-sex marriage; civil union | 34% | 63% | 39% | 27% |
| Allow civil union only | 24% | 16% | 18% | 25% |
| No gay antidiscrimination laws | 30% | 40% | 29% | 26% |
| No gays in military | 17% | 26% | 26% | 16% |
| No gay adoption | 47% | 68% | 50% | 43% |
| Friend or family member gay | 53% | 34% | 45% | 57% |
| Rate gays at 0 degrees | 10% | 25% | 15% | 11% |
| Women should not have equal role | 4% | 15% | 10% | 13% |
| Working mothers can't have as warm relationship | 23% | 24% | 30% | 21% |
| Better if woman tends home and man achieves | 26% | 33% | 42% | 31% |

*Source*: 2008 National Election Study

**TABLE 2.5** Other Issue Positions of Ethnic Religious Groups

|  | Black Mainline | Black Evangelical | Latino Protestant | Latino Catholic |
|---|---|---|---|---|
| Conservative self-identification | 25% | 33% | 41% | 30% |
| Republican partisanship | 6% | 5% | 31% | 20% |
| **Foreign/Defense Issues** | | | | |
| More defense spending | 34% | 38% | 36% | 41% |
| Iraq decreased terrorist threat | 9% | 13% | 20% | 18% |
| Iraq war worth cost | 5% | 8% | 23% | 15% |
| Decrease immigration | 50% | 56% | 30% | 28% |
| Approve torture of terror suspects | 21% | 20% | 21% | 24% |
| **Economic Issues** | | | | |
| Spend less on services | 10% | 8% | 15% | 13% |
| Oppose national health plan | 24% | 25% | 26% | 26% |
| Spend less on childcare | 11% | 11% | 11% | 9% |
| Spend less on science | 11% | 9% | 13% | 13% |
| Spend less on aid to poor | 7% | 8% | 14% | 11% |
| **Race/Crime Issues** | | | | |
| Government should not help blacks | 30% | 25% | 39% | 35% |
| Oppose more federal gun control | 36% | 32% | 37% | 38% |

*Source*: 2008 National Election Study

there is substantial opposition to adoption by same-sex couples among black evangelicals, as well as among other African American and Latino Protestants. As was the case with whites, African American and Latino evangelicals are less likely than others to have an openly gay or lesbian friend or family member, and African American evangelicals are as likely as white fundamentalists to rate gays and lesbians at 0 degrees.

Members of all four minority religious traditions are liberal on gender roles and not noticeably different from whites. The exception is whether it is best if a woman tends home while the man achieves and earns wages; here African American evangelicals are substantially more liberal than white evangelicals are, perhaps because African Americans are more likely to know strong women who have raised their children without support from their fathers.

Table 2.5 shows the positions of these religious constituencies on other political issues. Only a minority of all four groups identify as conservative, and a very small portion of African Americans are Republicans. Partisanship is a significant barrier to mobilizing these communities, because the

Christian Right has allied itself closely with the Republican party (Robinson, 2006).

All four groups are less supportive of the Iraq war, a difference that is again primarily explained by partisanship. All four groups are slightly less likely than whites are to support torture of suspected terrorists, although the differences are small.

On economic issues, there are large gaps between white evangelicals and all four religious communities. All four groups take generally liberal positions on economics, with Latino Protestants slightly more conservative than the other three communities. Finally, all four groups are more likely than white evangelicals (and whites more generally) are to support aid to African Americans, and less likely to oppose national gun control legislation.

African American Protestants are even more likely than whites to favor decreases in immigration, perhaps because they perceive immigrants as economic competition. In contrast, less than one-third of either Latino religious community takes this view.

### Issue Groups in the Target Constituency

How likely is it that the Christian Right might make significant gains among white and black evangelicals, white mainline Protestants, and white Catholics, or among African Americans and Latinos? In part this depends on the issue agenda of the movement. Taking positions on many issues allows any group or movement to perhaps find a few new members who care deeply about one issue but not others, but also risks losing members who disagree strongly on one or more issues.

One important barrier to engaging African Americans and many Latinos is the close connection between the Christian Right and the conservative wing of the Republican Party. In 2008 black support for George Bush was so low in most surveys that we could not be statistically confident that it was not 0 percent. In December Gallup showed 7 percent of African Americans approved of Bush's presidency, as did only 19 percent of Latinos. These ratings were partially based on Bush's policies, but are more generally deeply rooted in party images relating to civil rights and programs to help the disadvantaged. It is inconceivable that a sizable group of African Americans would rally to a movement that works exclusively within the GOP. But African Americans can and have worked with the Christian Right on specific issues.

There is considerable support in each religious constituency (except for the white unaffiliated) for some of the key values of the movement. A majority of all religious groups believed that newer lifestyles cause societal breakdown, and in other surveys general phrases such as "family values" garner very large majority support. A majority of Americans support other Christian Right positions not included in the survey, such as public displays of religious symbols and even teaching creationism in addition to evolution in public schools.

Within each of these communities there are many respondents who oppose abortions under at least some circumstances, and other surveys show that large majorities oppose funding abortions and support restrictions such as parental notification, waiting periods, and bans on "partial birth" abortion. But there is no majority support among any faith tradition to ban all abortions, even among those who attend church regularly. Similarly, a majority of all religious traditions oppose same-sex marriage, but only a minority would also ban civil unions, and smaller minorities oppose antidiscrimination laws and military service for sexual minorities. Thus the Christian Right would have a small potential constituency beyond fundamentalists if it took strong stands on abortion and gay rights, and larger support if it took more moderate positions.

Perhaps more troubling for the Christian Right is that in many of these religious traditions, younger Americans are more liberal than their elders on many key issues on the agenda, especially gay and lesbian rights. Table 2.6 shows the correlations between age and attitudes for each of the white religious groups. Positive correlations indicate that younger members of these traditions are more progressive.

The data in this table do not bode well for the contemporary Christian Right. Among white evangelicals, mainline Protestants, and Catholics, younger people are less likely to believe that new lifestyles lead to social breakdown, and among all four groups they are more likely to believe that we should tolerate those with different values.

In all four groups, younger people are more supportive of GLBT rights. Younger fundamentalists are more supportive than their elders were of allowing gays and lesbians to serve openly in the military, adopt children, and marry, and rate gays and lesbians more warmly on a feeling thermometer. The correlations are even higher among other evangelicals. Support for antidiscrimination laws protecting GLBT citizens is almost universal among younger evangelicals. The generational differences in affect are striking:

TABLE 2.6 Correlations Between Key Christian Right Issues and Age, White Religious Groups

| | Fundamentalist | Other Evangelical | Mainline Protestants | Catholic |
|---|---|---|---|---|
| Newer lifestyles cause societal breakdown | .02 | .19** | .14** | .18** |
| Tolerate those with different values | .19** | .27** | .21** | .32** |
| Gay/lesbian antidiscrimination | .01 | .29** | .03 | .08 |
| Gay/lesbian in military | .14* | .22** | .09* | .02 |
| Gay/lesbian adoption | .28** | .26** | .21** | .37** |
| Same-sex marriage | .21** | .38** | .23** | .31** |
| Affect for gays and lesbians | .25** | .27** | .24** | .28** |
| Better if man achieves | .30** | .44** | .33** | .23** |
| Affect for feminists | .02 | .10 | .02 | .09 |
| Abortion | .07 | .10 | -.01 | .20* |
| Abortion without oldest cohort | .05 | -.23 | -.21* | -.18* |

*= Probability of this result by chance is less than 5%.
**= Probability of this result by chance is less than 1%.

evangelicals under thirty years of age assign a feeling thermometer score of 58 on average to gays and lesbians, above the neutral 50 degrees. Those over sixty, in contrast, assign an average score of 32 degrees.

Among Catholics and mainline Protestants, younger people are also more supportive of GLBT rights, but older members of these traditions are so supportive of antidiscrimination laws and military service that the correlations are low.

Younger members of all faith traditions are less likely to believe that it is better if the man achieves outside the home while the woman tends the house. The correlation is again highest among evangelicals. Here nearly 50 percent of those over age sixty think that women should remain housewives, compared to only 10 percent of those under age forty-five. There are no generational differences in affect toward feminists.

The one key Christian Right policy about which the young are not consistently more progressive than their parents is abortion, and it is an important exception to the rule. Here the correlations are complicated, because younger and older citizens are less pro-choice than those who grew up during the 1960s and 1970s. The distinctiveness of younger Americans is especially apparent when abortion attitudes are measured not by a single question, but rather by a series of questions about particular circumstances such as rape, fetal defect, and poverty. The second set of correlations is for those under the age of sixty, using a more expansive battery of abortion questions. Among evangelicals, mainline Protestants, and Catholics, younger people are decidedly less pro-choice than are the middle aged. This is also true for the unaffiliated. We will return to the abortion issue in Chapter 5.

## Conclusion

Although there are potential supporters for the Christian Right among several different religious constituencies, there is opposition to its social agenda in all groupings as well. Clearly, groups such as Focus on the Family do not speak for all Christians or even for all white evangelicals, but their social issue agenda does appeal to many conservatives across religious traditions. If the Christian Right were to fully mobilize those potential constituents, it would be a powerful movement in American politics. But there are barriers to building a movement that appeals to these diverse constituencies.

Well-organized social movement organizations exist that seek to mobilize these potential activists. The next chapter introduces these groups.

# 3

..........................................................................................

# The Christian Right in American Politics

You are not some small special interest group, that's the other side. You are America. You are the heart of America.

**Gary Bauer,** speaking to more than 100,000 Christian Right activists at the Mayday for Marriage Rally in Washington, D.C., October 10, 2004

ALTHOUGH THE CHRISTIAN Right movements of the 1920s, 1950s, and 1980s all sought to influence public policy, the contemporary Christian Right is a far more sophisticated movement that pursues a variety of strategies to achieve a variety of goals. The Christian Right seeks to influence Republican nominations and to influence or control the party apparatus, help the Republicans control the White House and Congress, achieve legislative victories in Congress and state legislatures, influence decisions by the U.S. Supreme Court, win control of school boards in order to influence school curricula, and win referenda in states and counties to implement its agenda. Movement leaders are very ambitious, and their multifront initiative is clearly the most sweeping in the history of American Christian conservatism.

This chapter first describes the key organizations of the contemporary Christian Right and discusses the special role that each plays in the movement. It then focuses on the various political activities of the Christian Right and assesses their impact.

## The Christian Right in the First Decade of the New Millennium

To understand the activities of the Christian Right, it is first necessary to identify the key actors in the movement. Although it is relatively easy to identify the most important national organizations, defining the precise boundaries of the Christian Right is more difficult. Moreover, much of the action taken in the 2000s was by state and even local organizations, not all of which had ties to national groups.

Many organizations were active in conservative Christian politics, but three stand out as the largest, most professional, and best organized. Focus on the Family, the Family Research Council, and Concerned Women for America have built sophisticated infrastructures to mobilize and inform their members and bolster state and local affiliates.

## Focus on the Family

During the past decade Focus on the Family stepped up its political activity to become the Christian Right's dominant organization. Founded by psychologist Dr. James Dobson, it is a media ministry headquartered in Colorado Springs, Colorado. It is aimed at strengthening the traditional family structure through conservative principles, and many of its materials are apolitical. Focus's Web site includes advice on discipline for parents, ideas on how to spice up one's marriage, and reviews of movies and books.

As noted in Chapter 2, Focus on the Family has laid off several hundred staff in the past few years, and in 2009 it had a budget shortfall of $8 million. In June 2009 Focus sold "Love Won Out"—its department committed to helping individuals leave homosexuality—to another ministry organization. But the mission work of Focus is still substantial. The organization sends out 2.6 million pieces of mail each month, along with books, tapes, and videos to thousands of people daily without charge (although donation amounts are suggested). It also publishes a number of magazines, which reach a half million subscribers. Finally, Focus maintains a significant presence on the Internet and e-mails nearly 4 million newsletters a month in addition to nearly 6 million e-mails to its supporters.

Until early 2009, Focus was chaired by Dr. James Dobson. The liberal interest group People for the American Way has said that Dobson was "perhaps the most influential right-wing Christian leader in the country, with a huge and loyal following that he can reach easily through an impressive media empire" (www.pfaw.org). *Time* magazine named Dobson one of the twenty-five most influential evangelicals in 2005. Dobson's rhetoric is uncompromising and ideological and frequently at odds with the pragmatic language preferred by Republican operatives. "My goal is not to see the Republican Party prosper," he asserted, and if the party were to abandon its opposition to abortion and gay rights, he has said that he would "do everything I can to take as many people with me as possible."

In fact, in 2008 Dobson contemplated the idea of supporting a third-party candidate in the event that the Republican and Democratic parties both put forward pro-choice nominees. "You hear this a lot now, they talk about the lesser of two evils, choose the lesser. The only problem with that is if you choose the lesser of two evils, you've still chosen evil," he said at the Values Voter Summit in Washington, D.C., before the primary elections began.

Focus is a tax-exempt Christian ministry, but Dobson has long been politically active. Dobson was a perennial figure in the halls of Congress, lobbying with other Christian Right leaders. In 1998 he met with Republican leaders after threatening to "go nuclear" by encouraging his followers to sit out the 1998 election. After urging party leaders to focus on issues central to his group's agenda, he told a reporter for *U.S. News & World Report,* "I believe the leadership of the Republican party was listening."[1] His radio programs have long been loaded with political content and have featured Republican policymakers and candidates (Apostolidis, 2000). Numerous Republican heavyweights have made the pilgrimage to his office in Colorado Springs to seek his support, including 2008 presidential candidate Mitt Romney and former speaker of the House Newt Gingrich.

Focus has a network of forty state affiliates, many of which are also affiliated with the Family Research Council. The state affiliates are involved in public education and lobbying efforts. State affiliates vary in their activity; some produce ratings of state legislators, while others produce research reports on policy issues under debate in their state. These research reports are shared by state organizations, so a report produced in Michigan may be used by Virginia's Family Foundation to lobby state legislators, or it may be sent to activists in several states. In 2008 the California Focus affiliate was a crucial player in mobilizing voters on behalf of the ballot initiative that would amend the state constitution to define marriage as between one man and one woman. The national organization gave $657,000 to the cause. In many states the Focus chapter is the most effective Christian Right organization in the state. In some cases, current Focus affiliates were originally formed independently and were later invited to affiliate by Focus officials.

In the past several years Focus has launched major policy initiatives. In 1999 it helped sponsor a large campaign to change public opinion about homosexuality and to promote the "conversion" of gays and lesbians to heterosexuality. In 2004 and again in 2008, Focus took the lead in promoting efforts to ban same-sex marriage. During the George W. Bush administration, the organization also led the call for more conservative federal judges who might interpret the Constitution differently. However, its agenda is broader than these socio-moral issues, encompassing economic policy, environmental policy, welfare policy, and foreign policy.

In 2004 Dobson created Focus on the Family Action, a 501 (c)(4) for the parent organization. The branch has been active in elections ever since 2004 and conducts voter registration drives within churches. The organization supports candidates who oppose abortion rights and same-sex marriage. In 2004 Focus Action spent $256,025 to mail letters offering Dobson's endorsement of socially conservative GOP Senate candidates in four states: Mel Martinez in Florida, James DeMint in South Carolina, Thomas Coburn in Oklahoma, and John Thune in South Dakota.

It also distributed model sermons to churches to help pastors advise their congregants on how to properly vote their faith. In the 2005 fight over President Bush's judicial nominees, the group ran ads in sixteen states to pressure senators to support the "nuclear option" and bar filibusters of judicial nominees (Farrell and Mulkern, 2005). In late 2005 Focus on the Family Action ran newspaper ads across Michigan condemning Senator Debbie Stabenow (D-MI) for voting against the confirmation of John Roberts as chief justice of the U.S. Supreme Court.

During the 2008 election Dobson committed a radio broadcast to talking to the makers of Born Alive Truth, a 527 that aired anti-Obama advertisements on television. The ad featured a woman who was born after a failed abortion saying, "If Barack Obama had his way, I wouldn't be here." Focus on the Family Action spent $112,000 to air a radio version of the ad in Colorado.[2] Focus on the Family also posted on its Web page "Letter from 2012 from Obama's America," listing a series of predictions about Obama's first term in office that supporters of the religious right would find troublesome.[3] After Obama took office, Focus on the Family Action spent more than $400,000 on a media campaign aimed at defeating the Democratic Party's efforts to reform health care.

Focus became the center of attention in the period leading up to Super Bowl LXIV in 2010, when it was announced that it had purchased a thirty-second spot featuring Heisman Trophy winner Tim Tebow. CBS had previously rejected "advocacy" ads during the event, and liberals denounced the network in advance for what they assumed would be a strongly pro-life message. Tebow's mother had ignored medical advice to seek an abortion and was a strong pro-life advocate.

The actual ad did not engage in political advocacy, however. Tebow's mother called her son a miracle baby who "almost didn't make it into the world." She hugged her son, who then playfully "tackled" his mother. The $2.5 million spot did not mention abortion, and instead directed viewers to the Focus on the Family Web site for a more complete version of the story.

One survey after the Super Bowl reported that only 38 percent of viewers recognized the ad as having a pro-life message, and the advertisement did not significantly change viewer attitudes on abortion.[4]

After stepping down as chairman of Focus on the Family in 2009, Dobson ended his radio program at Focus in early 2010 and made plans to launch a new radio show, with his son as cohost. Some speculated the move was necessary because Dobson hopes to have his son take over his program, and his son's divorce makes it impossible for him to do this within the framework of Focus on the Family (Goodstein, 2010). Others suggested that Dobson was eased out by Focus's board of directors, who viewed Dobson's political activity as a distraction from the ministry (Barna, 2010).

Though Dobson and the new president, Jim Daly, have maintained that Dobson's departure was part of a transitional plan, the differences between the two men's public personas are stark. Although Dobson almost exclusively worked within the Republican Party, Daly has attempted a more inclusive approach, including praising Obama for his commitment to his family and attending a 2009 White House event celebrating fatherhood. Dobson routinely made public endorsements of candidates as a private citizen; when Daly was asked why he would not endorse candidates as Dobson did, he said, "I don't think that's helpful" (Simon, 2010).

Perhaps to ease Dobson's departure, Focus contributed $1 million to his new radio show. Under Focus, Dobson's program attracted about 1.5 million listeners on 1,000 radio stations worldwide. In addition to the radio program, Dobson writes a syndicated column that is carried by 400 newspapers. He also had plans in early 2010 to create a new tax-exempt charity. Both the charity and Dobson's new radio show would likely compete with Focus for financial contributions.

The future of Focus on the Family without Dobson is unclear. In 2010 Focus on the Family Action began an initiative to mobilize twenty-somethings into social conservative politics. As of this writing, the initiative consisted of a Web site designed to inform young people about political issues and solicit feedback about concerns facing the future generation. With Daly at the helm, Focus's political efforts are likely to be softer and more inclusive than under Dobson's tenure. In the short term, the organization as a whole has chosen to focus primarily on its ministry and to deemphasize politics. But many Focus on the Family supporters are political activists, and by the next presidential election, it is possible that Focus will be a major player.

## Family Research Council

Dobson helped create the Family Research Council (FRC) in 1982, and for a time the FRC was the political arm of Focus on the Family. In 1992 the FRC split from Focus because of IRS concerns, but the two organizations remained linked in many ways. The policy agenda of the FRC is very similar to that of Focus, and some state organizations are affiliates of both. Focus and FRC cooperate closely in their lobbying efforts.

The FRC is now a tax-exempt educational organization that is heavily involved in lobbying national and state governments. As a tax-exempt organization, the FRC cannot endorse or support candidates directly. Instead, it produces policy reports that are designed to shape the policy debate, help create a legislative agenda for Christian Right activists, and assist movement activists in lobbying government. It provides information on everything from stem cells and biotechnology to women's health to family economics.

In 2003 Tony Perkins became president of the Family Research Council. Perkins is one of the youngest Christian Right leaders currently on the scene and the only one to have held prior electoral office. Prior to heading the FRC, Perkins served as a state representative in Louisiana, where he authored and passed the nation's first covenant marriage law. His political skills make Perkins well suited to coalition building in the Christian Right movement, and the FRC is positioning itself as a key player in future Christian Right politics.

The Family Research Council played a pivotal role in the formation of the proposed federal marriage amendment in 2004 that would ban same-sex marriage. Positioned in Washington, D.C., the FRC strategically built a coalition to legally define marriage as between one man and one woman at the federal level and also led the Christian Right's efforts to ban same-sex marriage and civil unions in many states.

The FRC has a legislative lobbying arm called FRC Action, which helps coordinate grassroots activities and direct lobbying. In 2005 and 2006 FRC Action worked with Focus on the Family Action to host "Justice Sunday" events at churches across the nations, which were designed to place pressure on Senate Democrats threatening to filibuster conservative judicial nominees. During the debate over health-care reform in 2009 and 2010, FRC Action organized online town hall meetings, Webcasts with national leaders, and fund-raising efforts to oppose the Democratic Party's goals. FRC Action is also the chief sponsor of the Values Voter Summit held every fall in

Washington, D.C. Activists come from all over the nation to hear from candidates and conservative leaders. It has become a must-stop for prospective Republican presidential candidates. The format is very similar to "Road to Victory" conferences formerly held by the Christian Coalition in the 1990s. FRC Action also has a PAC, which was created immediately prior to the 2008 election to support pro-life candidates and oppose the Obama campaign. It is unclear how active the PAC will be in future elections.

## Concerned Women for America

The grandmother of the contemporary Christian Right is Concerned Women for America (CWA). Founded in 1979 by Beverly LaHaye, CWA today still resembles in some ways the fundamentalist organizations of the 1970s, as the messages of its direct mail and newsletters are those of a moral crusade rather than a political movement. Yet unlike those earlier groups, CWA has appealed beyond a narrow fundamentalist base; its local chapters include evangelicals, mainline Protestants, and Catholics. Moreover, from its inception CWA built grassroots organizations such as women's prayer meetings and Bible study groups, unlike most early fundamentalist groups, which focused exclusively on national direct-mail lists. Indeed, it is not uncommon to find several thriving local chapters without a state chapter to coordinate them. In 2010 CWA claimed to have 500 prayer/action chapters and a membership list of roughly a half million, although these numbers have not changed in several years, and some believe that membership numbers are much lower.[5] The special strength of CWA is grassroots lobbying. Its members meet with national, state, and local officials in district offices, write letters, and make phone calls to pressure policymakers.

CWA moved to Washington, D.C., in 1985 and established a national office and lobbying staff, but it remains a decentralized organization. Through matching grants from major corporations, the organization managed to maintain a focused presence in all congressional districts that enabled it to mobilize grassroots action in the 1970s and 1980s (Moen, 1992).

CWA once had a strong legal arm, and it provided legal assistance in many high-profile cases, including the Tennessee school textbook controversy, popularly referred to as "Scopes 2" (Bates, 1993), but it has discontinued this effort to focus on activities that use its grassroots resources more effectively. The organization has an affiliated research foundation called the

Beverly LaHaye Institute, whose president, Janet Crouse, is active in writing, speaking, and debating feminist leaders.

CWA has sought to position itself as the conservative Christian alternative to the National Organization for Women (NOW). On a few issues, such as trafficking in women and, to a certain extent, pornography, CWA actually cooperates with feminist groups. On most issues, though, the group takes strongly antifeminist positions and frequently depicts NOW as its political nemesis and NOW's agenda as being harmful to women. In 2005, in response to the nomination of Harriet Miers to the Supreme Court, CWA expressed concern that Miers had helped to initiate a women's studies lecture series at Texas Christian University Law School, where "the lecturers have been women who espouse a radical theory of feminism." The group questioned whether Miers might "share the feminist theory that lecturers have presented" (LaRue, 2005). Bush withdrew the nomination immediately after CWA officially announced its opposition to the appointment.

Over the years CWA has accumulated a staff of highly skilled women (and a few men) who run CWA's research, publicity operations, and lobbying. Wendy Wright, CWA's president since 2006, has become a strong media presence on national television and radio shows. *Washingtonian* magazine named her among "The 100 Most Powerful Women of Washington" in 2006. CWA has also been active in international politics and has been officially recognized by the United Nations as a nongovernmental organization (NGO). It has sent representatives to the World Summit for Children and the World Conference on Racism, hoping to shape policy consistent with its core principles (Buss and Herman, 2003). In the late 2000s CWA faced financial crises along with many other organizations. It reduced its staff, and especially curtailed the development of new material for its Web page.

CWA's founder, Beverly LaHaye, is the only Christian Right leader from the 1970s to have sustained a viable political organization that has become more effective over time. She has become one of the best-known figures of the movement and is the author of many books written for evangelical Christian women. Beverly is the wife of Timothy LaHaye, who is coauthor of the Left Behind book series. The series has sold more than 65 million books and made the LaHayes multimillionaires. Timothy LaHaye was instrumental in founding the Moral Majority and has taught classes at Jerry Falwell's Liberty University. Together the LaHayes have made a mark on the contemporary Christian Right movement and have been called the "evangelical power couple . . . [who] rank as four-star generals to many conservative Christians" (White, 2001). Their reputation contributes to the CWA's stature in Christian conservative circles. Although Beverly stepped down as president in 2005, she remains active in writing and lecturing.

U.S. Representative Michele Bachmann (R-MN), a conservative evangelical, gives credit to CWA and the LaHayes for much of her political knowledge. After being a supporter of CWA for many years, Bachman has said she was called by God to run for Congress in 2006. Christian Right groups mobilized their supporters for her 2008 reelection campaign, in which she received national attention for calling then-presidential candidate Obama's views "anti-American."

## *The Christian Coalition*

In the 1990s the most visible organization of the Christian Right was the Christian Coalition. Founded by televangelist Pat Robertson from the remains of his failed presidential bid in 1988, the group flourished under the astute leadership of Ralph Reed, a young Republican activist. The organization sought primarily to change policies by changing politicians and spent most of its resources on a massive voter mobilization effort. The organization claimed to distribute tens of millions of voter guides in 1992, 1994, and 1996, primarily in conservative white evangelical churches. The Coalition was more pragmatic than other Christian Right groups and generally supported Republican candidates regardless of their positions on social issues. It fielded an ecumenical and highly skilled lobbying staff in the early 1990s.

When Ralph Reed departed, the organization began a rapid decline. Without the restraining hand of Reed, Robertson quickly became embroiled in a series of controversial public statements that disillusioned key activists. When Robertson announced, without first consulting with state chairs, that it was impossible to impeach Bill Clinton, many resigned. When Robertson later appeared to partially defend China's forced abortion policy in a televised interview, most of the remaining state chairs resigned. With the hiring of Roberta Combs as the organization's president, many of the group's most talented personnel left. Many former employees credit Combs with destroying what remained of the Christian Coalition. Richard Cizik, then director of public policy for the National Association of Evangelicals, proclaimed the organization "moribund" in 2005 (Duin, 2005). By 2006 the national organization was reportedly $2 million in debt, and creditors from a number of states were pressing claims (Cooperman and Edsall, 2006).

In July 2006 Rev. Joel C. Hunter, pastor of a Florida megachurch, was named the group's president-elect. Wishing to appeal to a larger evangelical constituency, Hunter sought to expand the agenda of the group beyond social issues like abortion and same-sex marriage to include fighting global warming and combating poverty. But initial reports suggesting the organization would be receptive to such a change proved incorrect, and after meeting resistance from the board, Hunter left the organization that November. However, Hunter never left the national spotlight and went on to make a name for himself as a moderate evangelical willing to work across party lines. Though a social conservative, Hunter led a prayer at the 2008 Democratic National Convention and was appointed to President Obama's Advisory Council on Faith-Based and Neighborhood Partnership in 2009.

Meanwhile, the Christian Coalition as a national entity continued to flounder. The Christian Coalition of Iowa, one of the most active chapters, broke off relations with the national body, saying it "found it impossible to continue to carry a name that in any way associated us with this national organization" (Cooperman and Edsall, 2006). The organization is now known as the Iowa Christian Alliance, and it maintains relations with other former state Coalition affiliates, but not with the national headquarters. Yet in other states, such as Florida, the Christian Coalition affiliates remain active in elections, distributing voter guides and working on ballot initiatives.

### Other Organizations

Several other organizations are active, although they lack a strong grassroots presence. The Reverend Donald Wildmon founded the **American Family Association** (AFA), formerly known as the National Federation for Decency. His son, Tim Wildmon, is now chair and president. The AFA focuses on organizing boycotts of sponsors of television programs that contain excessive sex or violence or that contain an anti-Christian bias. It also became involved in battles over school curricula. The AFA has a radio program, a foundation, and a legal arm. Estimates of the membership of the AFA vary; it once claimed nineteen state affiliates but now lists only ten on its Web site. AFA runs on a $20 million budget and has 175 employees.

The group most active in battles over public schools is the Citizens for Excellence in Education (CEE), headed by Robert Simonds. The CEE's orig-

inal goal was to rid the public schools of texts that teach evolution and secular humanism by working within the system. It was active in elections,
supporting school board members who held conservative positions. But in
recent years the CEE adopted "Rescue 2010," a new strategy that calls all
Christians to exit the public school system and start a school in every church
facility by the year 2010 because "the price in human loss, social depravity
and the spiritual slaughter of our young Christian children is no longer acceptable (and certainly never was!)."[6] CEE's rhetoric is confrontational: in
a letter outlining the new strategy, Simonds explains, "We must go back to
what worked best for America. The only way to do this is to privatize all
public education. Secularists, atheists and homosexuals could have their
own schools, but they could not force tax-payers to subsidize their schools."[7]

**Vision America** is a group designed to inform and mobilize pastors. Baptist pastor Rick Scarborough founded the organization in 1994 and serves
as its president. Vision America provides pastors with the legal "do's and
don'ts" about political activity in the church and hosts Pastor Policy brief-
ings across the nation. The organization encourages pastors to be politically
active and to advise their congregants about public policy on a routine basis.
Scarborough is increasingly featured in media reports about Christian conservative activism. He was one of the few Christian Right leaders to endorse
Gov. Mike Huckabee prior to his winning the Iowa caucuses in 2008. He
hosts a daily radio program broadcast in his home state of Texas.

One of the oldest surviving Christian Right groups is **Eagle Forum**,
headed by Phyllis Schlafly.[8] Founded in 1972, Eagle Forum was quite effective in fighting the proposed Equal Rights Amendment (ERA) to the U.S.
Constitution. Throughout the 1970s a majority of Americans favored the
amendment, but through well-organized grassroots lobbying, Eagle Forum
and other groups managed to defeat the amendment in state legislatures
across the country. After that Eagle Forum shrank in size, but it remains active in opposing efforts to add equal rights amendments to state constitutions and in opposing legal abortion. Over the past several years Eagle
Forum has become increasingly involved in educational issues, opposing
sex education in schools. The group claims to have affiliates in forty-five
states, and its political action committee spent more than $200,000 in the
2008 election cycle supporting pro-life federal candidates. Schlafly is a longtime conservative activist who has spent much of her adult life traveling the
country arguing that women should remain at home with their children.
While not explicitly opposing President Bush's decision to select a woman

for the second Supreme Court vacancy in 2005, the Eagle Forum did not support the selection of Harriet Miers. Executive Director Jessica Echard asserted, "If it's going to be a woman, we expected an equal heavyweight to Ruth Bader Ginsburg and her liberal stance, and we did not get that in Miss Miers" (Baker and Balz, 2005).

The **Christian Defense Coalition** was established in 1991 in Washington, D.C., by Randall Terry, along with Dr. George Grant, Jay Sekulow, and the Rev. Patrick Mahoney, to challenge Christians to live out their faith in the public sphere through demonstrations and protests. The group is informal and works with a small number of activists across the country to stage demonstrations, similar to those first practiced by an earlier pro-life group, **Operation Rescue**. Known for its inflammatory techniques, in 2008 the group ran a campaign called "Barack Obama: The Abortion President" and conducted a news conference in front of the Senate office building where Obama's office was located.

The **Traditional Values Coalition**, headed by the Reverend Louis Sheldon, has centered its activity on issues relating to gay rights, although it also takes a pro-life position on abortion and is involved in attempts to alter public school curricula. The group was involved in the Oregon and Colorado initiatives that proposed constitutional amendments to limit antidiscrimination laws against gays and lesbians, and it worked to reject a health education curriculum for California public schools that discussed issues such as homosexuality and AIDS. In response to public opinion polls suggesting the public is becoming more accepting of gay rights, the group's executive director said in a news release, "Jesus didn't ask for a 'show of hands' at the Sermon on the Mount. We, His followers, should not ask America to vote on which of his teachings they choose to obey."

A number of groups have formed in recent years around the same-sex marriage issue. By 2010 two organizations had taken center stage at the national level. Founded in 2007, the **National Organization for Marriage** (NOM) is a 501(c)(4) nonprofit organization that lobbies and builds grassroots campaigns in support of traditional marriage—that is, in opposition to same-sex marriage—at the state and national levels. Through its political action committee, NOM Marriage PAC, the group is directly involved in elections and supports candidates opposed to same-sex marriage. Finally, the NOM Education Fund, a 501(c)(3), supports research in defense of limiting marriage to heterosexual couples and strives to make information available to religious and political leaders. NOM received significant media attention in 2009 when it ran an ad featuring Miss California expressing support for traditional marriage during the televised Miss USA pageant; she had been criticized in the media by gay activists, and the ad depicted her as a victim of mainstream media's bias in favor of same-sex marriage. (The ad was later pulled, however, after risqué photos of Miss California surfaced, calling her integrity into question. She was later fired for failing to fulfill the responsibilities of the position.)

The other prominent traditional marriage group is the **Alliance for Marriage**, founded by Matt Daniels. The Alliance for Marriage takes a similarly broad approach and seeks to strengthen marriage by supporting public policy that would reduce the tax burden on heterosexual married couples with children and eliminate aspects of welfare programs that penalize married recipients. The Alliance for Marriage has remained somewhat distinct from Christian Right groups thanks to Daniels, who is committed to remaining nonpartisan in his approach to increasing the number of "intact" homes. Daniels went out of his way to recruit an ethnically diverse board of directors, which has contributed to the racial diversity evident in the movement opposed to same-sex marriage.

The same-sex marriage issue has given Christian Right groups the opportunity to partner with racial minorities. The Freedom Federation is a coalition of multi-ethnic organizations committed to traditional values. It was created in 2009. Its founding document, "The Declaration of American Values," opposes abortion and same-sex marriage and defends traditional Judeo-Christianity in the public sphere. The federation includes many of the groups mentioned above in addition to groups not typically part of the Christian Right base, such as the National Hispanic Christian Leadership Conference and Brotherhood Organization of a New Destiny (BOND) and Catholic Online. It claims to represent 5 million people. It took on opposition to health-care reform as its first issue in 2009.

### The Fellow Travelers

Several organizations are best considered as being separate from the Christian Right, although they frequently share resources with Christian Right groups and back the same candidates. Most of these groups take strongly conservative positions on political issues and link those positions in some way to religious belief. Yet most political scientists would not classify them as part of the Christian Right, for various reasons.

One religious organization that shares some but not all of the Christian Right's policy goals is the National Association of Evangelicals (NAE), which represents sixty denominations and more than 45,000 evangelical churches. The NAE's mission is primarily religious and includes facilitating cooperative ministry among evangelicals in the United States. Although the NAE serves as something like a trade association of evangelical denominations, the organization has played an increasingly public role in policy issues. In 2005 the NAE brought together evangelical leaders to produce a document titled "For the Health of the Nation: An Evangelical Call to Civic Responsibility." The document outlined NAE's position on general policy issues, many of which overlap those of the Christian Right, and others, such as the evangelical brand of environmentalism known as "**Creation Care**," which do not. Similarly, the NAE published, "An Evangelical Declaration Against Torture: Protecting Human Rights in an Age of Terror" in 2007, a topic few Christian Right organizations were willing to address under the Bush administration.

The organization experienced internal turmoil during the 2000s. In 2007 Rev. Leigh Anderson was appointed president after Rev. Ted Haggard admitted to using illegal drugs and hiring a male prostitute over the course of many years. During this period Richard Cizik, director of public policy, pushed for stronger statements about environmental protection and sought to link the issue to defense of life. Cizik quarreled publicly with Dobson, who has declared global warming a liberal hoax. In 2008 Cizik resigned under pressure after endorsing civil unions for same-sex couples in an interview with National Public Radio. He has since formed a new association that seeks to mobilize moderate evangelical activism.

Perhaps the most numerous and intensely organized of the fellow traveler groups are the hundreds of national, state, and local pro-life groups. The National Right to Life Committee and hundreds of other pro-life groups oppose abortion rights and usually tie that position to religious belief. Yet pro-life groups are not generally identified with the Christian Right because a sizable minority of their supporters are not conservatives. In an effort to attract the widest possible audience, most pro-life groups focus their attention solely on abortion and take no official position on any other issue, including contraception, thus allowing liberals who oppose most of the Christian Right agenda to join pro-life groups. The most notable set of liberal pro-life activists come from the "seamless garment" network of organizations that oppose not only abortion but also the death penalty and nuclear weapons and advocate increased spending on child welfare programs.[9] Thus, although nearly all Christian Right activists are pro-life, not all pro-life activists support the Christian Right. Yet in elections in which candidates take divergent views on abortion, the two sets of organizations often work together, and their activists frequently mingle as they volunteer on behalf of pro-life candidates.

One large and growing segment of the public that provides substantial support to the Christian Right is homeschool advocates. Many Christian conservatives strongly object to elements of the public school curriculum, and some educate their children at home rather than send them to public schools. Like the pro-life movement, the homeschool movement tends to focus on a narrow set of issues to attract a wide diversity of membership. Moreover, there exists a small but important segment of the homeschool community that is politically liberal—indeed, some parents homeschool their children to prevent them from hearing nationalistic and pro-capitalist values in the classroom. Yet the homeschool constituency for the Christian Right is large and growing. In 1993 Michael Farris, a homeschool advocate, successfully mobilized this constituency in Virginia to win the Republican nomination for lieutenant governor before losing the general election.

Farris founded the **Home School Legal Defense Association** (HSLDA), which is a nonprofit advocacy group seeking to defend the right of parents to direct the education of their children as they see fit. HSLDA takes a particular interest in training young evangelicals to be politically active. A division of the organization, Generation Joshua, is aimed at direct political activism. According to its Web site, Generation Joshua equips homeschooled teens with the skills necessary to campaign actively for candidates who have been "prayerfully" selected by HSLDA's board of directors. Homeschoolers worked for President Bush in 2004 and for Gov. Mike Huckabee in the 2008 primaries. "We believe that some day homeschooled young people will help reverse Roe v. Wade [and] stop same-sex marriage," wrote then-HSLDA president Michael Farris in a statement that launched Generation Joshua (quoted in Grove, 2004). All candidate campaign activity is funded by the group's political action committee, HSLDA-PAC. Farris and the HSLDA's board of directors founded Patrick Henry College in 2000, a four-year college catering specifically to Christian homeschooled students. Farris now serves as its chancellor.

There is also significant overlap in the membership of the Christian Right and pro-gun groups. The National Rifle Association (NRA) had at one point a presence at Christian Coalition meetings—as exhibitor, advertiser, or both. Especially in the South, God and guns are forces often seen moving as one.[10] Strategist Chuck Cunningham was once the issues director for the Christian Coalition, and gun control issues appeared in Christian Coalition voter guides during that time. Yet many Christian Right activists, especially in the North, favor gun control, and many NRA activists take **libertarian** positions on social issues such as abortion and homosexuality.

The relationship the Christian Right has with the **Fellowship Foundation**— a group that sponsors the annual National Prayer Breakfast and hosts Bible studies and social events for political elites—is unclear, though there is likely overlap in their agendas and membership. The organization is known as "the Fellowship" and is incredibly secretive (Sharlet, 2009). It has no Web site, and employees (referred to as "associates") are reluctant to talk about the organization except to say its mission is to show the love of Jesus to world leaders. Those affiliated with the group generally subscribe to the evangelical faith and would agree with the Christian Right's position on abortion and marriage. Although the group does not have a registered lobbyist and is not concerned with grassroots mobilization, it clearly has inside access to politicians who attend Fellowship gatherings. The organization came under scrutiny in 2009 when it was revealed that South Carolina Governor Mark Sanford and Sen. John Ensign (R-NV) had engaged in extramarital affairs and had once lived in a house owned by the Fellowship.

The Christian Right is also distinct from the Tea Party movement, a somewhat inchoate mobilization whose final shape is difficult to see this early in its history. Many Tea Party activists are supporters of the Christian Right agenda and even members of those organizations, but there have been internal divisions within the Tea Party movement between libertarians and Christian conservatives. As one journalist remarked, you would be more likely to see activists waving "flags but not crosses" and interested in "reclaiming America for the Chamber of Commerce," rather than Christ (Waters, 2010). Nevertheless, Christian Right activists have used some Tea Party events for recruiting. For example, one state leader for Concerned Women invited fellow Tea Party activists to meetings to learn more about conservative thought.

A number of organizations combine right-wing religion and right-wing politics in ways that most Christian Right activists would find abhorrent. At the fringe of the gun community, the various militia groups that attracted attention after the Oklahoma City bombing frequently proclaim their Christian doctrine, but they are not part of the Christian Right movement, and most Christian Right activists oppose the militia groups. Many racist and anti-Semitic organizations claim a Christian grounding for their views, although their doctrine would be unpalatable to mainstream Christians. The Christian Identity Movement, for example, claims that Jews are the illegitimate spawn of Satan and that whites are the true Israelites (Barkun, 1994). The Christian Right leadership is unanimous in its condemnation of such extremist organizations.

## State and Local Organizations

Although national Christian Right organizations attract most of the media attention, each state has unique homegrown groups, which vary in their strength and longevity. In 1983 a local Ohio pastor founded Citizens for Community Values (CCV) as an antipornography group. Since then it has expanded to address other pro-family issues and serves as a model for other state organizations. There is now a CCV of Indiana and a Long Island CCV. The president of CCV, Phil Burress, ran the **Ohio Campaign to Protect Marriage** in 2004, an ad hoc coalition of Christian Right groups that worked to pass an amendment to the state constitution. He now has national name recognition as a Christian Right leader and advises groups across the country.

In many cases, state and local groups get significant aid from national groups. The American Family Association, for example, sent out mass e-mails to 60,000 supporters living in Ohio to encourage them to sign the petition needed to get same-sex marriage on the ballot in 2004 and to vote in November. Focus on the Family Action spent $20,000 on radio and newspaper advertisements against a civil-union bill at the Hawaii state legislature in 2009; the Hawaii Family Forum led opposition to the bill. The Hawaii Family Forum received Focus Action's "Family Champion Award" in 2009 for defeating the civil-union legislation.

Other examples of local groups advancing the Christian Right agenda include the Oregon Citizens Alliance (OCA), which spearheaded an effort to limit gay and lesbian rights by initiative and referenda.[11] The OCA played an important role in the state's Republican nomination politics for almost a decade and worked with the Christian Coalition and other groups to disseminate information before elections. It disbanded in 1998, but in 2004 a new group, the Defense of Marriage Coalition, formed and was successful in amending the state constitution to bar same-sex marriage. The contrast between these two Oregon organizations is instructive. OCA was primarily the tool of a single political activist and occasional candidate in Oregon, and this limited its possibilities. The Defense of Marriage Coalition, in contrast, sought to mobilize many churches across denominational and racial lines in Oregon and to downplay the personalities of the leadership. State-level organizations in the Christian Right, as in other movements, can flourish or wither depending on their leadership.

Often state groups are formed and then later become affiliates of national organizations. In Virginia the Family Foundation was created by Walter Barbee out of membership lists of a number of smaller local groups with diverse issue agendas. Barbee had fashioned a statewide organization and raised enough funds to hire a full-time state lobbyist when he was approached by Focus on the Family about becoming a state affiliate. In Michigan there are several strong, state-level Christian Right groups that have been active for many years, some of which have formed affiliations with national groups (Penning and Smidt, 2006).

In Fairfax County, Virginia, a dispute over the distribution of the gay advocacy newspaper *The Washington Blade* at public libraries led to the formation of a countywide organization. In 1992 Karen Jo Gounaud organized a local group of Christian parents to protest the *Blade* and demand its removal from public libraries. Her organization quickly drew advice and support from sympathetic Christian Right groups and expanded its agenda. The organization also sought to force libraries to provide parents with information on the books and tapes their children had checked out and to ban a gay library employee from wearing a pink gay pride triangle on his lapel, on the grounds that it advocated a criminal lifestyle.[12] In 1995 Gounaud founded Family Friendly Libraries, which incorporated her earlier group and expanded its reach.

The rapid development of this local organization headed by a previously apolitical homemaker is testimony to the solid grassroots networking of Christian Right groups. Gounaud received training from the Christian Coalition at a 1993 political activism seminar held in Manassas, Virginia. She also received advice from the American Family Association and support from key Republican county officials.[13] She soon had a large mailing list, access to a fax network, and other trappings of an institutionalized organization. Her organization is hardly unique, and indeed other local Christian

Right groups exist in Fairfax County. Across the country, many counties have affiliates of one or more of the three main Christian Right organizations, affiliates of one or more state-level groups, and one or more unique local organizations.

## Christian Right Social Movement Organizations and Leaders: Cooperation and Conflict

The Christian Right organizations described above all share a core of common issues and complaints, but they differ subtly in their explanation of events, their call for action, and their issue focus. Social movement organizations and leaders often cooperate on a particular issue, but they also compete; movement organizations seek to mobilize the same pool of potential supporters. That pool is large but finite, and although many activists join more than one group, their average financial contribution may decrease as the number they join increases. In a real sense, Christian Right groups compete for members and money. Perhaps more important, they compete for the attention of activists.

Each group offers a subtly different flavor of ideology, explanation, and agenda and seeks to form the movement around that vision. In the 1990s the Christian Coalition argued the case for pragmatism, for supporting all GOP candidates because the party is more likely to pass legislation favorable to the movement. The Family Research Council and Focus on the Family, in contrast, both promote a more uncompromising view and argue that Republicans have taken the movement for granted because it appears to lack an effective "exit strategy"—that is, the movement cannot threaten to leave the GOP coalition because its members are unlikely to support Democratic candidates, and third-party movements are seriously disadvantaged in American politics.

These fundamental differences carry over into legislative strategies, even when groups share similar goals. In 2004 there was disagreement over the wording of a national constitutional amendment to ban same-sex marriage. The FRC and Focus both argued that efforts to ban same-sex marriage would be derailed if the amendment also included language prohibiting civil unions. Although the leaders of Focus and the FRC oppose civil unions, they believed that the urgency of banning same-sex marriage necessitated a compromise. In contrast, CWA had long opposed civil unions and argued that the movement should not compromise in its opposition to all homosexual unions. They chose to support only an amendment that banned both same-sex marriage and civil unions.

Movement organizations and leaders do not always agree on the relative importance of various issues. Many Christian Right leaders in 2004 believed that the movement should focus primarily on stopping same-sex marriage because this was a relatively new issue, and they feared that gay rights groups might make rapid progress in the near future. Other Christian Right leaders continued to argue that abortion was a more important issue because they believe that abortion involves killing babies. In the end, money and volunteers flocked to newly formed groups that opposed same-sex marriage, and pro-life groups suffered a (perhaps temporary) decrease in resources.

The leaders of Christian Right groups also compete and do not always cooperate. When Pat Robertson ran for president in 1988, Jerry Falwell, head of the Moral Majority, endorsed then vice president George H. W. Bush. In 1999, when Gary Bauer sought the GOP nomination, Robertson made it clear that he backed Governor George W. Bush of Texas, and Falwell even refused to defuse a rumor linking Bauer with a sexual affair. And in 2008 there was substantial disagreement among organizations in supporting candidates in the GOP primaries.

This competition is not unusual in social movements—it happened in the civil rights and feminist movements as well. Moreover, competition does not mean that groups do not cooperate on many issues. In the late 1980s it was not unusual to see Ralph Reed traveling the halls of Congress with James Dobson, working together on an issue, even though the men disagreed on general strategy and tactics.

The **Arlington Group** is a coalition of Christian Right leaders that seeks to identify goals and coordinate strategy across groups. Members include James Dobson, Gary Bauer, Tony Perkins, and Phil Burress, among others. It was founded in 2002 and is primarily concerned with issues such as gay rights and abortion. Media credited the group for driving the effort beginning in 2004 to pass amendments to state constitutions banning same-sex marriage. Its meetings and deliberations are rather secretive, and in early 2010 the group had no active Web site.

## Members and Activists of the Christian Right

Although it is possible to estimate the membership for many of the groups just discussed, it is not easy to estimate combined total membership, because many of the same activists have joined several organizations. The Christian Right has formed a variety of organizations that specialize in particular tactics and particular issues. People most concerned with secular humanism in schools join the Citizens for Excellence in Education; those who want to combat the "radical gay agenda" might join the Traditional Values Coalition; those who wish to engage in electoral mobilization can do so through Focus on the Family Action; and those who wish to help prepare and disseminate research reports may choose to work for the Family Research Council.

But it is clear that many Christian Right activists are involved in more than one group, and a core of activists has multiple involvement. Thus the total number of activists is not as large as the sum of the membership totals of the various organizations. Political scientist John Green, who closely studies the Christian Right, estimated in 2000 that were as many as 4 million Christian Right members nationwide and possibly 150,000 activists who work in politics, but he believes the number of activists had decreased by as much as 25 percent in 2008.[14]

The activists themselves are generally well-educated, moderately affluent individuals who are distinctive primarily for their high levels of church attendance. They are disproportionately female, for there is a considerable talent pool of conservative Christian wives and mothers who remain out of the paid labor force for religious reasons. Many evangelical women who cannot justify taking on part-time employment find that political action is an important outlet for their energies and abilities.

Organizations communicate with their members in diverse ways. Most groups contact their members regularly by letter or e-mail, sharing information on pending legislation, the political process, activities of group leaders, and new issues being pursued, and usually asking for financial contributions in the process. Facebook and Twitter have also become popular means of communicating up-to-the-minute information to members. Dobson announced the decision to start a radio program with his son in 2010 as a status update on Facebook.

Most organizations also issue action alerts, which inform members of legislation under active consideration by some governmental body. Action alerts include explicit instructions and provide lists of officials to contact and talking points to argue. Most action alerts take the form of e-mails sent out two or three times a day when Congress is in session. These action alerts often contain links to longer Web page accounts, which may in turn contain information on contacting policymakers and links to allow members to contribute to the organization. Christian Right groups often maintain extensive Web pages, which provide research reports, video shorts, and information on a range of issues, along with ways to purchase materials and contribute to the groups (see Box 3.1).

Once members have been informed about issues, candidates, or events, they frequently share this information with others in their churches who may not be members or even necessarily supporters of the Christian Right. The frequent face-to-face interactions in churches provide an ideal opportunity to disseminate information, and in this way Christian Right arguments and issues have a much greater penetration than mere membership numbers would suggest (Wald, Owen, and Hill, 1988). Individuals who would never support the Family Research Council might nonetheless contact county school officials about the content of sex education classes or vote for a candidate whose views they shared. Moreover, many Christian conservatives receive information from a variety of Christian Right groups, although they are not members, and may use this information to guide their electoral behavior.

Compared with other social movements, such as the feminist and gay rights movements, the Christian Right has not paid particular attention to recruiting support from university students (Larson and Wilcox, 2005). None of the contemporary Christian Right organizations maintains chapters at college campuses, Christian or otherwise. Concerned Women for America has hosted student prayer groups, but they usually don't survive after the graduation of their leaders. The Christian Right appears to be depending on extra-collegiate programs to develop the next wave of the movement's leaders. The Family Research Council offers an internship program for college students and recent graduates, the Witherspoon Fellowship, which explores the philosophical roots of Christian involvement in the political process. Focus on the Family hosts a Focus Leadership Institute that includes courses on public policy. Focus on the Family Action launched Rising Voice in 2010 to mobilize young people into conservative political activism. A number of Christian Right leaders—Pat Robertson, Jerry Falwell, and Michael Farris—have actually started their own colleges with a commitment to teaching conservative principles, which may contribute to the future membership of the Christian Right. But with survey data suggesting young evangelicals as a whole are increasingly more liberal than older evangelicals, the movement's ability to mobilize young people remains questionable, which of course has implications for the strength of the movement in years to come.

BOX 3.1  The Christian Right and Technology

Although critics often charge that Christian conservatives are opposed to any form of modernism, the movement has always used the best technology available to spread its message. In the 1920s antievolution activists used printing presses to distribute fliers, published tracts and special newspapers, and held tent revivals. In the 1950s anticommunist groups used radio to communicate with fellow travelers. In the 1980s the Moral Majority used computers to organize a direct-mail campaign to fund its organization and used television to mobilize its base.

In the 1990s the Christian Right used technology as well as any movement in America. Its leaders used radio, television, and direct mail to reach their constituents, but their efforts were even more sophisticated than most. For example, direct-mail appeals were more carefully targeted to supporters based on their past responses to solicitations, and cable television provided programming for many market niches.

By 2010 Christian conservative groups had well-established Web sites, Facebook pages, and blogs designed to communicate with their constituents on a daily basis. For example, supporters of the Family Research Council can subscribe to "Action Alerts," weekly e-mails that inform recipients of the FRC's position on recent events in the nation's capital. Supporters can also subscribe to "Alerts" for their specific state. The organization's blog is updated multiple times a day when Congress is in session. And each fall the organization streams live footage of the annual Values Voter Summit online.

The Christian Right has successfully used the Internet to mobilize supporters, allowing constituents to "electronically" sign petitions and "attend" town hall meetings online, and urging them to e-mail their members of Congress. The Internet has also allowed Christian Right groups themselves to more quickly strategize and communicate with one another. Finally, most organizations now accept donations via the Web.

Web sites of Christian Right organizations:

| | |
|---|---|
| Focus on the Family | www.family.org |
| Focus on the Family Action | www.focusaction.org |
| Family Research Council | www.frc.org |
| Family Research Council Action | www.frcaction.org |
| Christian Coalition | www.cc.org |
| Vision America | www.visionamerica.us |

*(continues)*

---

(*continued*)

| | |
|---|---|
| Eagle Forum | www.eagleforum.org |
| American Family Association | www.afa.net |
| National Association of Evangelicals | www.nae.net |
| Citizens for Excellence in Education | www.nace-cee.org |
| Traditional Values Coalition | www.traditionalvalues.org |
| American Center for Law and Justice | www.aclj.org |
| Concerned Women for America | www.cwfa.org |
| Alliance for Marriage | www.afmus.org |
| National Organization for Marriage | www.nationformarriage.org |
| Freedom Federation | www.freedomfederation.org |
| Home School Legal Defense Association | www.hslda.org |
| American Center for Law and Justice | www.aclj.org |
| Susan B. Anthony List | www.sba-list.org |
| Christian Defense Coalition | www.christiandefensecoalition.com |

Web sites of anti–Christian Right organizations that monitor the movement:

| | |
|---|---|
| Interfaith Alliance | www.interfaithalliance.org |
| People for the American Way | www.pfaw.org |
| Americans United for Separation of Church and State | www.au.org |

---

## Christian Right Action in Electoral Politics

The Christian Right is active in a number of policy arenas and has pursued a variety of tactics to influence various kinds of governmental units. In general, the Christian Right has sought to influence the selection of political elites by working to help favored candidates win party nominations and then by helping them defeat their general election opponents. The movement has chosen a partisan strategy of working with the Republican Party instead of attempting to influence the policies of both parties. It has also sought to influence government leaders, including officials who are not supporters of the movement.

### The Nomination Process

Ever since the Christian Right reentered the political scene in the late 1970s, the groups have worked to help candidates win their party's nomination. In states where nominees are selected in caucuses or statewide conventions, these groups have had considerable success. In Virginia, for example, the Moral Majority sent hundreds of delegates to Republican nominating conventions in the early 1980s, and the Christian Coalition, Family Foundation (the local affiliate of the Family Research Council and Focus on the Family), and CWA did the same in the 1990s. In nearly all cases, the movement has been successful in helping nominate preferred candidates in Virginia. In states where nominees are selected by primary election, however, Christian Right groups have had mixed success (Green, 2000).

Christian Right involvement in nomination politics begins with candidate recruitment. Movement activists sometimes identify potential candidates from within their organizations and churches. They generally encourage a potential candidate to run for some local office and offer an array of services to help persuade the candidate to run. In the 1990s the Christian Coalition provided training for candidates, their campaign managers, and their campaign finance directors. The Madison Project trains campaign workers and state legislative candidates, and the Susan B. Anthony List trains pro-life women in many aspects of campaigning.

Candidate recruitment provides an invitation to struggle within the movement, for some activists prefer candidates who will take strong, uncompromising positions in support of the Christian Right agenda, whereas others prefer candidates who have a chance of winning. In general, movement leaders prefer the latter; many activists prefer the former. Thus movement leaders may recruit potential candidates who already serve in local or state office and have demonstrated a strong record of support for Christian Right policies, but who are not themselves members of the movement. These "outsider" candidates have a greater chance of winning than those recruited from within the movement.

Of course not all Christian Right candidates are recruited by movement leaders and activists. Some evangelicals say they hear a call from God to pursue public service, and over the past decade the movement has produced a number of "self-starter" candidates who hear a personal call to run for office. Although these individuals bring a great deal of enthusiasm to their candidacies, they generally bring little else. They lack experience in political office, assembling electoral coalitions, and raising money (Green, 2000). Generally they are extremely conservative and often unwilling to compromise their beliefs to win election. Self-starters therefore are prone to extreme statements or actions. For example, when the wife of Minnesota Republican Allen Quist died while she was pregnant, he had the fetus removed from her body and buried in her arms.[15] The gesture may have won him the undying support of some pro-life activists, but it surely alienated him from the majority of Minnesota voters. In recent years the Christian Right has begun to work to discourage candidacies by movement activists, preferring instead to back more experienced politicians who would support at least some of the movement's agenda.

After candidates are recruited, the movement can provide many resources for an intraparty nomination, including financial assistance, expertise, and access to a broad communication infrastructure. The most important resource, however, is voter mobilization. Voter mobilization in intraparty nomination contests is useful in all states, but statewide nomination rules make it more valuable in some states than in others. State parties can choose to select their nominees by primary election, convention, or caucus, and the Christian Right has far more success in influencing nominations in states that do not use primary elections. Statewide Christian Right groups, including CWA and the state affiliates of the Family Research Council and Focus on the Family, generally put together packets of information on how and where to vote in primary elections, where and when the caucus or convention will be held, and how to register to attend.

This information is crucial in states with caucuses or conventions, where few citizens know how to go about participating in the process. It is less useful in states with primary elections, where it is relatively easy to determine when and where to vote. Included in these information packets are profiles of various candidates, usually offered without an explicit group endorsement. However, a tacit endorsement is often signaled by the description of issue positions or even by the quality of the photos.

In the 2004 and 2008 elections, www.ivotevalues.com offered evangelicals, pastors, and church leaders easy access to such information. Run by Focus on the Family and FRC, a portion of the Web site's information was also mailed in convenient packets to local pastors. The packet included "a small-group and church leader's guide to a true patriotic legacy"—a five-point plan to influence government though the electoral process, each point supported by Bible passages.

Christian Right candidates may be opposed by party insiders, even if they have political experience. In Colorado in 2004, Republican congressman Bob Schaeffer and businessman Peter Coors squared off for the GOP nomination for the U.S. Senate. Both candidates took pro-life stances, and both endorsed a national constitutional amendment to ban same-sex marriage, but Christian conservatives rallied behind Schaeffer and were skeptical of Coors because his company, a brewery, offered benefits to partners of gay and lesbian employees and had insured abortions under the company's health plan. George W. Bush and other party insiders supported Coors, whose deep pockets were presumably a valuable asset. Coors won the primary election; however, Christian conservatives refused to help Coors in the general election, and he ultimately lost in a close contest (Larson, 2006).

In 2009 Family Research Council Action and Concerned Women for America joined with other conservative groups in backing a third-party candidate in a New York House of Representatives special election. The GOP nominee took moderate positions on the issues and eventually endorsed the Democratic candidate when it became obvious that she could not win. The Democratic candidate won the election, 49 to 46 percent, in a strongly Republican district.

In states with caucuses or conventions, the Christian Right not only can be a major player in nominations but can even dominate the process, for a determined voter mobilization campaign can swamp the opposition. In Virginia's open convention system, for example, Christian Right delegates were in solid control of the nomination process in both 1993 and 1994; however, in an open primary election for a 1998 Senate nomination they lost badly to moderate forces. In Minnesota in 1994, Allen Quist handily defeated the popular moderate incumbent, Arne Carlson, in the state convention. But Minnesota Independent Republicans ultimately selected their nominee by party primary, and Carlson defeated Quist by an overwhelming margin in the larger electoral arena.

In 2008 the Christian Right was a dominant force in the Republican Party in Iowa, a state famous for its early presidential caucus and particularly famous in 2008 for jump-starting Gov. Mike Huckabee's campaign. Christian conservatives in the state are known as savvy political operatives who rely on friendship networks to bring about strength in numbers (Conger and Ratcheter, 2006). Huckabee defeated Mitt Romney in Iowa despite being outspent by record margins and Romney's endorsement by many national party officials. Evangelical Christians constituted 60 percent of Iowa caucus goers, and they voted for Huckabee over Romney by a huge margin—in part because of Huckabee's roots as a Baptist preacher and in part because of their unease with Romney's Mormon faith (Campbell, Green, and Monson, 2009 ; Green and Silk, 2009).

Why is the Christian Right more influential in states with open caucuses and conventions than in states with primary elections? In most states the Christian Right represents a sizable Republican contingent but is clearly a minority. Participating in caucuses and conventions requires more effort than voting in a primary election, because caucus and convention meetings sometimes last for hours or even days, and participation requires knowledge of where the local meeting will be held. In states with caucuses and conventions, the Christian Right can win because its activists are more likely to make the extra effort to participate than are party moderates. In states with primary elections, however, voting is relatively easy, and moderate voters generally outnumber supporters of the Christian Right. Thus, the ongoing nomination struggles between Christian conservatives and party moderates often hinge on the party rules that dictate how candidates are chosen.

Because these rules are set by the state party committees, the Christian Right has frequently made efforts to gain working control of state parties. One way of measuring the influence of the religious right is to assess the percentage of each state's Republican Party committee who are members or supporters of the Christian Right *as perceived* by political elites. According to this methodology, in 2000 the Christian Right was dominant in eighteen states' Republican parties, and it was influential was twenty-six states (Conger and Green, 2002). By 2008 the number of state Republican parties with a strong Christian Right presence had decreased slightly, to fifteen, with another twenty-six state parties being moderately influenced by Christian Right groups.[16] (See Map 3.1.)

The Christian Right is influential in state Republican parties in parts of the South and Midwest but is far less influential in the Northeast. In part this reflects the presence of Christian conservatives, who provide the infantry for the intraparty battle. The Christian Right has also had great success in states in transition from Democratic to Republican majorities, perhaps because they contain fewer entrenched Republican elites, who resist its incursion into the party (Green, Guth, and Wilcox, 1998).

In states where the Christian Right has become an important party faction, party moderates and secular conservatives have reacted in diverse ways. Surveys of party activists have revealed that in some states, such as Minnesota and Virginia, the two factions have often expressed mutual hostility, with each preferring Democratic candidates to Republicans from the other

☐ – Low Influence    ▨ – Moderate Influence    ■ – High Influence

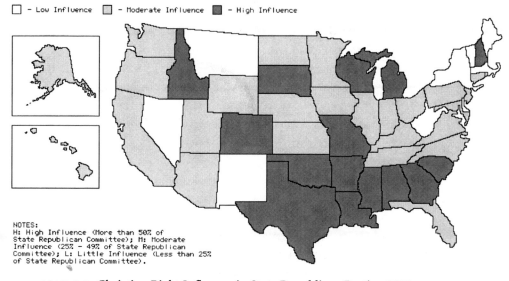

NOTES:
H: High Influence (More than 50% of
State Republican Committee); M: Moderate
Influence (25% – 49% of State Republican
Committee); L: Little Influence (Less than 25%
of State Republican Committee).

**MAP 3.1  Christian Right Influence in State Republican Parties, 2008**

faction of the party. In Colorado in 2004, for example, members of the Christian Right actually campaigned against a moderate Republican candidate for the state House of Representatives because she opposed school vouchers. Republican Rep. Ramey Johnson lost her seat to the Democratic challenger by only forty-one votes, so clearly the Christian Right campaign cost her the seat. After her loss, Johnson said the Republican Party in Colorado is participating in a "circular firing squad" (Bartels, 2004).

In Florida the Christian Right was described by one state Republican activist as a "necessary annoyance" (Wald and Scher, 2003). The movement has had success in electing social conservatives at the local level, but relatively little success in implementing its agenda statewide. Nonetheless, Christian Right groups regularly support primary challengers to moderate Republicans. In 2009 the outgoing head of the state Christian Coalition backed former state House speaker Marco Rubio's run against the more moderate Gov. Charlie Crist in the Republican primary for Senate. The intraparty battle grew so intense that the state Republican chairman resigned in early 2010, and Crist decided to leave the GOP to run as an independent after trailing badly a few months before Florida's primary election. Though the campaigns were primarily focused on the economy, Rubio nevertheless turned to social policy to mobilize the Christian Right base. At an event sponsored by the Christian Family Coalition of Florida, Rubio said Crist could not be pro-life, as Crist claimed, because he did not support overturning *Roe v. Wade*. In a news release, Rubio criticized Crist for refusing to get involved in the Terri Shiavo case in 2005 while attorney general of Florida. Rubio, a state representative at the time, did vote for a law giving the governor the authority to issue a one-time stay to prevent the withholding of nutrition and liquid from Schiavo. (The Schiavo case is described in detail later in this chapter.)

Sometimes national Christian Right figures contribute to factional disputes within a state's GOP. The 2010 Republican U.S. Senate primary in Kentucky received national attention when James Dobson initially endorsed Trey Grayson only to switch his endorsement to Rand Paul in May of that year. Dobson claimed senior members of the GOP had told him Paul was pro-choice, so Dobson immediately endorsed his opponent. After meeting with Paul and hearing from pro-life doctors in the state, he said he became convinced Paul was pro-life and decided to come out in favor of Paul, a Tea Party activist and the son of presidential candidate Ron Paul.

In other states, such as Texas and Washington, the factional disputes are more muted. Factional battles are more likely in states where the Christian Right activist core is large, but its popular support base is relatively small, and in states with convention systems that force activists into face-to-face confrontations (Green, 2000).

In some states the Christian Right dominates the Republican Party, and moderates complain that their party has been taken over. When Christian Right activists become the dominant force in a state party organization, they assume certain responsibilities and gain certain resources. The responsibilities include running the party on an ongoing basis, which requires time and considerable attention. In most states, however, movement activists have found the gains to be worth the investment in time and energy. First, the party has resources to help candidates, and these resources need not be divided evenly among all candidates running. The party makes direct cash contributions, has a corps of volunteers, and has connections with other interest groups that will work for and help fund candidates. Second, the party sets the rules for nominations, and control of the party means that these rules may favor insurgent groups like the Christian Right. Third, the state party writes its own platform, and this constitutes the core of the

**BOX 3.2** The Texas 2008 GOP Platform

Studying state GOP party platforms is one way to assess the influence of the Christian Right. Although some state party leaders have made efforts to phrase platforms in ways to maximize their appeals and minimize extreme rhetoric, other state platforms are more fundamentalist in nature, calling for the criminalization of sodomy and pornography and the required teaching of creationism. The Texas GOP platform includes the following elements, evidence of the Christian Right's presence in the state:

**Judeo-Christian Nation**—As America is a nation under God founded on Judeo-Christian principles, we affirm the constitutional right of all individuals to worship in the religion of their choice.

**Safeguarding Our Religious Liberties**—We affirm that the public acknowledgment of God is undeniable in our history and is vital to our freedom, prosperity, and strength. We pledge our influence toward a return to the original intent of the First Amendment and toward dispelling the myth of separation of church and state.

**Ten Commandments**—We oppose any governmental action to restrict, prohibit, or remove public display of the Decalogue or other religious symbols.

**Pledge of Allegiance**—We support adoption of the Pledge Protection Act. We also demand that the National Motto "In God We Trust" and National Anthem be protected from legislative and judicial attack.

**Family and Defense of Marriage**—We support the definition of marriage as a God-ordained, legal, and moral commitment only between a natural man and a natural woman, which is the foundational unit of a healthy society, and we oppose the assault on marriage by judicial activists.

**Marriage and Divorce**—We believe in the sanctity of marriage and that the integrity of this institution should be protected at all levels of government. We urge the Legislature to rescind no-fault divorce laws. We support Covenant Marriage.

**Marriage Licenses**—We support legislation that would make it a felony to issue a marriage license to a same-sex couple and for any civil official to perform a marriage ceremony for such.

**Homosexuality**—We believe that the practice of homosexuality tears at the fabric of society, contributes to the breakdown of the family unit, and leads to the spread of dangerous, communicable diseases. Homosexual

*(continues)*

*(continued)*

behavior is contrary to the fundamental, unchanging truths that have been ordained by God, recognized by our country's founders, and shared by the majority of Texans. We oppose any criminal or civil penalties against those who oppose homosexuality out of faith, conviction, or belief in traditional values.

**Texas Sodomy Statutes**—We oppose the legalization of sodomy. We demand that Congress exercise its authority granted by the U.S. Constitution to withhold jurisdiction from the federal courts from cases involving sodomy.

**Choose Life**—We ask the Legislature to provide Texans opportunity to purchase "Choose Life" license plates.

**RU-486**—We urge the FDA to rescind approval of the physically dangerous RU-486 and oppose limiting the manufacturers' and distributors' liability.

**Morning After Pill**—We oppose sale and use of the dangerous "Morning After Pill."

**Unborn Child Pain Protection**—We support legislation that requires doctors, at first opportunity, to provide to a woman who is pregnant, information about the nervous system development of her unborn child and to provide pain relief for her unborn if she orders an abortion.

**Unborn Victims of Violence Legislation**—We urge the State to ensure that the Prenatal Protection Law is interpreted accurately and consider the unborn child as an equal victim in any crime, including domestic violence

**Theories of Origin**—We support objective teaching and equal treatment of strengths and weaknesses of scientific theories, including Intelligent Design. We believe theories of life origins and environmental theories should be taught as scientific theory, not scientific law. Teachers and students should be able to discuss the strengths and weaknesses of these theories openly and without fear of retribution or discrimination of any kind.

party's agenda. When Christian Right activists took control of the Washington State Republican Party in 1992, they wrote a platform that included opposition to the teaching of "New Age Movement Philosophy, including reincarnation, mystical powers, Satan worship, etc., as introduced in the textbooks of our education system," opposition to "mind-altering techniques for public school students," and the endorsement of parental control of textbook adoptions.[17] Few party moderates believed that the Washington state public school curriculum taught Satan worship.

In 2008 the Washington State platform was more moderate in tone but still included language reflecting some Christian Right influence, including protection of the sanctity of life and a definition of marriage as between one man and one woman. Moreover, the cover page of the document included the oft-quoted phrase by the Puritan leader John Winthrop: "For we must consider that we shall be as a City upon a Hill, the eyes of all people are upon us." In recent years party leaders have made efforts to word policy in a way to maximize appeal and minimize extreme rhetoric.

The GOP platform in Texas has far stronger Christian Right overtones. In a long document rich in detailed policy prescriptions, the platform addresses almost all issues of importance to the Christian Right, along with many other issues of interest to conservatives (see Box 3.2).

## Presidential Nominations

Presidential nominations are politically distinctive in many ways. They entail national campaigns that are contested state by state, they are lengthy processes that involve a rapid winnowing of the field, and they are extremely expensive. The Christian Right plays an important role in the process of presidential selection because the movement controls state party committees in many states, some states select among the nominees through caucuses or conventions, and the movement has ample financial resources to support a candidate.

Although movement leaders backed Ronald Reagan in the 1980 primaries and caucuses, the Christian Right was at the time a fledgling movement, and at least some who would eventually join it were still registered as Democrats in Southern states. In 1984 Reagan ran unopposed, so the first real test of the strength of the Christian Right in nomination politics came in 1988, when Pat Robertson sought the presidency.

The 1988 campaign revealed that the movement had considerable resources. Although Robertson's father had been a U.S. senator and Robertson had been involved indirectly in politics for some time, he lacked experience in elected or even appointed office and was at the time an ordained minister.[18] Despite these liabilities, Robertson's campaign was surprisingly successful. He won most of the states that hold caucuses and raised more money than any previous presidential candidate.

Yet the campaign also showed some of the weaknesses of the Christian Right. Robertson lost badly in all primary elections, despite spending huge sums of money. Religious particularism, especially fundamentalist antipathy toward charismatics, hampered his campaign, and ultimately his support was narrowly based among pentecostal and charismatic Christians. As noted in Chapter 2, he made wild statements that attracted widespread derision and in other ways behaved like an amateur candidate.[19]

Robertson suffered because of his lack of experience, general public distrust of preachers who want to be president, and religious divisions among his evangelical constituency. Yet when the Christian Right supports presidential candidates who lack these liabilities, it is a formidable force in nomination politics. The movement can provide volunteers, infrastructure, and lots of cash for favored candidates.

In 1996 the movement was courted by several candidates with at least passable credentials as social conservatives. Alan Keyes, Bob Dornan, and Patrick Buchanan all had established records as social conservatives, and Phil Gramm and Bob Dole also made strong appeals. As the campaign unfolded, movement activists divided their votes between Dole and Buchanan. Buchanan's fiery rhetoric excited many of the movement's purists. At one rally he claimed that the founding fathers would have had one response if they had learned that public schools did not teach the Bible but taught about homosexuality: "Lock and load!"

But Buchanan's candidacy came with baggage—many Christian conservatives found evidence of racism and anti-Semitism in his speeches, and others objected to his extreme nativism. Some fundamentalist activists may have opposed Buchanan because of his Catholicism. More pragmatic Christian Right activists backed Dole, whom they saw as the only candidate with a real chance to defeat President Bill Clinton.

In 2000 the field of candidates vying for Christian Right support in the primaries was large. Longtime movement activist Gary Bauer took leave from the Family Research Council to run. Senators Bob Smith of New Hampshire, John McCain of Arizona, and Orrin Hatch of Utah sought the nomination, along with former vice president Dan Quayle. Perennial candidates Alan Keyes and Patrick Buchanan resumed their quixotic quests. Multimillionaire candidate Steve Forbes, who ran in 1996 as a social moderate, campaigned with the zeal of a born-again social conservative, although many movement activists questioned his sincerity.

Yet party moderates and conservatives ultimately united behind the candidacy of George W. Bush, governor of Texas and son of the former president. By summer 1999 Bush had received more than 100 endorsements from House GOP members and had the support of most sitting governors as well. Christian Right leaders like Pat Robertson worked openly to help Bush win the nomination, in part because they believed that only Bush could beat Gore in November. Robertson recorded a phone message that was dialed to many registered Republicans in South Carolina, which suggested that Bush was a far stronger pro-life candidate than Senator McCain, a move that brought an angry rebuke from the senator.

In South Carolina Bush spoke at Bob Jones University and failed to use the occasion to chasten the school for its openly anti-Catholic message and its ban on interracial dating. During the primaries Bush professed that Jesus was his favorite philosopher and the Bible was his favorite book. In private, he reassured Christian conservative leaders in each state of his commitment to Christ and to Christian conservative policies. Overall, Bush campaigned hard for the Christian Right vote, and ultimately it was critical to his primary election victory (Rozell, 2002; Wilcox, 2002).

In 2008 the Republican field was again wide, including liberal Republicans such as former New York City mayor Rudy Giuliani, and Christian Right favorites such as Sen. Sam Brownback (KS). The Christian Right leadership was unusually divided in 2008. Pat Robertson endorsed Giuliani because of his campaign emphasis on Islamic terrorism, but as noted above, James Dobson warned he would support a third-party candidate if Giuliani got the nomination. Many pro-life groups endorsed Sen. Fred Thompson, even though he had labeled himself pro-choice when he first ran for the Senate and had been involved with lobbying for a pro-choice organization. Mike Huckabee, a favorite among many rank-and-file members, won few endorsements, both because he was seen as unelectable and because he had raised taxes to provide more health insurance for poor children as governor of Arkansas.

Former Massachusetts governor Mitt Romney posed the most interesting temptation for Christian Right leaders. Romney had strongly endorsed gay and lesbian rights, as well as abortion rights, as a candidate and governor in Massachusetts, but he now claimed to have changed his mind on these issues. The greatest problem for Romney was his membership in the Church of Jesus Christ of Latter-day Saints, which opposes abortion and same-sex marriage, but whose theology is seen by many as outside the Christian tradition. Richard Land of the Southern Baptist Convention, who was personally somewhat supportive of Romney, offered the measured opinion that Mormons were not Christians, but they were "people of the book"—as closely related to Christians as Jews and Muslims are. Huckabee was able to subtly exploit evangelical hesitations about Mormons by stressing the importance of electing a "Christian" president without commenting on Romney's faith. Romney gave a major speech about his faith that was widely touted as a sharp contrast to John F. Kennedy's promise not to allow his faith to influence his politics, but he was ultimately unable to persuade evangelicals (Campbell, Green, and Monson, 2009; Green and Silk 2009).

Huckabee's victory in Iowa did not increase enthusiasm among those who distrusted his economic conservatism and feared he was unelectable. Ultimately the nomination went to John McCain, who was possibly the least favored candidate of national Christian Right leaders.

Christian Right activists have also played an active role in drafting presidential nomination platforms. Republicans select delegates to platform committees through procedures that allow organized activists a disproportionate voice, and the movement has "owned" various sections of the platform since 1980. In 1996 Bob Dole worked hard to insert a "tolerance" plank in the platform, which proclaimed that the Republican Party welcomed support from those who did not share the pro-life position of the platform. Ultimately he lost this effort. Dole promptly announced that he had not read the platform and did not think he would have time to do so. In 2000 and 2004 Christian Right leaders won key platform victories, such as support for a constitutional ban on same-sex marriage, but they did not press Bush to campaign on abortion or other issues.

Despite (or perhaps because of) the Christian Right's doubts about his candidacy, McCain and the GOP accommodated the Christian Right in significant ways when writing the 2008 platform. The McCain campaign hired movement leader Gary Bauer to consult on the formation of the platform. The final draft asserted the country's Judeo-Christian heritage and supported voluntary prayer in schools, abstinence education, a continued ban on gays and lesbians serving openly in the military, and constitutional amendments banning same-sex marriage and abortion. Interestingly, as a U.S. senator, McCain in fact opposed an amendment banning same-sex marriage, calling it "un-Republican," and has said abortion should be allowed in cases of rape, incest, and threat to life.

## General Elections

The Christian Right does not always win its intraparty struggle over nominations, but in the November general election, movement activists usually decide that the Republican candidate is closer than the Democrat to their views and that their policy objectives will fare better in a Congress or state legislature dominated by Republicans.[20]

In the 1990s the Christian Coalition worked hard for relatively moderate Republican candidates, and most pragmatic activists realize the benefits that come with Republican majorities. In 1996, and again in 1998, the Coalition supported many vulnerable Republican incumbents in the House and Senate, regardless of their ideology, in an effort to help the Republicans retain control of the U.S. Congress. The Family Research Council and Focus on the Family are less pragmatic than the Christian Coalition of the 1990s and do not go out of their way to support moderate Republicans, even when they are in a close race with a Democratic challenger. The 2004 Colorado Senate race between Republican Pete Coors and Democrat Ken Salazar is a case in point. Likewise, in the 2004 Pennsylvania Senate race, Focus and the FRC supported the conservative Republican Pat Toomey over the more moderate Republican incumbent Arlen Specter. After Toomey lost, these organizations did not rally the troops for Specter in the general election, and after he won, they actively opposed his chairmanship of the Senate Judiciary Committee.

Nonetheless, the Christian Right does focus much of its efforts on electing Republican presidents, even moderately conservative candidates such as George H. W. Bush in 1992 and Bob Dole in 1996. These centrists may not be the first choice of movement activists, but they are far more likely to pursue conservative policies than are their Democratic opponents. Clinton's veto of a bill banning late-term abortions helped mobilize the Christian Right against him, and its activity was generally more focused on defeating Clinton than on electing Dole.

The Monica Lewinsky scandal in the Clinton administration, coupled with Clinton's victories in many battles with Congress, led many movement leaders and activists in 1999 to believe that a GOP victory in 2000 was essential to the success of their agenda. Moreover, public support for the GOP Congress coming out of the impeachment process was extremely low (Andolina and Wilcox, 2000). As a consequence, Pat Robertson and other leaders worked hard in early 1999 to make George W. Bush acceptable to

Christian Right activists; Robertson believed that Bush could win the 2000 general election, whereas other Christian conservative candidates such as Bauer and Buchanan could not. In 2004 Bush had the strong support of Christian Right leaders.

The centerpiece of Christian Right activity in the general election is voter mobilization. Christian Right groups often distribute large numbers of voter guides in churches and publish them in religious media. The Christian Coalition voter guides of the 1990s attracted widespread attention; the Coalition claimed to have distributed more than 40 million guides in 1992 and more than 30 million in 1996. Christian Right voter guides are supposed to be nonpartisan because of tax law, but in the case of the Christian Coalition there was little doubt that the group backed GOP candidates. In Virginia's 1994 Senate election, for example, the Christian Coalition guide distorted the record of Democratic senator Chuck Robb and included a very unflattering picture of him (Rozell and Wilcox, 1996).[21] Moreover, the Coalition issued two quite divergent ratings of incumbent Republican senator John Warner—one in the primary when he was opposed by a social conservative within the party, and another, much higher rating when he ran in the general election against a Democrat. In 1999 the Internal Revenue Service denied the Christian Coalition of Virginia tax-exempt status, but other groups distributed similar voter guides in later elections.

Many pastors in conservative churches allow these voter guides to be distributed before, after, or even occasionally during services on the Sunday before the election. Many pastors make a few brief remarks about the candidates at this time, but some go further. In many cases, candidates are invited to speak directly to congregants, and although pastors are prohibited by tax law from endorsing candidates, they often make it abundantly clear that the candidate has their support.

These voter contact efforts are important because many evangelicals retain a suspicion of politics and a belief that it is better to remain pure than to compromise with "the world." Although it is difficult to assess the scope of these efforts, a survey conducted by the Pew Research Center revealed that 30 percent of white evangelicals said they encountered election materials in their church during the 2006 midterm elections. These figures are higher than for Americans in most other religious traditions (only black Protestants are higher, at 50 percent) and are far higher than for other white Protestants. This suggests that there is substantial voter contact in white evangelical churches, mostly by Christian Right groups and activists.

As described above, in 2004 and 2008 Christian Right groups distributed sample sermons to pastors, and in states with marriage amendments there was extensive church-based mobilization around that issue. In 2004 Dobson and other religious leaders participated in weekly conference calls with the White House to help coordinate campaign strategies, and some activists found the Christian Right's get-out-the-vote efforts to be much more effective than the Bush-Cheney campaign (Cooperman and Edsall, 2004). In battleground states, Christian Right groups distributed videos and DVDs to pastors featuring Bush's faith, which were frequently shown in churches. Let Freedom Ring distributed a video in Pennsylvania and Ohio that portrayed Bush's faith in a flattering light. In other states, pastors were provided with a copy of the DVD *George W. Bush: Faith in the White House*. The tone of the video is captured by the statement on the back cover: "Like no president in the history of the nation, George W. Bush boldly, publicly, and genuinely lives his faith on the job. . . . The Bush administration hums to the sound of prayer. Decide for yourself whether President Bush's faith has been good for America! But whatever you decide, his faith will change and inspire you."

But in 2004 the Bush administration believed that the Christian Right would not be sufficient to mobilize evangelical Christians to the extent that they believed necessary to win the election. The Bush team therefore sought to duplicate some of the Christian Coalition's tactics used in the 1990s within the presidential campaign and within the Republican Party. The Bush reelection team identified church liaisons who would turn over church membership lists. The campaign then used those lists to contact potential voters and urge them to vote. Although this tactic drew stern rebukes from religious leaders, including many who supported Bush, it did yield valuable lists of potential supporters in several key states. In addition, the Republican National Committee mailed persuasion pieces to potential voters in battleground states, copying themes that had been used by Christian Right groups. In West Virginia, for example, an RNC letter warned that liberals wanted to take away Christians' Bibles.

There was markedly less Christian Right mobilization for the presidential ticket in 2008, in part because the McCain campaign did not encourage it, and in part because movement leaders were lukewarm toward McCain. The most interesting effort was the Focus on the Family "Letter from 2012 in Obama's America," which was posted on the group's Web page with e-mails alerting many activists to the URL. Though not a voter guide, the document is clearly intended to mobilize evangelical turnout for McCain.

The letter purports to be a letter from the future, warning Christians in 2008 of the dangers of allowing an Obama victory. It does not profess to be genuine religious prophecy, but it does quote Jesus in the first paragraph. And its predictions allow some ability to test the Christian Right's statements—at least in the year 2012. Some of the key predictions include

- The Boy Scouts of America are forced to hire gay scoutmasters.
- All first-grade classes have *compulsory* gender identity courses, with parents forbidden to opt out their children. Christian teachers have been fired for their unwillingness to do this.
- Radio and television can no longer broadcast sermons deemed offensive.
- Doctors are ordered to provide artificial insemination for lesbian couples.
- Churches are required to allow gay and lesbian couples to marry in their buildings.
- All state and national restrictions on abortion are overturned, and doctors and nurses are required to participate in abortions.
- All restrictions on pornography have been overturned, and prime time TV now depicts explicit sexual acts.
- In many cities and states, those who own guns are subject to large fines.
- Homeschooling has been virtually abolished, with some parents fleeing to New Zealand.
- Terrorists have detonated large bombs in U.S. cities.
- Russia occupies Poland and most of the former USSR territory.
- National health insurance means that everyone must wait three years for surgery, and all medical care is cut off for those over eighty.
- Talk radio has been essentially abolished by the requirement that any conservative program must allow a free liberal response.
- Christian book publishers can no longer distribute books through large chains.

The Christian Right is also a source of campaign funds for candidates. The organizations of the 1980s used political action committees to raise and distribute money, but throughout the early 1990s the new generation of groups did not form national PACs.[22] Gary Bauer's Campaign for Working

Families raised more than $7 million in 1997–1998 and contributed or spent more than $1 million on behalf of federal candidates, including a few Democrats. The PAC also served to help Bauer prepare for his presidential campaign, including paying for consultants and helping him refine his e-mail solicitation lists. Later years saw a decline in fund-raising and subsequent contributions. In 2004 the PAC had receipts of less than $1.5 million and gave less than $250,000 to federal candidates. Similarly, in 2008 the group gave $230,000 to federal candidates and spent only $1 million overall.

The Susan B. Anthony List is a pro-life PAC that has a special focus on Christian conservative women candidates. Styling itself as a conservative counterpart to EMILY's List, the group recruits, trains, and helps fund pro-life women candidates in both political parties, but it also makes substantial contributions to male candidates. In 2008 the committee made contributions to federal candidates totaling $333,000, all of it to Republicans in that year, and spent another $300,000 on independent expenditures.

Another organization that raises and distributes funds for socially conservative candidates is Michael Farris's Madison Project, which contributes money to congressional candidates who support the Christian Right agenda. The Madison Project endorses only pro-life Republicans. The group also trains grassroots volunteer operatives (especially students) and encourages its members to make direct contributions to specific pro-life candidates in close races across the nation. The PAC spent over $925,000 during the 2008 election cycle, but only $7,000 went directly to federal candidates.

More important, candidates for Congress or the presidency can use mailing lists from Christian Right organizations to send campaign literature directly to members asking for funds. Activists have shown a great willingness to give to candidates who espouse their cause. Many are willing to volunteer time and money, providing candidates backed by the Christian Right with what has been called an "army that meets every Sunday."

## School Board Elections

States may dictate that local school board members be appointed or elected, or they may leave these decisions to counties or other local government units. Some states also have elected statewide school boards that set policy for the entire state. The Christian Right has in recent years made a major effort to increase the number of states and counties that elect school boards and to encourage conservative Christians to seek election. School board elections are usually low-information contests; few citizens bother to vote, and those who do typically can recognize only a few names on the ballot. This makes it possible for a well-organized minority to have great success.

Yet in many of these elections, the Christian Right faces well-organized, well-funded opposition from national teachers' unions and groups of progressive parents who oppose the Christian Right agenda for public schools. Whenever officials of the National Education Association (NEA) or other teacher groups recognize an attempt by the Christian Right to control a school board, they frequently mobilize supporters in opposition. Christian Right slates have been defeated in many high-profile elections, including in Virginia Beach, Virginia, home of Pat Robertson's business empire. It is therefore advantageous for Christian Right candidates to avoid recognition by opposition groups, and stealth candidacies persist in school board elections in some areas.

In 1993 the Christian Coalition led a move by conservative Christians to oust Joseph Fernandez, the chancellor of the New York City public schools, and to end a multicultural "rainbow curriculum" that included such controversial books as *Heather Has Two Mommies*, a story about a girl raised by lesbian parents. The Christian Coalition and other groups helped to assemble slates of conservative Christian candidates for many of the city's thirty-two school districts and prepared 550,000 voter guides for distribution in 1,300 white evangelical, Catholic, and black churches (Reed, 1994a). The Christian conservative slates won about as often as those backed by the liberals, and the curriculum was revised under the directorship of a new school board leader (Dillon, 1993a, 1993b; Randolph, 1993).

In one study of Christian Right school board candidacies, Melissa Deckman (2004) found that although there have been many candidacies by conservative Christians for school board positions, few candidates reported that they had been recruited by Christian Right groups. Instead, many were motivated by their religious beliefs and concerns over curricular matters—concerns perhaps intensified by information provided by Christian Right groups.

Although Christian Right candidacies are increasing rapidly in school board races, Christian conservative majorities in school boards remain relatively rare across the country. However, a minority of Christian conservatives may work in coalition with other conservative board members to enact policy changes. For example, in Charles County, Maryland, two Christian

Right activists held key positions (including chair) of the school board in 2005. Although both chose to homeschool their own children rather than send them to public schools, they worked to remove books they considered to be offensive from the curriculum and optional reading lists.[23]

A string of policy shifts has changed the way evolution is being taught to students in several states. In some states, references to evolution in statewide tests have been scaled back, virtually assuring that it will receive less attention by teachers who generally "teach to the test." In several school districts across the country, evolution is now presented as a controversial theory.

In 2005 opponents of teaching evolution concentrated on promoting the teaching of "**intelligent design**"—a theory that asserts that life on earth is too complex to have evolved through random mutation and must have been designed by a supreme being. The push was aided by President Bush, who stated publicly that he supported presenting both theories to students.

Eighty years after the Scopes "monkey trial," a similar debate about evolution erupted in Dover, Pennsylvania, this time over intelligent design. In 2005 the local school board required biology teachers to read a four-paragraph statement about intelligent design in the classroom that also referred to evolution as a theory with gaps. The school district was the first in the nation to require the teaching of intelligent design. Eleven parents sued the board, claiming the requirement was simply a dressed-up form of biblical creationism and violated the separation of church and state. The trial gave advocates of intelligent design, such as scientists at the Seattle-based **Discovery Institute**, media attention and the chance to keep the debate on the agenda. But the U.S. District Court for the Middle District of Pennsylvania agreed with the parents and said the requirement violated the establishment clause of the First Amendment. The school board members who voted in favor of the intelligent design requirement were voted out of office in November 2005.

In 1999 the Kansas statewide school board, dominated by the Christian Right, announced that the state's recommended science curriculum would no longer include core teachings in biology, astronomy, and geology that were inconsistent with creationism. Soon thereafter, moderates won a majority of the board positions. By 2005, however, Christian Right candidates had regained a majority on the board, and in November voted to adopt a new standard that although students must understand evolutionary concepts, they should also be taught that Darwin's theory has been challenged by recent findings in biology. The state school board also revised the definition of "science," which no longer includes the search for natural explanations for phenomena.

### The Christian Right as Target: Countermobilization

Although the Christian Right has impressive abilities to mobilize on behalf of candidates in nomination contests and general elections, it also serves as a potent symbol against which to rally secularists, liberals, and even religious moderates. In Virginia in 1994, Christian Right activists won the GOP Senate nomination for Oliver North, only to see him lose despite a nationwide GOP landslide. In Washington State, Christian Right activists helped Linda Smith win the Republican Party primary for a Senate bid in 1998, but she ultimately lost in the general election because many voters saw her as too closely tied to the Christian Right. In many states, candidates with close ties to the Christian Right have lost when those who oppose its agenda have mobilized to defeat them.

Democratic candidates often attempt to paint Republican candidates as tools of the Christian Right. The Christian Right has dealt with this problem in several ways. Some candidates sought to deflect this countermobilization by hiding or denying their ties to the movement. However, as the movement's more unpopular leaders, such as Jerry Falwell and Pat Robertson, have passed away or taken a less visible role, some candidates have instead responded to such attacks with counterattacks accusing Democrats of antireligious bigotry.

More recently, movement leaders have encouraged candidates to run on a broad array of issues and to speak the secular language of politics at most campaign events. Overall, however, the backing of the Christian Right is a mixed blessing. Candidates do best when they win the support of the Christian Right without being perceived as part of the movement. A candidate who can successfully appeal to Christian conservatives without appearing to most voters to be a Christian Right activist can benefit from the quiet voter mobilization by Focus on the Family and CWA and other organizations without prompting a countermobilization of moderates and liberals. When voters believe that a candidate is part of the Christian Right, however, countermobilization efforts are frequently (though not always) successful.

George W. Bush is a good example of a candidate who has run with the blessings of the Christian Right without prompting a countermobilization. Although liberals and Democrats attacked Bush as a pawn of the Christian Right, a majority of voters saw a candidate who was open about his personal faith but not inordinately influenced by Christian Right leaders. Bush himself intentionally used very ecumenical language in his 2004 campaign, emphasizing his acceptance of all faiths and his willingness to pray with Sikhs and Hindus (Larson and Wilcox, 2006).

In comparison, had former Arkansas governor Mike Huckabee, an ordained Baptist minister, won the Republican presidential primary in 2008, he would have struggled to silence critics in the general election. During the primaries Huckabee included explicit religious imagery in his campaign ads and accepted endorsements from numerous Christian Right leaders. In 2008 there was a countermobilization against Sarah Palin's vice-presidential bid, but it is unclear if the effort was in response to her association with the Christian Right or simply a response to her qualifications for the White House more generally. Had the election been closer, however, her close ties to the movement might have evoked more scrutiny.

In Virginia in 2009, Republicans successfully captured the governorship and elected an attorney general who had close ties to the Christian Right. Both candidates ran primarily as economic conservatives, and their campaigns built on promises to unite Virginians on common values. The gubernatorial candidate, Robert McDonnell, faced down controversy about some very conservative views expressed in a master's thesis, saying that his views had changed and that his views on family life were represented by a bill he had sponsored to make it easier for working mothers to find childcare. McDonnell's campaign showed how movement candidates can win election, but it remains to be seen whether he will pursue Christian Right policies or focus more centrally on economics.

## Initiatives and Referenda

The Christian Right has also been active in promoting state and local initiatives and referenda, usually on matters dealing with homosexuality. In some cases, these efforts have sought to amend state constitutions in ways that might permanently disadvantage gays and lesbians (Reed, 1998). In Colorado in the early 1990s, Christian Right activists promoted a successful statewide initiative to overturn all city laws banning discrimination against gays and lesbians and to prohibit the state from adopting such laws in the future. The U.S. Supreme Court overturned the Colorado measure by a six to three vote in May 1996, primarily because it would have permanently barred a group from future political participation.

The Oregon Citizens Alliance placed an even more radical initiative on the state ballot in 1992, which was narrowly defeated. It would have included language in the state constitution labeling homosexuality "abnormal, wrong, unnatural, and perverse" and would have required public schools to teach children that homosexuality should be avoided. The year after the defeat of the initiative, thirteen cities and counties in Oregon voted to prohibit antidiscrimination legislation in their local jurisdictions (Gamble, 1995).

Although the leaders of the Oregon Citizens Alliance promised to work to place similar initiatives on the ballot in a number of states in 1994, they were unsuccessful in doing so. In many states political elites maneuvered to keep these issues off the ballot, and in other states the petition drives simply failed to attain the requisite number of signatures.

In Maine a group called Concerned Maine Families succeeded in 1995 in gaining ballot access for a referendum that would have prevented the state or any locality from passing legislation to ban discrimination against homosexuals. A similar bill had passed the Maine legislature in 1993 but was vetoed by the governor. Other statewide organizations formed to join the campaign, and Focus on the Family provided some assistance (Hale, 1995). Ultimately the referendum was defeated 53 to 47 percent.

In 2004 the Christian Right movement had great success in amending state constitutions to ban same-sex marriage. In all, thirteen states amended their constitutions by referendum in 2004, including eleven states that voted on the referendum on the day of the presidential election. The Marriage Amendment Project, the name given to a coalition of Christian Right groups at the time, helped coordinate strategy between each of the eleven states and the national Christian Right organizations. By mid-2009 a total of thirty states banned same-sex marriage in their state constitutions, and six others had statutes prohibiting same-sex marriage.

The most newsworthy same-sex marriage ban came from the citizens of California in 2008. In 2005 and 2006 California lawmakers passed bills allowing same-sex marriage, but Republican governor Arnold Schwarzenegger vetoed both. Then in 2008 the California Supreme Court issued a ruling declaring marriage between two people of the same sex was a guaranteed civil right. In the wake of that decision, Christian Right groups mobilized, and with the financial support of the Church of Jesus Christ of Latter-day Saints and high turnout among African American Protestants who came out for Obama but voted for the referendum to ban same-sex marriage, the proposition passed. In 2009 voters in Maine overturned a law passed by the state legislature to allow same-sex marriage. Both referenda were close, but as of early 2010 every state that has voted on same-sex marriage has voted to ban it.

Finally, the Christian Right has worked to pass or oppose initiatives and referenda in other policy areas, including abortion. The movement has had less success on abortion referenda; efforts to require parental notification or consent failed in two consecutive elections in California. In 2006 state voters in South Dakota rejected an amendment that would have banned all abortions and made it a felony to perform one. Two years later pro-life forces offered a less radical measure that would have banned all abortions in the state except for those performed because of rape or incest or to protect the woman's health, and this measure was also defeated handily. If approved, the measure would have faced a test in the Supreme Court, because its restrictions violate the core tenets of *Roe v. Wade*. Seven states have launched formal "personhood" initiatives for 2010 and have pending ballot measures that would recognize the personhood of the unborn from conception. As of this writing, however, no state had gathered enough signatures or legislative support to place the measure on the ballot.

## Lobbying Government

Although much of the focus of the contemporary Christian Right has been on electing socially conservative candidates, these organizations lobby government using the same techniques and tools as other organizations. They approach members of the national executive, legislative, and judicial branches in different ways, seeking to advance their policy agendas. The Christian Right is especially active in lobbying state and local governments.

### The Presidency

In every presidential election since 1980, the Christian Right has concentrated its efforts on electing the Republican candidate. There are several reasons for this focus. First, the president has ready access to national media and thus is ideally situated to participate in a moral crusade. The "bully pulpit" is an important resource in efforts to persuade the public of particular goals. America's civil religion seems to require that the president assume the role of national spiritual leader, and if that were to entail assuming a prophetic stance on behalf of a conservative agenda, the Christian Right would surely benefit. Second, the president controls many key appointments in the bureaucracy and therefore has substantial influence on the way the bureaucracy makes rules and interprets laws. Third, the president selects the men and women who fill the nation's judiciary and therefore indirectly shapes the types of decisions made by the courts. Finally, for most of the 1980s it appeared unlikely that the Republicans could ever capture control of Congress, so the presidency was the only realistic national electoral goal. The Christian Right has lobbied all three Republican presidents since 1980, but it has focused its efforts more on the Reagan and George W. Bush administrations.

In 1980 the Christian Right celebrated the election of Ronald Reagan. Although Reagan was the only divorced man ever to win the White House and seldom attended church services, he ran as a pro-family candidate and openly courted the support of conservative evangelicals. Although he had once, as governor of California, signed the most liberal abortion law in the nation, Reagan ran as a pro-life candidate in 1980, and his supporters promised privately that he would appoint only pro-life judges to the Supreme Court. Reagan supported the elimination of a longtime GOP platform plank endorsing the Equal Rights Amendment and the insertion of a pro-life plank.

Reagan appointed Christian Right activists and supporters to visible posts in his administration. A Moral Majority leader, Bob Billings, assumed a post in the Department of Education, and antiabortion activist C. Everett Koop became surgeon general. James Watt, Reagan's choice to head the Department of Interior, reportedly argued that the imminent second coming of Christ meant that there was little need to preserve the environment (Wald, 1992). Gary Bauer, who later became head of the Family Research Council and a presidential candidate, served in Reagan's second term as the head of his domestic policy team.

Reagan (and later his successor, George H. W. Bush) also ordered the bureaucracy to interpret laws in ways that pleased Christian Right activists. Perhaps the most famous example was the "gag rule" on abortion, which barred the disbursement of public funds to any family planning organization that discussed abortion with its patients. Moreover, Reagan provided many symbolic benefits to conservative Christians: He addressed pro-life rallies in Washington remotely from the White House and mentioned Christian Right issues in his televised speeches.[24]

Yet ultimately many Christian Right activists became disenchanted with the Reagan administration. They argued that Christian conservatives received primarily symbolic gestures, while Reagan concentrated the energies of his administration on satisfying economic conservatives by providing tax cuts for corporations, and foreign policy conservatives by undertaking a massive military buildup. Reagan's first Supreme Court appointment was Sandra Day O'Connor, who did not vote to overturn *Roe v. Wade*, and his administration did not work to help pass a constitutional amendment that would have allowed prayer in public schools, despite heavy lobbying by the Moral Majority.

This disenchantment grew during the Bush administration, as key Christian conservatives criticized the president's moderation on social issues, exemplified by his inclusion of openly gay activists at the ceremonial signing of the Hate Crimes Act. Michael Farris blasted both the Reagan and George H. W. Bush administrations for giving nothing more to Christian conservatives than "a bunch of political trinkets." He argued that the Republican presidents provided "very little real progress in terms of advancing our public policy goals or getting our kind of people appointed to positions of real influence" (Farris, 1992, 43). Although his views represented those of many Christian conservatives, Christian Right activists nonetheless worked hard to reelect Bush in 1992.

Though Christian conservatives may have been disappointed in the slow pace of policy change in the Reagan and Bush administrations, the election of Bill Clinton illuminated the stark differences between the two parties. Within weeks of his inauguration, Clinton signed executive orders lifting restrictions on abortion rights and appointed feminists to key administration posts. More important, the first major policy challenge for his administration involved the president's effort to lift the ban on gays and lesbians serving in the military. Clinton quickly became the focus of intense Christian Right attacks and a very successful fund-raising foil. Suddenly the Bush presidency seemed like the good old days, and the movement became focused on electing a GOP president. In 1996 the movement worked hard for Bob Dole, and some leaders such as Ralph Reed argued that the GOP should nominate Dole instead of Buchanan (whose views were more compatible with most movement activists) because Dole was more electable.

Soon after Clinton's reelection, the story broke of his affair with a White House intern. Clinton initially denied the story publicly and under oath, but eventually admitted to an "inappropriate relationship" with Lewinsky when the evidence of the affair became irrefutable. Christian Right activists and supporters were outraged by what they saw as public immorality by a figure who is supposed to play a key role in American civil religion. Many sermons compared Clinton to immoral kings in the Old Testament, and Christian Right leaders pushed hard on Congress to impeach and remove the president.

Yet the general public did not abandon Clinton, choosing to frame his behavior as personal, not professional. Indeed, popular support for Clinton reached its apex during his trial in the Senate (Andolina and Wilcox, 2000). Eventually Pat Robertson backed away from the impeachment effort, leading many Christian Coalition leaders to complain that the organization had urged them to push hard for impeachment and then had not given them any warning of the retreat from that position.

Christian Right leaders made electing a GOP president in 2000 their top priority, confident that a Republican president would work with the Republican Congress to pass significant portions of their issue agenda. It is difficult to exaggerate the enthusiasm the Christian Right had for George W. Bush after he won the Republican nomination in 1999. He was immediately viewed by activists as a welcome change from the questionable morality of the Clinton years. Christian conservatives saw Bush as one of their own, in large measure because his personal testimony resonated with the evangelical experience. In his presidential campaign, Bush credited his relationship with Christ for his ability to quit drinking and win public office in the state of Texas. Although previous presidents also have spoken of their faith, Bush intentionally spoke about his faith in a way that would trigger evangelical support. He told Doug Weed, a former pastor and family friend, "As you said, there are some code words. There are some proper ways to say things and some improper ways." He added, "I am going to say that I've accepted Christ into my life. And that's a true statement."[25]

Bush linked his faith to policy positions, especially abortion, on which he did not lay out a concrete position but instead proclaimed his support for a "culture of life." Moreover, in a televised presidential debate in 2000, when asked who his favorite philosopher was, Bush replied, "Jesus, because he changed my life." Pundits were quick to criticize Bush; he was "playing the Jesus card," or "running with Jesus" according to national media outlets.

If it was strategy, it was a successful strategy. The Christian Right pledged its support to Bush in 2000 and contributed to his narrow victory over Vice President Al Gore in a number of swing states.

The Christian Right had great expectations for Bush's presidency, but few of these were realized. Although Bush had promised to defend a "culture of life," he did not use the bully pulpit to push for restrictions on abortion. He did sign bills sent to him by Congress, such as the Unborn Victims of Violence Act, which allows a pregnant woman's murder to be tried as double homicide in federal murder cases, and another banning "partial-birth" abortion.[26] However, it is likely that past Republican presidents such as Bush's father and Ronald Reagan would also have signed these bills. Bush also struck a compromise on federal funding for embryonic stem cell research and threatened to veto any congressional legislation on the question. During his tenure abstinence programs received more than $100 million per year in federal funding and about $50 million in federal money distributed via the states.

Bush also supported the use of federal funds to aid religious charities, and his administration reimbursed religious groups that aided survivors of Hurricane Katrina in 2005. This program did not win universal support from the Christian Right, however, and some who supported the policy complained that the administration preferred to use it as a campaign issue rather than strike a bipartisan compromise. Aside from these minor policy positions, Bush's political agenda focused more on tax cuts, the repeal of a variety of regulations on corporations, the privatization of Social Security, and the war in Iraq.

On gay rights Bush was particularly disappointing for many movement activists. He declined to reverse the "don't ask, don't tell" policy that applies to gays serving in the military and publicly announced that his administration would not discriminate against gays and lesbians in hiring. Indeed, Bush hired an openly gay man to head the White House Office of National AIDS Policy, to the great ire of the Christian Right.

After some delay, Bush did endorse a national constitutional amendment barring same-sex marriage but allowing civil unions. Yet his endorsement came only after considerable pressure from CWA and other groups; he pointedly avoided mentioning the issue during most of the 2004 campaign. Moreover, although he occasionally used language about the need to defend the institution of marriage, it was activist judges and not "radical homosexual" groups that he identified as the threat. In the third presidential debate in 2004, Bush noted: "I think it's very important that we protect marriage as an institution between a man and a woman. I proposed a constitutional amendment. The reason I did so was because I was worried that activist judges are actually defining the definition of marriage." When asked later in the debate if homosexuality was a choice, Bush replied, "I don't know." Moreover, in other statements Bush has said that states should be allowed to offer civil unions and other protections for gay and lesbian couples.

Although voter turnout among evangelicals and mobilization within churches played a key role in Bush's victory over Senator John Kerry in 2004, issues of concern to the Christian Right quickly took a back seat to energy policy, the war in Iraq, and Social Security reform in his second term. Many Christian conservatives protested Bush's lack of support for their agenda in his second term, but support for Bush among the Christian Right's rank and file remained high even late into his second term. And if Bush's appointments to the Supreme Court—Chief Justice John Roberts and Justice Samuel Alito—one day result in a reversal of key Court decisions on abortion and gay rights, Christian Right activists will remember him as one of their strongest supporters in the White House. But in 2010 many activists expressed the same disappointment with Bush as they had with Reagan.

Though President Barack Obama spoke candidly about his Christian faith during the 2008 campaign and paid numerous visits to evangelical heavyweights such as Rick Warren, Christian Right groups warned of dire consequences if he were elected and have been united in their opposition to his policies. The movement has been especially mobilized against national health insurance. Gary Bauer's Campaign for Working Families urged its supporters to "stop Obama's socialism." The Traditional Values Coalition called for a stop to "Obamunists'" attempt to destroy private health care. The Christian Right suggested health care reform would lead to taxpayer-funded abortions and "death panels" supporting euthanasia. Meanwhile, FRC Action ran an "Expose and Oppose Campaign" aimed at President Obama's judicial nominees, including Supreme Court Justice Sonia Sotomayor.

Notably, however, President Obama has used the Office of Faith-Based and Neighborhood Partnerships—a carryover of an office first created under President George W. Bush—to reach out to Christian Right leaders. The director of the office, Pentecostal pastor Joshua DuBois, met with religious conservatives, including representatives from Concerned Women for America and the Family Research Council, to speak about abortion reduction. Moreover, Obama appointed Francis Collins, an orthodox evangelical

Christian, to head the National Institutes of Health; Christian Right groups took issue with this appointment, however, because Collins approves of embryonic research if embryos are created artificially.

After one year in office, Obama had yet to deliver on his pledge to end the "don't ask, don't tell" policy that bars gays and lesbians from serving openly in the military but promised the law would be repealed by the end of his second year. And although he announced support for a repeal of the Defense of Marriage Act, which allows states to refuse to recognize same-sex marriages performed in other states, he had not yet asked Congress to move forward on the proposal.

## Congress

The president is the most visible figure in American politics, but Congress drafts and passes legislation, passes the budget, and approves treaties and appointments. No matter how enthusiastically a president may support a bill backed by the Christian Right, there are real limits on his ability to steer it through the legislature. Christian Right groups have fielded full-time congressional lobbyists since 1980, but they have had only limited success.

Until 1995 Christian Right lobbyists faced a Democratic majority in the House of Representatives, and Democrats controlled the U.S. Senate between 1987 and 1995 and again briefly in 2000 and 2001. Democratic Party leaders were not receptive to Christian Right policies, but even the Republican-controlled Senate in the early 1980s defeated a proposed constitutional amendment to allow prayer in public schools and failed to pass the tuition tax credit that Christian Right activists sought.

During the 1980s Christian Right lobbying was generally unsophisticated and frequently alienated even supporters of the movement's policy goals. This was especially true of the Moral Majority, which succeeded in angering even Republican Senator Orrin Hatch, a conservative Mormon sympathetic to the organization's objectives (Moen, 1989). Once important legislation such as the Equal Access Act was under consideration, Moral Majority activists did not participate in the bargaining as the legislation was being rewritten, and their public comments were widely seen by even their allies as harmful (Hertzke, 1988).

The strength of the Christian Right in the 1980s was clearly grassroots, outsider mobilization. The Moral Majority frequently mobilized its members to bombard Congress with mail and phone calls. Often these appeals were misleading. While Congress was considering legislation to reverse Supreme Court decisions on civil rights, Falwell mobilized his followers by telling them that the bill would classify sin as a handicap and then force churches to hire as youth counselors "active homosexuals, transvestites, alcoholics, and drug addicts, among others" (O'Hara, 1989, 13).

In the 1990s the Christian Coalition, Focus on the Family, and Family Research Council proved far more sophisticated than the Moral Majority in their lobbying efforts. All three organizations, along with CWA, were skilled not only at grassroots pressure but also at the subtle art of the inside strategy— contacting and persuading congressional members. The Christian Coalition employed an ecumenical staff of professional lobbyists who established a reputation for providing accurate information, playing by the rules, and building effective if sometimes unusual coalitions. The FRC specialized in providing detailed policy analyses to staffers and sympathetic members.

Concerned Women for America built a special network for more sophisticated grassroots lobbying. Its "535 Program" focused on developing a core group of women to track legislation and the voting intentions of members of Congress. The women would communicate this information to women in each congressional district, and in turn they would contact the member's home office, organize prayer chains, and otherwise focus pressure on the member if needed (Hertzke, 1988; Moen, 1992).

When the new Republican majority took office in the House and Senate in January 1995, Christian Right lobbyists suddenly had access to the majority party. Active evangelical Christians constituted a significant portion of the new GOP majority (Guth and Kellstedt, 1999). Moreover, because many observers credited the Christian Right with increasing turnout among white evangelicals and thereby helping elect Republicans in close contests, Republican leaders openly promised a "payback time" to vote on items from the Christian Right agenda. House Speaker Newt Gingrich promised a vote on a school prayer amendment by July 1995, but he did not deliver on that promise. The first months of the legislative session were taken up with passing the Contract with America and dealing with budget issues, and the Christian Coalition played an active role in helping promote the Contract, waiting patiently until after the House had dealt with these matters before pursuing congressional action on its agenda.

By spring 2000, however, the GOP Congress had given the Christian Right few policy victories. The Defense of Marriage Act (DOMA) was an important symbolic victory for the movement, allowing states to refuse to honor marriages between two gay men or two lesbians performed in another state. At that time, no state allowed gays or lesbians to marry, but by 2004 officials in Massachusetts were performing same-sex marriages, and thus DOMA took on more importance.

With the election of George W. Bush and a Republican-controlled Congress in 2000, many activists were hopeful that Congress would move more quickly on key Christian Right agenda items. But when the Republicans lost their majority status in 2006, Congress had done far less for the Christian Right than its leaders had hoped. Congress had passed legislation that barred partial birth abortion and that made the murder of a pregnant woman during a federal crime a double homicide, but the law had little impact because few murders are covered by federal law.

The furor over the Terry Schiavo case in 2005 made clear both the symbolic power of the Christian Right with Congress and its substantive weaknesses. Schiavo suffered a heart attack in 1990 and was diagnosed as being in a persistent vegetative state, a diagnosis later confirmed by autopsy. A legal battle ensued between her husband, who argued that Schiavo had requested that she not be kept alive under such circumstances, and her parents, who maintained that Schiavo had cognitive abilities and would respond to therapy. With legal options exhausted, the parents appealed to Christian conservative leaders and the federal government.

In March 2005 the Republican-dominated Congress passed a personal bill for Schiavo's parents, allowing them to appeal her case to federal courts. Bush interrupted a vacation to fly back to Washington to sign the bill. But although this was a significant symbolic victory for the Christian Right, its substance was limited by two important points. First, the bill applied only to Schiavo, not to any other individual in similar circumstances. Second, the bill did not change the underlying law, and thus Schiavo's parents' appeal was ultimately refused by federal courts.

Despite the intense mobilization behind an amendment to bar same-sex marriage, the Republican-majority Senate did not vote on it while they had majority status. Bush did not press Congress for a vote, claiming that it was impossible to win on the issue, but he continued to press for changes in the Social Security system long after congressional leaders had informed him that there was too little support to bring the bill to the floor. In 2005 the Republican-controlled House of Representatives passed a bill that would further expand federal funding for embryonic stem cell research, although Bush promised a veto.

During the 2004 campaign Republican strategists and Christian Right activists endorsed a Houses of Worship Free Speech Restoration Act. The legislation would essentially allow pastors to endorse political candidates from the pulpit without jeopardizing their church's tax-exempt status. Current IRS law prohibits tax-exempt organizations from making political endorsements, although they can take positions on issues during the campaign. Even with the FRC, Focus on the Family, CWA, and the Christian Coalition throwing their weight behind it, the House bill received only 178 votes in favor in the 107th Congress.

After Democrats took control of both chambers in 2006 and reached a filibuster-proof majority in the Senate in 2008, the Christian Right had little hope of influencing legislation through inside negotiations. The goal featured in one FRC newsletter mailed to supporters in 2009 was to "win an impressive number of 'no' votes from senators on judicial nominees." Dobson told his supporters in early 2009 that conservative Christians had entered "the most discouraging period." A few months later, in response to the House of Representatives passing a "hate crimes" bill that broadened the law to include attacks based on sexual orientation, Dobson told his radio listeners, "I want to tell you up front that we're not going to ask you to do anything, to make a phone call or to write a letter or anything. There is nothing you can do at this time about what is taking place because there is simply no limit to what the left can do at this time. Anything they want, they get and so we can't stop them."[27] Dobson's response signaled to many that he did not believe the Christian Right could be successful without the GOP.

The Tea Party movement that rose in opposition to health care reform in 2009 did not originate in the Christian Right, though there was overlap in the activism. Christian Right state affiliates urged their members to attend "tea parties" held in their states. The president of the Minnesota Family Council described Obama's plan for health care reform as against God's design, saying, "In Obama's worldview, our trust is in government not in God. A denial of how God designed and created our economic and social systems to actually work in the real world."[28] The Southern Baptist Convention sent an open letter to Congress opposing health care reform. Other groups attempted to secure funding for abstinence education. When Congress began debating whether or not abortions would be covered by government-run health insurance at the end of 2009, Christian Right groups urged their members to call their representatives, believing that federal funding would increase the number of abortions.

## The Courts

Although Christian Right activists have focused much of their attention on electing presidents and members of Congress, U.S. Supreme Court rulings are the most frequent focus of their anger. The 1962 decision *Engel v. Vitale*, in which the Court ruled that daily classroom prayer violated the establishment clause of the First Amendment, and the 1973 *Roe v. Wade* ruling that overturned state laws banning abortion, convinced Christian conservatives that they needed to work to change the composition of the U.S. Supreme Court. President Reagan appointed several new justices, and yet the Court still upheld the basic abortion right in *Webster v. Reproductive Health Services* in 1989. And despite the fact that President George H. W. Bush was able to appoint still more new justices, the Court struck down "voluntary" prayer at a high school graduation ceremony in *Lee v. Weisman* in 1992. In a further blow to the Christian Right, the Supreme Court ruled in the 2003 case *Lawrence v. Texas* that state laws barring sodomy between consenting adults in the privacy of their homes are unconstitutional.

Many Christian conservatives perceived the Rehnquist Court as a very liberal institution. Although seven of the nine justices were appointed by Republicans, Christian Right leaders hoped and even openly prayed for vacancies on the Court, so that moderate justices could be replaced by strongly conservative ones. Pat Robertson attracted controversy in noting that several justices were quite old and some in ill health, and then announcing Operation Supreme Court Freedom, in which he and others would pray for God to create vacancies on the Court that President George W. Bush could fill. The image of a religious leader praying for the imminent death of these justices outraged many moderate and even conservative Americans.

President Bush's appointments to the federal trial and appeals courts generally pleased Christian Right leaders. All of his appointees were strong economic conservatives, but many were also strong social conservatives who were pro-life and opposed expanding gay and lesbian rights. The movement was pleased with nominees such as Janice Rogers Brown, Priscilla Owen, and William Pryor. Although Christian Right leaders framed their support for these candidates as being for their judicial restraint, in fact all social movements (including the Christian Right) are more concerned with results than judicial philosophy. Priscilla Owen, for example, consistently rejected petitions from minors who sought judicial bypass of the state's parental consent law, inviting some sharp rebukes from Alberto Gonzales, a conservative judge who later served as Bush's attorney general. Gonzales characterized her decisions as "activist." This made Owen very popular with the movement, who saw her decisions not as judicial activism but as principled pro-life activism.

In the summer and fall of 2005 two Supreme Court vacancies were created when centrist justice Sandra Day O'Connor resigned and Chief Justice William Rehnquist died. Bush chose John Roberts, an appeals court judge from the Washington, D.C. Circuit, to replace Rehnquist as chief justice. Roberts won strong support from Christian conservatives, although some worried about his public statements that *Roe v. Wade* was settled precedent. NARAL and other groups opposed him, but he won confirmation by a wide margin.

Bush selected White House counsel Harriet Miers to replace O'Connor, but Miers's nomination met with opposition from conservatives. Some focused on her lack of experience in dealing with constitutional matters, but Christian conservatives worried that she was not a committed opponent of liberal precedents like *Roe v. Wade*. James Dobson of Focus on the Family endorsed Miers after reassurances from White House political director Karl Rove; other Christian Right groups withheld judgment. After criticizing liberals for questioning Roberts on his faith and judicial views, Bush sought to reassure conservatives that Miers attended a pro-life evangelical church. But remarks by Miers that implied a pro-choice position in the 1980s surfaced, and almost immediately some Christian Right groups called publicly or privately for her withdrawal. She withdrew in late October 2005.

Bush next nominated Court of Appeals judge Samuel Alito. Alito's nomination was greeted with enthusiasm by Christian conservatives, because his dissent in favor of spousal notification in abortion cases and his writings appeared to indicate that he was strongly opposed to *Roe v. Wade*. The movement's support appeared justified when in 2007 Alito, as well as Roberts, voted with the majority in a 5–4 decision to uphold a ban on partial-birth abortions passed by Congress. The decision was controversial because opponents argue that the procedure is sometimes necessary to save the life of the mother. It was the first time since *Roe* that the Court had allowed Congress or the states to ban a specific procedure used to perform an abortion.

Unlike the Bush administration, Christian Right groups did not have much hope for judicial nominees during the Obama presidency. With Democrats initially holding a filibuster-proof majority in 2009, the movement could only sit back and hope for the largest number of "no" votes possible. Obama's nomination of Sonia Sotomayor to the Supreme Court was particularly challenging for the Christian Right to oppose. Although her record indicated she would be a moderately liberal judge and support abortion rights, the Christian Right was reluctant to be a focal opponent, as Sotomayor would be the first Latino on the high court and likely have the support of Hispanics, a constituency the Christian Right has tried to attract. Apart from one pro-life protestor disrupting her hearings for the Senate Judiciary committee, the Christian Right was relatively quiet as Sotomayor was confirmed 68–31. At the time of this writing, it is too soon to say how Christian Right groups will respond to Obama's nomination of Solicitor General Elena Kagan to the Supreme Court in 2010. In the initial days following her nomination, the Christian Right joined other conservative groups in criticizing her effort as dean of Harvard Law School to ban military recruiters on campus due to the "don't ask, don't tell" policy. Kagan is generally known as a centrist, however, and with only 41 Republicans in the Senate, many pundits expected Kagan to easily win confirmation.

Christian Right groups have also formed special organizations designed to change public policy through litigation. Pat Robertson formed the **American Center for Law and Justice** (ACLJ) in 1990, and he promotes the group as the Christian counterpart to the American Civil Liberties Union. The ACLJ is especially active in cases involving church-state issues. The American Family Association Law Center, founded by Rev. Donald Wildmon in 1990, has been active in cases defending state and local obscenity and sodomy laws and Operation Rescue protesters. The Home School Legal Defense Association devotes much of its time to defending the rights of home-schooling parents nationwide.

The Alliance Defense Fund (ADF) is one of the largest Christian Right organizations committed to working through the courts to ensure religious freedom and defend the traditional family structure. ADF was founded in 1993 by a number of Christian leaders, including James Dobson and the late D. James Kennedy, and has grown exponentially since then. In 2003 the organization raised $18 million—up from $4.7 million in 1997 (Peterson and Matthews, 2005). ADF has a legal team of 23 full-time attorneys and 750 lawyers working on a pro bono basis, putting in roughly 450 hours a year. Many of their cases involve the issue of gay rights. In 2000 ADF supported the Boy Scouts of America in a U.S. Supreme Court case about whether state antidiscrimination laws applied to this private organization. The Court upheld the right of the Boy Scouts to bar boys who are gay or atheist from joining the Scouts and to bar gay and atheist men from serving as leaders. ADF also worked to invalidate marriage licenses issued to same-sex couples who were married in San Francisco in 2003.

In the 2004 elections ADF promised legal support to pastors who showed videos produced by Let Freedom Ring that highlighted Bush's personal faith, or who gave sermons about the importance of the election and how congregants could vote their values in the 2004 election. Similarly, in 2008 ADF led a legal effort to assert "First Amendment Rights" of pastors to speak about politics from the pulpit, known as the Pulpit Initiative; in truth, the effort was designed to defy IRS regulations prohibiting places of worship from supporting or opposing candidates. ADF sponsored Pulpit Freedom Sunday in late September 2008 and asked pastors to deliver sermons that applied the Bible to the subject of candidates for government office and then send the sermons to the IRS. Thirty-three pastors participated. As of early 2010 the IRS had sent a letter to one pastor saying the probe was closed due to a procedural matter, but it "may commence a future inquiry."

In recent years the number of Christian Right legal groups has grown, and all groups have become more active (Brown, 2004; Hacker, 2005). These groups have frequently engaged in litigation against public school boards. Some cases involve students who were allegedly prevented by school officials from reading their Bibles or praying; others involve public school curricula.[29] Attorneys for these groups frequently argue that their clients have endured discrimination because of their religious beliefs or that their right to free exercise of religion has been denied. In many cases the threat of a lawsuit is sufficient to change school board policy; in others the threat of suit by the Christian Right balances that by the ACLU, and the counterthreats enable board members to vote their own religious preferences.

There are many other conservative legal groups, such as the Rutherford Institute, which take cases of interest to the Christian Right such as parents' rights, religious freedom, and sexual harassment. The Rutherford Institute provided free legal counsel for Paula Jones in her sexual harassment lawsuit against President Clinton. Although a federal judge dismissed the Jones lawsuit, material from the discovery portion of the case eventually led to the Lewinsky scandal and impeachment. The Rutherford Institute does not as a rule provide free counsel for sexual harassment cases, and most observers believe that the group did so in this case because of the potential political damage to President Clinton.

## State and Local Governments

Today Christian Right groups focus much of their attention and energy on state and local governments, because many of the issues of greatest concern to the Christian Right are decided at those levels. State and local governments decide what kinds of regulations to impose on Christian schools, what kinds of books to assign in public schools, and whether and how to teach about human sexuality. State governments can impose some kinds of restrictions on abortion access, including banning abortions in public hospitals, insisting that teenage girls obtain parental consent before having an abortion, and requiring doctors to inform women considering abortion about the development of the fetus and the alternative of adoption. State governments define marriage and consider any other legal protections that might be offered to same-sex or unmarried heterosexual couples.

In many states Christian Right organizations employ lobbyists and mobilize grassroots pressure on governors, state attorneys general, members of the state legislature, and local government officials. Frequently Christian Right groups try to create ties to governors. In Virginia, for example, the Christian Right had strong ties with Governor George Allen in the 1990s. Allen's top advisors in education (including the state secretary of education) were Christian conservatives who opposed sex education and favored prayer in schools. His secretary of health and human services was Kay Coles James, a prominent pro-life activist who had worked in the first Bush administration and had blocked the release of an AIDS pamphlet aimed at teens because it advocated the use of condoms. The head of Virginia's Family Foundation became the director of the governor's personnel and training operation (Rozell and Wilcox, 1996). As noted above, the movement now has close ties to Governor McDonnell and especially to Attorney General Ken Cuccinelli, but it is too soon to know what policies might come out of the new administration.[30]

In a striking testament to the limits to the Christian Right agenda, the movement did not mobilize in 2004 when the legislature accidentally reinstated an old law that required Virginia businesses to allow all workers one day off on every weekend for religious observance and family time. The business community quickly mobilized to demand a special session to repeal this law, and the Christian Right did not oppose them (Larson, Madland, and Wilcox, 2006).

Christian Right groups also focus on county and city governments. In August 2009 the Goshen, Indiana, City Council issued a preliminary 4–3 vote in favor of a "gender-identity" ordinance that would extend housing and employment rights to homosexual, bisexual, and transgendered individuals. Local Christian Right groups worked with ADF and Focus on the Family to oppose the measure, and the ordinance was defeated on the second vote. From county government the Christian Right often seeks policies relating to schools and libraries. In many counties Christian Right groups push for "adults only" sections in public libraries that would include all books they find objectionable; in others, they seek to remove objectionable books and magazines or force library boards to buy materials published by Christian Right organizations. In many counties groups are pushing to install pornography filters on public computer terminals at libraries and public schools. In some counties Christian Right activists have sought to end after-school child care in the public schools, arguing that such programs make it easier for women to work outside the home.

## Conclusion

The Christian Right is composed of a set of national, state, and local social movement organizations that compete and cooperate in political action. These groups vary in their issue agendas and tactics and attract different sets of activists. Overall, the movement employs a wide variety of tactics to influence elections and public policy.

The diversity and growing power of the Christian Right are a source of great solace to its supporters but of great concern to those who oppose its agenda. It is precisely because of the growing effectiveness of the Christian Right that the movement generates such controversy. Different conceptions of the Christian Right are explored in the next chapter.

# 4

........................................................................

# Assessing the
# Christian Right

Christians, when they have lived up to the ideals of their faith, have defended the weak and vulnerable and worked tirelessly to protect and strengthen vital institutions of civil society, beginning with the family. We are Orthodox, Catholic, and evangelical Christians who have united at this hour to reaffirm fundamental truths about justice and the common good, and to call upon our fellow citizens, believers and non-believers alike, to join us in defending them. These truths are 1) the sanctity of human life, 2) the dignity of marriage as the conjugal union of husband and wife, and 3) the rights of conscience and religious liberty.

**"The Manhattan Declaration: A Call of Christian Conscience,"**
statement by conservative evangelical and Catholic leaders, 2009

Pretending that all moral questions can be boiled down to two hot-button issues profoundly misrepresents the moral questions Christians encounter in America today. Seeing that every American has the health care they deserve and access to a quality education are not peripheral to our struggle for justice and righteousness—they are absolutely central to it. Many Christians of every denomination support health coverage for all people, high-quality public education in every community, and, yes, reproductive choice for women and marriage equality for all. . . . Americans of all faiths and no faith at all are engaged in serious issues that affect all of our lives. That debate requires honesty, mutual respect, and an understanding of the complexities that surround us. This document serves none of those virtues.

**Reverend Timothy McDonald,** founder of the African American Ministers Leadership Council and board member of People for the American Way Foundation, November 24, 2009

THE CHRISTIAN RIGHT is a deeply controversial element of American politics. Its activists depict a movement that seeks to defend the rights of conservative Christians to freely exercise their religious beliefs, whereas its opponents describe a movement of moral censors who would impose their interpretation of biblical law on all Americans. At their most extreme, these divergent views of the Christian Right paint a picture of stalwart Christians battling satanic forces for the soul of America or neo-Nazi storm troopers rounding up homosexuals and roasting marshmallows in the flames from the books they have culled from the public library.

Christian Right direct-mail solicitations and Web pages sometimes allege that Christians may soon be forbidden to carry Bibles to work, wear a religious lapel pin or necklace, or even worship on Sunday, and that liberals want to take away their Bibles. Christian Right groups have warned pastors that their churches are in danger of losing their tax-exempt status and that their sermons might be considered hate speech. Despite this extreme rhetoric, there is no real controversy about the right of religious conservatives to worship or to mobilize their beliefs into political action. No one is proposing that preachers be forbidden to talk about politics or that Christians be prosecuted and fed to the hungry lions at the National Zoo.

Instead, the real dispute is whether Christian Right involvement in politics is good or bad for America. The question posed by opponents of the movement is whether the Christian Right is a dangerous force that might eventually undermine constitutional freedoms in an effort to impose its interpretation of biblical law on the United States. The question posed by Christian conservatives is whether government and society are so biased against religious faith that Christians must band together to protect their way of life, and whether society is so damaged by liberal morality that they must fight to redeem America.

This chapter examines the dilemma of the Christian Right. The first section explores the question of whether support for the Christian Right is rational. Many scholars in the 1950s argued that supporters exhibited pathological personalities or were deeply alienated from society, but more recent scholarship has challenged that view. The next section poses two important questions: Does the Christian Right promote democratic participation, and does it promote democratic values? The final section considers the policies the Christian Right seeks to implement, using proclamations by movement elites, data from surveys, and in-depth interviews with movement activists. The section includes a discussion of the disagreements among Christian Right leaders and activists about precisely what policies to pursue in each area and an analysis of what the public thinks of those policy proposals.

## Why Do People Support or Join the Christian Right?

Opponents of the Christian Right portray its members as irrational, suffering from a variety of social and even psychological deficits. Public statements by Christian Right leaders sometimes seem bizarrely divorced from reality, as when Pat Robertson proclaimed in 2010 that a devastating earthquake in Haiti occurred because that country had made a "pact with the devil." Rank and file Christian Right members may also strike nonsupporters as irrational. Christian conservative parents initially objected to an English textbook in Hawkins County, Tennessee, in 1983 because they believed a short story by Ray Bradbury was teaching their children to use telepathy to control their minds; later the parents expanded their objections to include illustrations of cats, which they noted were satanic symbols (Bates, 1993).

When sociologists who studied the Right in the 1950s and 1960s wrote about the movement, they used terms such as "paranoid style" and referred to activists as "authoritarian," and "dogmatic." Scholars argued that support for the Right in the 1950s came largely from individuals who had personality disorders, had anxiety about their social status, or were alienated from society.[1] If these explanations are valid, then there might be reasons to fear a Christian Right coming to power. But most studies of membership in other types of interest groups and movements do not portray members as irrational; instead, they suggest that individuals support groups that promote their values and join those groups if the incentives offered fit with their motives.

### Personality Explanations

A number of social psychologists in the 1960s wrote that support for the Right (and sometimes for the extreme Left) came from individuals with distinctive, distorted personalities. The most prominent charge was that supporters of the Right had authoritarian personalities. In a massive tome published in 1950, several psychologists described the authoritarian personality as involving displacement of self-hatred into aggression toward out-groups and support for right-wing figures (Adorno et al., 1950). People with authoritarian personalities were said to have hatred for certain out-group and reverence for strong right-wing leaders. Subsequent writers have attributed other personality disorders or cognitive styles, especially dogmatism and the inability to tolerate ambiguity, to supporters of the Christian Right.

Why would the Christian Right appeal to such authoritarian or dogmatic people? Those who argue for a personality link suggest that the Christian Right encourages hatred for feminists, gays and lesbians, and other liberal groups, and provides a vehicle for its supporters to enhance their self-worth by fighting against these insidious forces. Surveys show that many Christian Right activists view these groups as almost satanic and see their crusade as rescuing America from evil (Wilcox, Jelen, and Linzey, 1991). Many Christian Right activists are extremely hostile toward liberal groups and perceive them to be very dangerous and powerful in their communities.

In addition, the Christian Right offers a straightforward portrait of a struggle between the forces of darkness and light, symbolism that has strong appeal to those who dislike ambiguity. Biblical interpretations of the struggle between God and Satan might invite Christian Right activists to see conspiracies and collusion among forces opposed to the movement. This is consistent with what some have called dogmatic personalities. Finally, authoritative pronouncements from ministers who interpret the inerrant word of God enable the Christian Right to offer strong leaders, who are especially appealing to those with authoritarian personalities.

There are within the Christian Right activists and members who seem to fit personality explanations. When one of us asked a Moral Majority county chair why he was involved in the movement, he responded in a serious voice that he was worried about "rampant bestiality" in the high schools. His account revealed more about his personality than about the behavior of the adolescent boys in his rural farming community. In some surveys that we have conducted, some activists have penciled in extremely hateful language in the margins of questions about gays and lesbians. (Other activists have penciled in Bible verses about God's love for sinners.)

TABLE 4.1  **Personality Traits Among Indiana Moral Majority Activists**
(percent of respondents, N = 162)

| Authoritarianism | |
|---|---|
| Strong leaders are better than laws and talk | 58 |
| Disobeying orders is inexcusable | 38 |
| Obedience is the most important virtue in children | 75 |
| I feel guilty when I question authority | 27 |
| I sometimes question authority | 78 |
| **Feelings of inadequacy** | |
| I do not have much to be proud of | 12 |
| I take a positive attitude toward myself | 39 |
| I wish I respected myself more | 21 |
| **Alienation** | |
| I am alienated or on the fringe of society | 40 |
| I never feel useless since joining the Moral Majority | 39 |
| Membership in the Moral Majority makes me feel worthy | 43 |

*Source*: Survey data provided by Sharon Georgianna Linzey, 1983.

All movements, however, attract on their fringe individuals with disordered lives. Anyone who has interviewed activists in almost any political movement can point to a few whose personalities fit these theories—and this holds true for liberal groups such as environmentalists and feminists as well. The real questions are whether the Christian Right has any special appeal to such personalities and whether they constitute a sizable number of movement adherents.

There are few surveys that directly seek to assess the personality characteristics of Christian Right members, along with others who are not members. One survey of Moral Majority activists in Indiana showed that a sizable minority exhibited signs of authoritarianism and feelings of inadequacy (see Table 4.1). A majority felt that strong leaders would be preferable to laws and talk, and more than a third found it inexcusable to disobey an order. Nearly a third felt guilty when they questioned authority, and another 28 percent felt no guilt because they reported that they never questioned authority. There was evidence of feelings of personal inadequacy as well. The data show that those individuals with the strongest evidence of authoritarianism were the least active in the Moral Majority, which suggests that the organization succeeded in keeping maladjusted members at the margins (Wilcox, Jelen, and Linzey, 1995).

These results are difficult to interpret without a comparison with the larger public or with activists in other organizations, and it is likely that some Americans who oppose the Christian Right would give similar responses. Yet the data do suggest that the Christian Right attracts some individuals with a predisposition to defer to strong leaders. Similarly, Owen, Wald, and Hill (1991) reported that members of the Christian Right differed from others in the community and even in the same congregation by their authority-mindedness, which they characterize as a cognitive style. They conclude that "we must at least entertain the suggestion that the Christian Right is attracting those more conservative Evangelicals who require authoritative guidance in all areas of their lives and who are potential candidates for manipulation by authoritarians who couch their message in Christian rhetoric. If there is a real danger associated with authority-mindedness, it lies in a propensity to be controlled, not in a desire to dominate" (1991, 90).

Similarly, data confirm that Christian Right activists may see political issues as having one side and political conflicts as a battle between good and evil. In one survey of Republican donors, over half of Christian Right activists agreed that on most issues there is a single correct view; more than two-thirds agreed with the statement that the attack on Christian schools is led by Satan, and also that God works through political parties and elections. These views are evidence of some dogmatism. Yet neither these results nor those on authority are clear evidence of personality disorders, because each of these views is consistent with what many hear in their churches. That is, we might conceive of Christian Right attitudes toward authority, the rightness of their own positions, and the potential evil of their opponents as beliefs, not as core personality constructs.[2]

A number of studies suggest that Christian Right activists show no evidence of having disproportionate personality problems (Wilcox, 1992), but none of the data is definitive. In our judgment, based on in-depth interviews with activists in the Christian Right, environmentalist, feminist, and other movements, most Christian Right activists are as well adjusted as most activists in other movements. At a minimum, it is fair to say that a majority of Christian Right activists whom we have interviewed show no evidence of unusual personality disorders. Moreover, many groups make an effort to exclude potential activists who seem unbalanced. The terrorists who have killed abortion providers and bombed clinics are typically not members of Christian Right or pro-life groups and often have been expelled from such organizations.

What is striking about Christian Right activists, however, is the extent of their fear of their political opponents. The rhetoric of many Christian Right leaders, especially in fund-raising appeals, portrays a coalition of liberals, feminists, gays and lesbians, and others bent on destroying America and limiting religious freedom for Christians. Although the feminist, environmental, and civil rights activists we have interviewed dislike their political opponents, Christian Right activists are far more likely to truly despise many liberal groups (Jelen, 1991a), and a substantial minority of activists rate these groups at 0 degrees—the lowest available score (Wilcox, 2010).

## Group Membership as a Rational Choice

The most parsimonious explanation for why people join the Christian Right is that the organizations of the movement represent their political and religious views. In this way the Christian Right is like all social movements, mobilizing a group of people with shared identities, ideologies, and grievances (Wilcox, 1992). In this sense, joining the Christian Right is as rational for Christian conservatives as is joining the Sierra Club or National Organization for Women for environmentalists or feminists.[3]

Those who support the Family Research Council or similar groups do so because these groups articulate their religious, moral, and political sensibilities. Most activists in the Christian Right are orthodox Christians with very conservative political views. The movement appeals to them because it connects their religious beliefs with their political positions. Christian Right groups offer packages of incentives for individuals to join, including newsletters and strongly worded letters warning of the dangers facing America if they do not act. Interest groups across the political spectrum recruit their members in the same way.

Among Republican donors in 2000, the best predictors of Christian Right membership were conservative positions on social issues, conservative religious identities, and belief in a literal interpretation of the Bible. But Christian Right members were also much more likely than other Republican donors to say that Satan was behind the opposition and God was on their side. This apocalyptic world view is especially important in predicting who will actually join a Christian Right group instead of passively supporting the movement.

Nevertheless, the conclusion that support for the Christian Right is rational does not mean that the movement is not dangerous or that it is good for America. Well-adjusted, rational citizens can limit the civil liberties of others and even destroy democracies. Among social issue attitudes in the donor survey, one that predicted Christian Right membership most strongly was the belief that known homosexuals should be jailed. To know whether the Christian Right is good or bad for America, we must consider its support for civil liberties and its policy agenda.

## The Christian Right and American Democracy

Critics of the Christian Right charge that it is a dangerous movement that would undermine basic civil liberties, strip rights from unpopular cultural minorities, and possibly impose a right-wing theocracy on America.[4] Of course, what appears dangerous to one American may seem perfectly reasonable to another. Direct-mail appeals by groups that oppose the Christian Right routinely begin with a warning in bold red letters that the Bill of Rights is in danger, and the fine print reveals that this danger is from a proposal to allow a moment of silence at the beginning of public school sessions in which children could pray if they wished or meditate on a book or video game they had seen if they preferred. To some, such a moment of silence is seen as the dangerous first step down a slippery slope toward a theocracy; to others it is a basic element of religious freedom. To a pro-choice activist, the Christian Right is dangerous because it seeks to sharply limit women's reproductive freedom; to someone opposed to abortion, the abortion providers are a danger to "unborn children."

Supporters of the movement claim that the Christian Right enhances democracy by mobilizing previously apolitical Christians into active citizenship. Opponents argue that the Christian Right is dangerous because its activists do not share basic democratic norms and are not supportive of basic civil liberties. There is some truth in both claims.

### Democratic Participation

The Christian Right may have had a positive impact on democracy if it provided a voice for a previously disenfranchised community. Many theorists hold that democracy works best when all groups participate fully in a range of political activity. The American political system is frequently described as pluralistic—a system in which multiple, competing social and political groups bargain together within the framework of government to set public policy. When a group is disenfranchised for whatever reason, the voices of its members are not heard by the political system, and the policies produced by that system will not reflect their preferences. This is especially troubling if the members of a group hold distinctive policy positions, for if they do not participate in politics, their views do not even help shape the debate, much less public policy.

Evangelicals, pentecostals, and especially fundamentalists have traditionally been less likely to participate in politics than other citizens. In the 1972 National Election Study, white evangelical voters turned out at a rate nearly 17 percent lower than other whites, and in 1984 the gap was still 13 percent. One reason white evangelicals voted less often than other whites is that they had lower levels of education and income, but that is only part of the explanation. Even among those with the same level of education—for example, evangelicals and nonevangelicals who have college degrees—evangelicals voted less often than did other whites.

Evangelicals were less active in politics because their religious doctrine holds that Christians should not compromise with the secular world but should remain apart from it. This is especially true for fundamentalists, whose separatism is more extreme than that of other evangelicals. The fundamentalist organizations of the 1980s faced a substantial barrier in mobilizing their constituency, precisely because many activists believed that politics was a dirty business that would inevitably corrupt those who engaged in it. One survey of members of the Indiana Moral Majority revealed that fully one-quarter had been taught to shun politics, and more than two-thirds believed that "this world belonged to Satan." Although these activists were involved in a political organization, 42 percent were bothered by that involvement in politics, and an additional 15 percent had been bothered at one time. Fully 96 percent believed that Christ could come again at any time, an idea that made voting in the next election seem considerably less urgent.

Yet the National Election Studies show that evangelical turnout rate began to approach that of other whites in the years when the Christian Coalition and other groups mounted massive voter registration and turnout drives. In 1992, when the Christian Coalition claimed to have distributed 40 million voter guides in evangelical churches, white evangelicals voted only 5 percent less often than other whites. In 2008 white evangelicals voted as often as, or perhaps even slightly more often than, other whites.

This matters because white fundamentalists and pentecostals have a distinctive set of policy preferences, as seen in Tables 2.2 and 2.3. If white evangelicals have traditionally been less likely to participate in politics, and if they hold a distinctive set of issue positions, then a social movement that mobilizes them into political action might produce a more balanced and fruitful policy debate. The Christian Right may therefore have had a positive democratic influence by helping a previously disenfranchised constituency gain a voice.

But it is not clear that the increase in voter turnout among evangelicals is primarily because of the Christian Right. Although some studies have shown that evangelicals who received voter guides in their churches were more likely to vote, other research has reported that evangelical turnout since the formation of the Christian Right can be almost entirely explained by changing demographic characteristics, especially the increased education of evangelicals (Claasen and Povtak, 2010).

Perhaps more important, Christian Right activists hold very different attitudes than most white evangelicals do, and on many issues are more conservative than even white fundamentalists. One recent survey of Christian Right activists, for example, showed that more than two-thirds would ban abortions for any reason, a far higher number than evangelicals and fundamentalists shown in Table 2.2. Other surveys suggest that activists in the Christian Right (like those in many other movements) are far more politically extreme than their target constituency. Thus the Christian Right may have exaggerated the voice of the most conservative evangelicals at the expense of the far larger and more moderate mainstream, instead of representing a previously disenfranchised constituency.

### The Christian Right and Democratic Values

The American political system was designed to work by negotiation and bargaining. Factions within each body of Congress must bargain with one another, the House must bargain with the Senate, and Congress must bargain with the president. Critics charge that the Christian Right has mobilized a horde of uncompromising activists whose incivility and intolerant attitudes pose a danger to democracy. They suggest that movement activists cannot engage in civil deliberation because they have a moral certitude that brooks no disagreement or compromise. Flyers distributed in Virginia before the 1992 presidential election warned churchgoers that "a vote for Bill Clinton is a vote against God." In 2008 the pastor of one California church told his congregation that it was impossible for a true Christian to vote for

Barack Hussein Obama. Christian Right publications and fund-raising letters warn that the agenda of the opposition is evil, and that compromises will only help opponents gather momentum.

Studies have shown that Christian Right activists are more likely than other political elites to express certainty about the truth of their views. Surveys have shown that about half of members of the Indiana Moral Majority in 1984, of Virginia Republican convention delegates who were members of Christian Right groups in 1990, and of presidential donors who were members of Christian Right groups, agreed that there is a single correct point of view on most political issues. Many of the remaining members were uncertain, so that few members disagreed with the statement (Rozell and Wilcox 1995b).

Of course, members of many groups are certain that their side is correct—gay rights activists are certain that there is only one correct position on same-sex marriage. What is striking about Christian Right members, however, is their tendency to view political issues in apocalyptic terms. In the survey of Indiana Moral Majority members in 1984, fully 99 percent agreed that "the devil exists" and nearly three in four agreed that "this world belongs to Satan." More troubling was the fact that 92 percent agreed that "the attack on Christian schools is an attack by Satan."

Among Republican presidential donors in 2000, two-thirds agreed that Satan led the attack on Christian schools, and two-thirds also agreed that God works through parties and elections. The figures were even higher among the donors of small amounts, who are far more numerous in Christian Right organizations. This apocalyptic cognitive style does not lend itself to support for democratic civility and compromise, which for some is literally a "deal with the devil."

More than three-fourths of respondents to the survey of the Indiana Moral Majority disagreed that compromise was necessary. Among members of Christian conservative groups who attended the Virginia Republican conventions of 1993 and 1994, only 43 percent agreed that compromise was sometimes necessary in politics, and nearly half agreed that on most matters of public policy, there was only one correct Christian view. There is more support for compromise among Christian Right GOP donors in the 2000 survey, but far less than among other GOP donors.

Table 4.2 shows democratic values of Christian Right group members compared to those of other Republican donors. Included in the category of nonmembers are a substantial number of evangelicals who support the Christian Right but are not members of organizations. There are two im-

**TABLE 4.2 Republican Presidential Donors: Democratic Values**

| | Member of Christian Conservative Group (N = 709) | Not a Member (N = 1144) |
|---|---|---|
| Attack on Christian schools is by Satan | 65% | 22% |
| US is a Christian nation, should make laws consistent with Bible | 94% | 66% |
| God works through parties and elections | 69% | 22% |
| Can understand why others disagree on abortion | 58% | 79% |
| Compromise is important part of American politics | 65% | 84% |
| On most issues, one correct view | 53% | 23% |
| Should be tolerant of others who live by different moral standards | 26% | 42% |
| **Demonstrate** | | |
| Feminists | 80% | 85% |
| Environmentalists | 86% | 87% |
| Atheists | 72% | 78% |
| Homosexuals | 59% | 75% |
| **Teach** | | |
| Feminists | 42% | 58% |
| Environmentalists | 64% | 72% |
| Atheists | 42% | 58% |
| Homosexuals | 24% | 50% |

*Source*: Survey of Republican presidential donors in 2000 elections.

portant points to make from these data. First, Christian Right members are not universally uncompromising and intolerant. A majority say they can understand why some people disagree with them on abortion, and nearly two-thirds agree that compromise is necessary. Only a small majority believe there is a single correct view on most issues.

Yet on each of these questions, Christian Right activists are significantly less supportive of democratic values than other GOP donors, the second important point. They are also less willing to allow those who disagree with them to teach in public schools. The survey of Republican presidential donors asked whether members of various groups should be allowed to demonstrate "if there was no threat of violence" or should be allowed to teach in public schools assuming that they maintained professional conduct. Table 4.2 shows that substantial majorities of Christian Right members and nonmembers would allow members of these groups to demonstrate in the community, although many would not allow homosexuals to demonstrate.

When it comes to teaching in public schools, however, Christian Right activists show surprising levels of intolerance. Nearly 60 percent would not allow feminists or atheists to teach in public schools, more than 75 percent would bar homosexuals, and more than one-third would bar environmentalists. These numbers are surprisingly high for a survey of well-educated political activists. Allowing those with abhorrent views to teach children prior to college is a hard test of tolerance; imagine, for example a white supremacist teaching an eighth grader that you know on Martin Luther King Jr. Day. The same survey revealed that among secular Democratic donors in 2000, fully 38 percent would not allow Christian fundamentalists to teach in public schools. The numbers for feminists, atheists, and homosexuals are very high, and suggest that many Christian Right activists would consider significant curbs on civil liberties.

One reason that Christian Right activists are so intolerant on educational issues is that they perceive public schools as hostile to their values and believe that they will tempt their children away from their faith. Christian Right groups stoke the flames by warning of dangerous ideas in public schools. One of the most frequent themes of Christian Right direct mail in the 1990s was that public schools teach "witchcraft." The label has been especially applied to guidance counselors who attempt to implement programs that improve student self-esteem or help students clarify their values, but also to teachers who tell their students that a girl can grow up to be president. This accusation takes on more chilling overtones because the Bible counsels "suffer not a witch to live."[5]

But other studies have shown that Christian Right intolerance is not limited to teachers in public schools. One large study of religious activists found that Christian Right members most often identified liberal groups such as the National Organization for Women, the American Civil Liberties Union, and People for the American Way as the most dangerous to the country, and they were not especially willing to let members of such liberal groups take part in the political debate. Only 61 percent would allow them to speak in their communities, 57 percent would allow them to run for public office, 53 percent would allow them to demonstrate, and a disconcerting 14 percent would allow them to teach in public schools.[6] In contrast, although religious liberal activists frequently named the Christian Right as the greatest threat, they were far more willing to accord its adherents basic civil rights.

These data provide some support for the alarmist view that the Christian Right might pose a danger to civil liberties. Two factors may mitigate that danger, however. First, Christian Right activists, like all Americans, have internalized abstract basic democratic values and a great respect for the Constitution. They therefore hold two conflicting values: support for freedom and equality on the one hand, and an eagerness to act to protect America from moral decay on the other. This ambivalence is not uncommon—most Americans hold conflicting values on many issues. But if an actual law were proposed to limit free speech or to fire environmentalist public school teachers, at least some activists would doubtless pull back because of their commitment to the abstract ideal.

Second, the mere process of involvement in politics might instill in Christian Right activists a greater willingness to compromise and help to humanize their political opponents. Many political theorists have argued that the very process of participating in politics effects personal transformations among citizens. By engaging in political discourse and action, Christian conservatives may enhance their political abilities, especially what some have called their "deliberative capacities" (Warren, 1993; 1996). John Stuart Mill argued that participation provided moral instruction because the citizen is forced to "weigh interests not his own; to be guided, in case of conflicting claims, by another rule than his private partialities; to apply, at every turn, principles and maxims which have for their reason of existence the general good" (Mill, 1862, 89). Samuel Barber suggested that by debating together, citizens discover their common humanity (Barber, 1984). They may also increase their overall support for the political system and their trust in government. One study of participation in urban areas concluded that increased participation led to greater efficacy, information, and tolerance for diverse viewpoints, especially among those with lower levels of education and income (Berry, Portney, and Thomson, 1993).

Pluralists also have argued that active involvement in interest group politics tempers political passion and increases the commitment to democratic norms, such as bargaining and compromise. An activist from the Family Research Council may work with a member of the National Rifle Association to support Oklahoma Senate candidate Tom Coburn, for example, and come to understand the latter's libertarian views on social issues. If that NRA member is also a member of the Sierra Club, repeated interactions may sensitize the Family Research Council activist to the logic of environmental activists.

If these theorists are correct, the mere process of political engagement may lead to greater tolerance among Christian Right activists and greater support for democratic norms. As Christian Right activists bargain with moderate Republicans in party meetings, they learn the value of compromise. As they spend time in face-to-face dialogue with moderates, they may discover they share a concern for their children, their communities, and their country. As Christian conservatives enter public office, they will be forced to bargain with Democrats and in the process learn that liberals may share many of their concerns, if not their policy positions.

The Christian Right seeks to mobilize a constituency that enters politics with a deficit in civic virtues. Studies have shown that fundamentalists and Pentecostals in general are less tolerant than other Americans—they are less willing to allow atheists, homosexuals, socialists, militarists, and racists to speak in communities, teach in colleges, or have their books available in public libraries (Wilcox and Jelen, 1990). This lack of tolerance is directly related to belief in the literal truth of the Bible. Although religious liberals and secularists may believe that all voices should be heard and tested in the marketplace of ideas, fundamentalists and other evangelicals believe that they already have the inerrant truth and that other ideas are simply wrong. They are therefore less likely to be willing to allow those ideas to be voiced, because they might confuse or tempt vulnerable Christians. One study concluded, "It is not religion per se that generates intolerance, but fundamentalist theological perspectives. . . . Thus, the very motivation for [fundamentalist] political action reduces the civility of their work" (Green et al., 1994, 191).

Thus it could be simultaneously true that Christian Right activists are less willing to deliberate and compromise and less tolerant than other political elites on the one hand, *and* that the Christian Right has increased their civic virtues. One recent study of Christian Right organizations concludes that "civility is easily the most universally taught deliberative norm in the Christian Right." Drawing on his own interviews with activists, Shields claims these groups "labor diligently to moderate and inform the passions they have provoked by encouraging activists to embrace deliberative norms, especially the practice of civility, the rejection of theological appeals, and moral reasoning. . . . To violate these deliberative norms, then, is not just impolitic; it is also unfaithful" (Shields 2007). Shields's results are especially compelling for small pro-life groups that seek to persuade women not to have abortions, although some of the larger Christian Right organizations have also trained their most active members in the art of compromise.

Some of our previous research suggests that membership and especially activism in the Christian Right may at least allow for greater tolerance of other conservative religious groups. Within the Christian Right, century-old hostilities between fundamentalists and Catholics have weakened considerably as members of these two religious groups work together stuffing envelopes and planning strategies. One Catholic activist in Fairfax County found he was welcome in the home of fundamentalists who never would have spoken to him a decade earlier. Another Catholic activist described the way women in the Farris campaign exchanged their views on religion and politics and how each side came away with a renewed respect for the other's faith (Rozell and Wilcox, 1996). A more recent study shows that fundamentalists in the Christian Right now look at Catholics as positive cues for politics, something that was definitely not true in the Moral Majority formed in 1978 (Robinson, 2008).

Moreover, some (but not all) studies show that Christian Right members who have been active the longest are the most willing to compromise (Rozell and Wilcox, 1996; Layman, forthcoming; but see also Wilcox, 2010). Those who have been newly mobilized are far more likely to reject the necessity of political compromise and to believe that there is one correct Christian view than are those who have been active for ten years or more. Presumably, two separate processes are at work: Those who remain in politics learn the norms of the process, and those who cannot compromise leave the political arena. It seems likely that some Christian Right activists from the 1980s are no longer involved in Republican politics because they were unwilling to compromise. Debra Dodson noted that "the unconventional, anticompromise style may be ill suited to sustain involvement in heterogeneous organizations that must legitimize compromise" (1990, 138).

Robert Putnam has distinguished between "bonding" and "bridging" social capital. Bonding capital refers to social trust and reciprocity among those who share a common identity, and bridging capital extends those bonds to those who are in some way outside of the social group (Putnam, 2001). In this sense, the Christian Right has done some bridging by expanding which groups fundamentalists and Pentecostals share a bond with. But this may not extend to greater tolerance for political opponents. In the 2000 donor survey, Christian Right activists were more likely to say that working in politics helped them understand different political views, *and* that working in politics helped them see just how dangerous some ideas are. This probably means that fundamentalists have come to understand how

Catholics think of the death penalty and immigration, but also to fear and dislike feminists, gay rights activists, and others who oppose them.[7]

The direct-mail solicitations of the Christian Right seek to drum up fear and hatred among potential donors. One direct-mail fund-raising letter sent out by the Moral Majority in the early 1980s warned that schools that receive federal funds would "be forced to hire known, practicing and *soliciting* homosexual teachers." It also warned that the courts and Congress would protect smut peddlers, "so that they can openly sell pornographic materials *to your children*" (emphasis added).

Nearly two decades later, a fund-raising appeal by Concerned Women for America began by warning that "Your right to think and live as a Christian is in deadly danger because of Tom Dashcle, Ted Kennedy's new 'hate crimes' bill. You and I must do everything we can to stop this evil bill TODAY." The letter goes on to warn that "your pastor could be jailed," "Christian schools could be shut down," "the whole pro-life movement could be outlawed," and "Like a scene from Nazi Germany, bonfires would fill the streets as liberal activists destroy Bibles and other sources of 'intolerance' and 'hate speech.'" The mailing was enclosed in an envelope with a picture of the Bible, covered with the word CENSORED in bold red letters, and "CONTAINS HATE SPEECH" printed below that (Berry and Wilcox, 2007).

Of course, all direct mail warns of the dangers of not immediately sending $25, and liberal groups frequently warn of great dangers to America if the Christian Right were to "win." Yet survey data show that Christian Right activists perceive a greater threat from their political enemies than do religious liberals, and that they are more likely to want to limit the civil liberties of groups that they see as threatening. Consequently, Christian Right activists are more likely than others to want to deny their opponents basic civil liberties.

It may well be that the many Christian Right members and supporters whose primary contact with the movement is through direct mail, Internet documents, and other publications become less tolerant as a result of membership in the organization, and those who are more involved in face-to-face negotiations with other political factions become more tolerant. What is clear, however, is that Christian Right activists today include a substantial group that is certain of the righteousness of their positions and sees the opposition as evil and dangerous. These views make civil deliberation difficult.

# The Christian Right Agenda: Is It Radical or Mainstream?

The Christian Right, like all social movements, is characterized by decentralization and has competing leaders and social movement organizations, each with somewhat different complaints and policy solutions. Not all members of Concerned Women for America agree on all issues, any more than all members of the Sierra Club agree on all issues. Nevertheless, it is possible to describe in general the shared agenda and to consider the range of positions that movement organizations and activists take. On each issue there are some activists who take positions that are likely to be considered moderate and others whose positions are quite radical.

## *Abortion*

Almost all Christian Right activists believe that abortion is murder, and they ardently seek to ban most or all abortions. Surveys show that when asked if they favor a ban on all abortions, between 80 and 90 percent of Christian Right group members say "yes" (Brown, Powell, and Wilcox, 1995; Rozell and Wilcox, 1996; Green, Jones, and Cox, 2009). It is a measure of just how strong the pro-life consensus is in the Christian Right that some activists will voice their reservations on the issue only off the record. One activist in Ohio asked one of us to turn off the tape recorder and promise never to reveal her responses to other Moral Majority members; she then said that she supported an exception for rape because she had been raped a few years earlier and had worried for weeks about a possible pregnancy. A Virginia man with a wife in uncertain health privately endorsed an exception for maternal health, but he too repeatedly asked that we tell no one else in the movement about his views.

But these hesitant voices are not as isolated as they believe. If Christian Right activists are asked whether abortion should be legal under various circumstances, substantial numbers favor allowing abortion in certain restricted circumstances. The survey of Indiana Moral Majority members in 1982 found that nearly one in five approved of abortions in cases of rape, and more than half approved of abortions when the woman's life was in danger. A survey of the membership of Concerned Women for America conducted in the 1980s showed that 65 percent of the organization's members would allow abortions to save the life of the mother, and 21 percent would allow abortions in cases of rape and incest (Blakeman, 1996). These exceptions provoke heated debates in Christian Right circles, and the movement does not want those debates to be held publicly. Perhaps for this reason, Christian Right speakers use consensual language such as "protecting the life of the unborn" rather than focusing on any specific exceptions that should be granted.

Most activists regard abortion as the slaughter of innocents and would therefore ban abortion altogether except in those few instances when the life of the mother is truly in danger. Many would not allow abortion even then and would argue that God should make the ultimate decision.[8] For a few more radical activists, abortion is murder, and abortion providers (and for a few, also the women who get abortions) are murderers who should be treated as such. One prominent fundamentalist Bible study guide, in its discussion of Exodus 21, reached the dubious conclusion that the Bible called for the death penalty for abortion providers. During his 2004 Senate campaign in Oklahoma, Tom Coburn (R) said it would be appropriate for abortion providers to receive the death penalty if abortion were made illegal.[9]

The Republican Party embraced a pro-life plank in its 1980 presidential platform and has kept it in all elections since; in some elections this has hurt Republicans (Abramowitz, 1995), and in others it may have helped them, especially when Republicans have managed to frame elections around "partial birth" abortion instead of whether abortions should be generally legal. For that reason many Republican candidates use phrases such as "a culture of life" to signal their support for abortion restrictions. But few candidates openly oppose abortions under all circumstances, and those who do often lose if the election turns on the issue (Cook, Jelen, and Wilcox, 1994). President George W. Bush did not oppose all abortions, nor did he use his office to try to convince the public to oppose abortions.

Movement leaders are divided in their approach to the abortion issue, with some insisting that elections should be fought over a ban on abortion, but a majority preferring to support candidates who will impose modest procedural restrictions on abortion. Many Christian Right leaders promote the latter in the belief that it is possible in the United States today to win passage of restrictions on abortion access but not possible to ban abortions. In a November 4, 1993, appearance on ABC's *Nightline*, Pat Robertson explained: "I would urge people, as a matter of private choice, not to choose abortion, because I think it is wrong. It's something else, though, in the political arena to go out on a quixotic crusade when you know you'll be beaten continuously. So I say let's do what is possible. What is possible is parental consent."[10]

Restrictions such as parental consent, a waiting period, and informed consent are very much in the mainstream of American politics and supported by sizable majorities. Roughly half of Americans would also limit abortions to a few circumstances that are physically traumatic: danger to the life or health of the mother, rape, or severe fetal defect. But few Americans favor a ban on all abortions, and they are greatly outnumbered by those who would always permit abortions. The death penalty for abortion providers, or for the women who seek abortions, is on the radical fringe of American debate on this issue.

Most Americans are ambivalent about abortion. They place some emergent value on fetal life, but also are uncomfortable with the government banning abortion. Surveys show that the youngest cohort of Americans is less pro-choice than their parents are, a topic explored more fully in Chapter 5. Christian Right activists hope that the U.S. Supreme Court will overturn *Roe v. Wade*, which will return the regulation of abortion to the U.S. states. With two new pro-life justices on the court, an overturn of *Roe* seems possible, although both new justices indicated in Senate testimony that *Roe* is a precedent deserving of respect. Meanwhile, movement leaders work diligently to pass statewide restrictions, which they believe will both lower the abortion rate and help to change public opinion. Concerned Women for America president Wendy Wright says "the law is a teacher," a statement of the belief that restrictions on abortion will lead the public to see abortion as immoral. Among the core policy issues of the Christian Right, abortion is the only one about which the public is demonstrably closer to the Christian Right position in 2010 than they were in 1978.

## Education

Educational issues rival abortion and gay marriage in their ability to mobilize Christian Right enthusiasts. In Ohio in the early 1990s, the leading organization advocating for Christian schools was far larger than the Moral Majority. In Virginia, Michael Farris surprised many observers by mobilizing thousands of homeschool advocates to attend the 1993 state Republican nominating convention and select him as nominee for lieutenant governor. Battles over sex education, school textbooks, and other issues arouse almost as much heat as abortion.

At the heart of the Christian Right criticism of American education is the charge that it promotes anti-Christian values and threatens the ability of conservative Christians to inculcate their values in their own children. The specifics of this critique are diverse. Many argue that the schools promote a religion called secular humanism, a doctrine that places humans at the center of the universe with no room for God. Others single out multicultural curricula, which promote tolerance for non-Christian lifestyles. Still others decry classes that invite students to clarify their values, for they fear that this activity may lead some to reject their orthodox Christian views. Many Christian Right activists focus their attention on school psychologists, who they believe "brainwash" students away from their Christian values. All bemoan the absence of prayer and religious content in the schools.

For some Christian Right activists, the public schools are a lost cause, and Christian parents must educate their children at home or in religious schools. Michael Farris, for example, exasperated after a court ruling against parents who sought to remove their children from parts of the public school curriculum, proclaimed, "It is time for every born-again Christian to get their children out of public schools."[11] The alternatives promoted by the Christian Right are religious schools, often associated with fundamentalist or Catholic churches, and homeschool education, and both of these options have become more common over the past two decades.[12]

Christian Right activists who promote homeschooling and Christian schools have their own agenda. The central objective is tax relief, because they resent paying taxes to support public schools and then paying to educate their children outside those schools. They also vehemently resist state regulation of the content of this education or any state requirement that teachers in religious schools be required to have minimal credentials. All enthusiastically support proposals for tuition tax credits and especially for educational vouchers, which would give each family with school-aged children money to be used to purchase whatever kind of education the family desires.

Other activists keep their children in the public schools and fight battles to alter the curriculum. In recent years Christian conservatives put significant money and effort behind a push to teach "intelligent design" as an acceptable scientific alternative to evolution in public school textbooks, an effort that was ultimately thwarted by the courts. Others seek to teach creationism instead of evolution, teach only the virtues of abstinence in sex education classes, and teach the Bible as literature. Others attempt to excuse their children from reading certain books or attending sex education classes. In 2009 Focus on the Family unveiled www.TrueTolerance.org, a Web site designed to help parents respond to "homosexual advocacy" in the public schools. It includes advice from legal experts about parental rights and counterpoints to "pro-gay" lesson plans.

Most activists seek to include prayer in public schools, although some would have only a moment of silent prayer, others a voluntary spoken prayer, and a small minority a mandatory spoken prayer. All seek more local control of the school curriculum, because a small number of motivated activists can often greatly affect the outcome of educational battles at the local level. Most Christian Right organizations have opposed efforts to establish national educational standards, although George W. Bush's strong support for the No Child Left Behind Act did win support from some activists. But others in the movement believe that these programs would establish a national curriculum that promotes secular humanism and values clarification.

Many Christian conservatives believe that educational policy at the national level is set by a group of liberal counterculture activists whose values are outside of the American mainstream. On the campaign trail in 1999, presidential candidate Patrick Buchanan got great cheers from Christian Right activists by railing against policymakers from the Department of Education who wore "beads and sandals," a reference to the attire of the "hippies" of the 1960s. Because these liberals are seen as dominating the educational establishment, activists believe that it is essential that Christian parents get some control of local school boards. As a result, many Christian conservatives have run for county school boards across the country (Deckman, 2004).

Some elements of the Christian Right agenda for education are quite popular with the public; others strike most Americans as extreme and perhaps dangerous. A clear majority of Americans favor a moment of silence during which children may pray if they wish, though most Americans oppose a chosen, spoken prayer in schools. A majority of Americans also favor teaching creationism along with evolution, although not always teaching them as equally plausible (Berkman and Plutzer, 2010). And a majority of Americans want high school sex education courses to encourage abstinence and discourage homosexual behavior. Nonetheless, a substantial majority of Americans favor teaching about birth control in classrooms and teaching ways to prevent the spread of AIDS and other sexually transmitted diseases. They also want their schools to encourage independent thinking on politics, economics, and moral issues.

## Opposition to Gay and Lesbian Rights

For the past twenty-five years Christian Right groups have made opposition to gay and lesbian rights a central part of their policy agenda and a key theme in their direct-mail fund-raising efforts. With the legalization of same-sex marriage in Massachusetts in 2003, however, the issue moved to the top of the movement's agenda (Wilcox, Merola, and Beer, 2006). Many saw same-sex marriage as undermining the very fabric of civilization and, in the words of Dr. James Dobson, hurtling the nation toward Gomorrah. Christian Right activists interpret the Bible to say that God destroyed Sodom and Gomorrah for their rampant homosexuality, although liberal religious activists see God's judgment as a result of attempted rape and sexual harassment.

However, same-sex marriage is far from the only GLBT issue on the Christian Right agenda. Christian Right activists perceive that educators, the media elite, and other liberals are trying to legitimate a "radical homosexual rights agenda." Activists believe that homosexual conduct is sinful and should be at least discouraged and possibly even criminalized. For many, it is far more sinful than adultery or fornication, what political scientist Ted Jelen has called "an inconceivable sin"—that is, one that Christian Right activists cannot imagine tempting them.

The intensity of Christian Right opposition to gay and lesbian rights strikes many outside of the movement as unusual. But movement activists believe that sexual orientation is a voluntary choice: God would not create someone who is predisposed to this kind of sin. They teach their children that homosexual behavior is a grievous sin, and yet most know other conservative Christians who have gay or lesbian children. Indeed, one son of a prominent Christian Right leader came out in the early 1990s. But the Bible promises that children raised in the faith will not stray from it, and this leads many activists to believe that gays and lesbians seduce heterosexuals and that the gay and lesbian lifestyle is powerfully attractive. As a result, activists oppose any public legitimation of homosexuality. They object to sympathetic portraits of gays on television, in books, and especially in the classroom. Some have gone so far as to seek to remove from school libraries any books that mention homosexuality without condemning it, under the assumption that if adolescents are exposed to even the idea of homosexuality, they will be strongly drawn to experiment.[13]

In addition, Christian Right organizations universally condemn any national, state, or local laws that prohibit discrimination against gays and lesbians in housing and employment. Currently, in many states it is legal to fire an employee discovered to be gay, regardless of the quality of the person's work, and to refuse to rent to or in some cases even to evict gay and lesbian tenants. But many states, and an increasing number of cities and counties, have recently adopted laws that ban such discrimination, and Congress has debated the Employment Non-Discrimination Act (ENDA).

The Christian Right opposes these laws. The antidiscrimination laws are usually referred to within the movement as conferring "special rights" on gays and lesbians. Activists argue that Christians should be free to discriminate in hiring and especially in renting property to those who engage in sinful lifestyles. They thus reframe these laws from protections of gays and lesbians to discrimination against conservative Christians. As public support for antidiscrimination laws has grown even among conservative evangelicals, Christian Right groups have shifted to a defense of workers who condemn homosexuality in the workplace. In January 2010 Concerned Women for America had posted on its Web site a story of how Christians were being discriminated against for anti-gay rights statements and postings on their cubicle walls. But religious groups that refuse to provide services to gay people are losing a growing number of legal fights (Salmon, 2009).

Many Christian Right activists argue that homosexual behavior is sinful but that Christians should "hate the sin, love the sinner." They strongly reject the implications of recent research that there may be a genetic component to homosexuality and believe instead that sexual orientation is entirely a voluntary choice.[14] The group Christian Regeneration Ministries seeks to "convert" gays and lesbians to heterosexuality, and many Christian Right activists believe that such ministries offer a "solution" to the "gay problem" (Erzen, 2006). Focus on the Family maintained for many years a ministry called "Love Won Out," which also sought to convert gays and lesbians to a heterosexual life. Recently some organizations have launched Web sites to guide gays and lesbians through the process of sexual conversion. These sites require the participant to choose a mentor, who must also log onto the site and receive training (Rankowitz, 2009). Such efforts may seem offensive to gay and lesbian citizens, but to those who believe that gays and lesbians will be eternally tormented in hell, such actions are positive.

Other activists clearly hate the "sinner" as well. One segment of the Christian Right is strongly homophobic. When Mark Rozell and one of us surveyed Republican activists in Virginia, some Christian Right activists penciled in vicious comments beside our questions about gay rights. Three

quoted Old Testament proscriptions of homosexual behavior that man-
dated death by stoning for homosexuals. At the May Day for Marriage Rally
in October 2004, a participant told one of us that he had taken his son to a
gay pride parade in Pittsburgh the previous weekend so he "could learn the
enemy." In Virginia's gubernatorial campaign of 2009, many activists
pushed Republican candidates to attempt to recriminalize homosexual relations, in violation of Supreme Court rulings. In the 2000 presidential
donors survey, more than a third of Christian Right group members agreed
that "sodomy is a crime, and known homosexuals should be jailed."

Although there is a consensus among Christian Right activists that the
culture should not promote homosexuality as a legitimate lifestyle, there
are divisions in the movement about just how central the issue should be
to the Christian Right agenda and how far to go in discouraging homosexual conduct. Fully 98 percent of members of the Indiana Moral Majority in
the early 1980s wanted to fire public school teachers if they were discovered
to be homosexual. But a recent national survey of Christian Right activists
showed that 12 percent would allow civil unions or same-sex marriage. The
issue of same-sex adoption has to some extent divided Catholic activists
from Protestants, who strongly oppose it. In Florida, Christian Right activists opposed a request by a gay man to adopt two children for whom he
had provided foster care for years, despite clear evidence from county officials that the children loved him and that he had created one of the best
foster care homes in the county (Anderson-Morshead, 2009).

Since the formation of the Moral Majority in 1978 the public has become far more progressive in attitudes toward GLBT issues. When President Bill Clinton sought to allow gays and lesbians to serve openly in the
military, the public was evenly divided. In 2008 large majorities of Americans favored allowing sexual minorities to serve openly in the military and
supported antidiscrimination laws as well. More than half supported allowing same-sex couples to adopt children, and a majority favored some
legal recognition for same-sex couples, either marriage or civil unions. But
a majority in 2010 opposed same-sex marriage, and in every state that has
ever voted on the issue, a majority has supported barring same-sex couples
from marriage.

On GLBT issues the Christian Right has fought and retreated over the
past two decades. In a relatively short time, the central issue on the public
agenda has moved from laws that criminalized homosexual criminal acts
to allowing same-sex couples to marry. Family Research Council president

Tony Perkins acknowledged that the Christian Right has failed to convince younger evangelicals to oppose all gay rights, and that some younger people have come to reject organized religion because they see it as intolerant toward gays and lesbians. He called on Christian Right leaders to develop a new approach to discussing GLBT issues.

## Traditional Families

Many Christian Right leaders prefer to refer to their organizations as "pro-family," for obvious reasons. Families are positive symbols to Americans, and most people, liberal or conservative, believe that the policies they favor would help American families. Many Christian Right activists go further and advocate policies that would promote "traditional" families. The central issue is the role of women in society and the rights of children and parents.

The ideal family for many Christian conservatives is a married couple with children, the father working for wages outside the home and the mother working as a homemaker. Christian Right activists charge that government policy encourages women to work, both by providing tax breaks for childcare for working mothers and by allowing homemakers to contribute only a small amount toward individual retirement accounts (IRAs). Moreover, they charge that high taxes are the primary reason that women enter the workforce, and many argue that lowering taxes would encourage women to stay at home and tend to their children.[15] Many are critical of county-funded after-school childcare, charging that it encourages women to work outside the home.

For some fundamentalists and other conservative evangelicals, the Bible prescribes specific roles for women and men in families, with the man as the head of the household (Ammerman, 1987; Griffith, 2000). Women and men are thought to have different abilities and strengths, which make each specially suited to certain tasks. Televangelists frequently preach on the theme of a woman's role in the family as mother, homemaker, and supporter of her husband and as one who submits to her husband. Some Christian Right activists take this division of labor very seriously: Among the delegates who supported Michael Farris in his bid for the Virginia GOP nomination for lieutenant governor were a number of men whose wives were not delegates because they believed that this was not a proper role for women. Instead, many of these women arranged babysitting for other Farris delegates. Fully a third of Farris delegates believed that men are better suited for politics than women, and 90 percent of the members of the Indiana Moral Majority indicated that they believed in male-dominated families.

In recent years a larger number of Christian Right activists have proclaimed that women should play an active and equal part in politics, but that because they also have special abilities as mothers, they should remain in the home while their children are young. Among 2000 presidential donors who belonged to Christian Right organizations, more than 80 percent agreed that women should have an equal role in business and politics, and only one in four agreed that men are better suited for politics than women. But most believe that women who work outside the home must put their roles as mothers and wives first. Interestingly, the presidents of both Concerned Women for America and Eagle Forum are single women with no children who do not personally face the need to achieve this balance (Solon, 2009).

Christian conservatives also object to any government interference in how they raise their children, including matters of discipline. Although many fundamentalists and other evangelicals believe that God has prescribed physical punishment as the optimal form of discipline, courts in many states are drawing increasingly strict definitions of child abuse. The Christian Right objects to such limitations and also seeks to overturn state laws and policies that might force disturbed children to receive counseling or remove children from homes under a variety of circumstances. Michael Farris has written a novel depicting the dangers of such laws when the state tries to remove a child from a Christian home because of an anonymous accusation of child abuse. A few Christian conservatives have also objected to laws that specifically criminalize spousal abuse, including rape within marriage and spousal beating, and have urged the government to stop funding spousal abuse centers.[16] These activists oppose spousal rape and abuse, but believe the government should not intrude into families.

An overwhelming majority of Americans agree that America would be better off if there were more attention to family values, and a sizable minority believe that it is better for children if mothers remain at home, at least until the children enter school.[17] Yet there is now almost universal support for an equal role for women in politics and the larger society. The success of Hillary Clinton in the Democratic primaries and of Sarah Palin in the 2008 general election shows that the public has come to accept the idea of a woman president. The public also increasingly supports gender equality in families: A clear majority of Americans disagree that the man should be the achiever outside the home while the woman takes care of the home and family, and that the husband's career is more important than the wife's career. A majority believe that working mothers can establish just as warm and secure a relationship with their children as can homemakers, and that preschool children do not suffer if the mother works. The pro-family label of the Christian Right deeply angers liberals, who complain that many of the economic policies advocated by Christian Right leaders, including privatizing welfare programs and reducing spending on Medicaid, hurt working families. They also complain that the Christian Right's definition of a family is far too narrow and that single mothers and nontraditional families can provide loving environments for children. Finally, they argue that the Christian Right's strong opposition to gay and lesbian rights and the opposition by some in the movement to laws that protect women and children from physical abuse clearly harm some members of some families. A bumper sticker frequently seen in the Washington, D.C., area is "Hate Is Not a Family Value." As Focus on the Family has become more powerful, a new bumper sticker advises Christian Right activists to "FOCUS ON YOUR OWN DAMN FAMILY."

## Pornography

Conservative Christians have long sought to limit access by children and adults alike to erotic literature and images, and the Christian Right today wants to restrict the distribution and possession of "pornography." The greatest issue for many activists is the easy access to hard-core pornography provided by the Internet. Many parents worry that their children will stumble across hard-core images or video by accident or will search for it on a whim and be exposed to harmful materials. Most groups advocate stronger legislation on child pornography and have backed proposed legislation to ban pornography from the Internet. In addition, countless local groups seek to remove books and newspapers that they find offensive from their public libraries and to stop the sale of adult magazines in their community.

It is often argued that pornography is difficult to define but easy to recognize. This may be true in some instances, but pornography is also in the eye of the beholder, and Americans in general vary widely in what they label pornographic. Some find *Playboy* magazine pornographic. Others might reserve such a label for *Hustler*, and still others might object only to hard-core Web sites that actually depict sexual acts. Some feel library books that sympathetically portray a lesbian romance are pornographic, and others object to any books that contain pictures of nude men or women, even reproductions of paintings in art books.

Christian Right activists are also divided on these matters and advocate differing policies. Some would limit all kinds of erotic materials and ban not only their production and distribution but also their ownership. Others would limit only the sale and distribution of hard-core sexual materials, such as XXX-rated movies and magazines and Internet video that depict explicit sex acts. Still others seek primarily to keep adult materials out of the hands of children.

The public is ambivalent about limitations on pornography. A majority favor banning the distribution of pornographic materials to those under eighteen, and a sizable minority favor banning distribution to adults as well. Majorities believe that sexual materials lead people to commit rape and lead to a breakdown in public morals, but a majority also believe that sexual materials provide an outlet for bottled-up sexual urges. Surveys show substantial popular support for Internet filters in public schools that bar pornographic access and more limited support for filters in public libraries.

Interestingly, the pornography issue is one on which the Christian Right finds common ground with many feminists, who believe that sexually explicit films and magazines exploit women and may lead to sexual violence. But many libertarian conservatives oppose the Christian Right on this issue, holding that adults should have the right to read or view whatever they choose. Proposals by the more ideological elements of the Christian Right movement to remove any book from the public library that describes a sexual encounter, including many best-selling novels, lead many to charge that the Christian Right is a movement of book-burning moral censors.

### A Christian Nation

Christian Right activists believe that the United States is a Christian nation, and that its laws should reflect God's will. Some go further and believe that the country is specially chosen and blessed by God, but that if national policies do not conform to God's laws, he will punish the nation much as the Old Testament describes his punishment of Israel. At the 2004 Christian Coalition Road to Victory conference, Arkansas governor Mike Huckabee, a Baptist minister, compared the state of the United States with that of Rome before its fall and urged attendees to weep for the "sins of the country."

Christian Right activists seek to restore a more public role for religion in general and Christianity in particular in American life. Most Christian Right activists believe that their faith is denigrated by modern society, government, and the media, and that God will not continue to smile on a nation that marginalizes Christianity. They note that born-again Christians constitute more than one-quarter of the national population but do not appear as sympathetic characters on network programming, in movies, or in mass media.[18]

The Christian Coalition's **Contract with the American Family** included as its first plank a proposed Religious Equality Amendment to the U.S. Constitution. Its pamphlet on the contract cites a variety of "wrongs" the amendment is intended to correct, many stemming from misinterpretations by overly zealous school administrators of court rulings about separation of church and state. The pamphlet cites several examples: a schoolgirl in Nevada banned from singing "The First Noel" at a Christmas pageant; bans on religious celebrations in Scarsdale, New York, public schools; children told they cannot read the Bible during study time; nativity scenes barred from post offices; and courthouses banned from displaying the Ten Commandments. More recently Christian Right activists, along with Fox News commentators, have suggested that there is a "war on Christmas" being waged by liberals and secularists, who wish one another "Happy Holidays" instead of "Merry Christmas." In 2009 Focus on the Family's *Citizen* magazine asked readers to visit its Web site to rate retailers on their treatment of Christmas as "friendly," "negligent," or "offensive." *The Colbert Report* has also decried the war on Christmas, tongue firmly in cheek. Colbert's Christmas special includes a video with Santa and Jesus dodging missiles and bombing their opponents.

Most activists clearly intend for prayers in schools to be Christian prayers and the public displays of religion to be Christian ones. Although many Christian Right activists would allow displays of the menorah in December and might accept secular symbols such as Santa Claus as well, they are primarily interested in displays of the nativity scene. Some admit that they are not especially comfortable with displays of the menorah, much less a statue of Buddha or Vishnu, on the courthouse lawn, and that if the price of displaying the nativity scene is to also allow displays of the Buddha at a later time, they might prefer that neither be displayed.

Many opponents charge that the Christian Right seeks to create a truly "Christian nation" in which religious minorities would be marginalized. Some Christian Right leaders have sought to build common ground with orthodox Jews, and in some cases morally conservative Hindus and Muslims as well. But more commonly Christian Right activists seek to establish Christianity, not religion more broadly. Many Christian Right leaders have been especially critical of Islam after the 9/11 terrorist attacks, often using very harsh language to disparage the faith.

In Arizona, Christian Right activists who attended a Republican state convention passed a floor resolution declaring that the United States was a Christian nation and that the Constitution created "a republic based upon the absolute laws of the Bible, not a democracy."[19] A previous version of the Texas Republican Party platform also declared the United States a Christian nation. The Rev. Tim LaHaye, a prominent movement writer, has repeatedly argued that humanists are not fit to hold positions in government and should be removed.

At the fringe of the Christian Right is a group of theorists who adhere to the doctrine of **Christian reconstructionism**. Also known as dominion theologists, kingdom theologians, or theonomists, these reconstructionists are postmillennialists who believe that Christians must work to recover control of America from the forces of Satan in order to establish the millennium and allow Christ to come again. To do this requires that society be reconstructed from the ground up, generally in keeping with Mosaic law (the laws of Moses) as detailed in the first five books of the Bible.

Rousas John Rushdoony, the most influential reconstructionist thinker, said that a reconstructed America would have no room for Jews, Buddhists, Muslims, Hindus, Baha'is, or humanists. There might not even be room for nonreconstructed Christians, for Christian reconstructionists seek to dominate society. According to Gary North, a leading reconstructionist writer, it is important to adopt the language of liberalism until the reconstruction has begun, but after that time, there is no reason to tolerate dissent.

Perhaps most controversial is the reconstructionists' call for capital punishment to be meted out according to Mosaic law—to those who murder, commit adultery, engage in homosexual behavior, act incorrigibly as teenagers, blaspheme, or commit acts of apostasy. North has claimed that death by stoning not only is an important part of the Mosaic code but also has certain advantages: Stones are plentiful and cheap, no single "killing blow" can be traced to any individual, and group stone-throwing underscores the community norms being enforced.[20]

It must be noted that Christian reconstructionists are but a tiny fringe of the Christian Right, but their arguments are being increasingly incorporated into mainstream writing, including in books by Pat Robertson (Shupe, 1989). This does not mean that many Christian Right activists advocate stoning incorrigible children, but it does indicate that serious discussions are taking place among some Christian Right activists on how to go about restructuring society to conform with biblical law.

Public opinion polls suggest that Americans are very supportive of a greater role for religion in public life and are at least somewhat willing to accommodate the needs of non-Christian groups. Large majorities of Americans favor a prayer to open sessions of Congress and before high school sporting events, a moment of silence in schools, displays of nativity scenes and menorahs on public land, allowing student religious groups to meet on school property, and teaching creationism in addition to evolution in schools (Jelen and Wilcox, 1995).

Yet focus groups conducted by Ted Jelen revealed a more complex picture. Most of those who participated in these groups were initially unable to imagine why issues such as prayer in schools were controversial. When asked how children from minority religious traditions might react, they suggested nonsectarian prayers. When asked how Buddhist or Muslim children might react, they expressed more discomfort but indicated that these children could simply leave the room. Yet when other participants pointed out that this would stigmatize the students, many became uneasy. And when Jelen suggested that a truly neutral prayer might need to rotate across religious traditions, no parents were willing to have their children sit through a Buddhist prayer (Jelen and Wilcox, 1995).

Nonetheless, the Christian Right's agenda on public accommodation of religion is generally popular—more so than any other issue cluster. Once again, however, the policy proposals of the more radical elements of the movement frighten not only Jews and other non-Christians, but many evangelicals as well.

### An Economic Agenda?

The Christian Right in the 1920s did not focus on economic issues, but it did embrace William Jennings Bryan, perhaps the most liberal presidential nominee in the twentieth century, as its standard-bearer. Beginning with the fundamentalist groups of the 1980s, however, Christian Right leaders have staked neoliberal positions on economic issues. Although the target audience for the movement is less affluent than other Americans, various

Christian Right groups have endorsed subminimum wages, a return to the gold standard, protectionist trade policies, privatizing the welfare system, cuts in Medicaid and other social spending, a flat income tax, and an end to the estate tax. Christian Right groups in 2010 all opposed national health insurance, with a variety of justifications. The Concerned Women for America posted a Web page claiming that "Obamacare" would lead to forced abortions, an unusual claim since Obama had not in fact proposed a health care plan, and the House had voted a day earlier to make it harder for all women to pay for abortions through their private health insurance.

A number of internship and summer programs offered by the organizations discussed in Chapter 3 address economic issues and provide a biblical justification for a free-market society. Summit Ministries, a Christian worldview training center for high school and college students, assigns a reading that cites a passage in the New Testament—Acts 2:44–45—as an endorsement of capitalism: "And all that believed were together, and had all things common; And sold their possessions and goods, and parted them to all men, as every man had need." The author concludes from this passage, "The student will recognize that whenever modern capitalism is practiced 'with a heart' it showers blessings of wealth, generosity, good will, and happy living on every community it touches" (Larson and Wilcox, 2005). Economic liberals note instead that early Christians took from each person according to his or her ability and gave to each according to his or her need, a distinctly noncapitalist principle.

Many Christian Right activists, and much of their target constituency, hold conservative positions on economic issue. But some are uncomfortable advocating them within the context of organizations with a religious mandate. These activists argue that the social issue agenda on abortion, gay rights, and school curricula should be central to the movement. Others are neutral toward the policies and take a pragmatic stand: They will support the policy concerns of economic conservatives if the economic conservatives will in turn back the social agenda of the Christian Right.

Yet a number of Catholic activists are troubled by the economic positions of the Christian Right. One Catholic activist in northern Virginia told one of us that she interpreted the Bible to indicate a great sympathy for the poor and that cuts in welfare spending might lead to more abortions by poor women. Another activist told one of us that he believed the Christian Right had become too enamored of policies that help the rich, even though Christ had warned that "a rich man shall hardly enter into the kingdom of heaven. . . . It is easier for a camel to go through the eye of a needle than for a rich man to enter into the kingdom of heaven."[21]

Surveys show that white evangelicals have a mixed reaction to the economic agenda of the Christian Right. Calls to eliminate welfare and to scale back other poverty programs appeal to the economic individualism rooted in the Calvinist heritage of evangelicals, but even those who take conservative positions on these issues do not see them as essentially religious questions. Other white evangelicals favor government action to provide aid to the poor. It should be noted that a significant minority of evangelicals favor greater government action to help the poor. Most prominent of these is the Sojourners, whose leader carries a Bible with all references to the poor clipped out; the resulting confetti is designed to show the economic sensibilities of the text.

The economic agenda may pose a barrier to greater expansion of the Christian Right among Catholics, because their communitarian ethic does not mesh well with calls to cut back on programs that provide food and health care for the poor. Moreover, many Catholics believe that the danger of such cuts increasing abortion among poor women is sufficiently great that they oppose any reductions in aid for the poor. The economic agenda is an even greater barrier to mobilizing black evangelicals, who generally support government aid to the poor.

One area of economic policy that has divided evangelicals is protection of the environment. James Dobson and many other older Christian Right leaders continue to oppose environmental policies, and some decry global warming as a liberal hoax. Premilleniallists have frequently argued that there is little need to conserve the environment, for Christ will come again soon. In testimony before Congress in 1981, then interior secretary James Watt stated that "God gave us these things to use. After the last tree is felled, Christ will come back" (quoted in Harden, 2005). Christian Right leaders like Michael Farris have called for the repeal of the Endangered Species Act.[22] In 2008 Tony Perkins called Earth Day "a calculated attack on the sanctity of human life," calling the environmental and pro-choice movements a form of population control.

But some evangelical leaders have supported environmental protection policies, including the National Association of Evangelicals, which has endorsed a program of "Creation Care" to distinguish itself from more secular environmentalists. Former National Association of Evangelicals vice president Richard Cizik has argued strongly that protecting the environment is pro-life. He suggested testing pregnant women for lead poisoning and once marched in a pro-life march carrying a sign that read "stop the mercury poisoning of the unborn." Younger evangelicals appear to hold greener attitudes, and this creates the possibility that Christian conservatives might break with the business community within the Republican coalition on some issues. Moreover, there have been negotiations between Christian Right activists who oppose cloning and environmentalists who oppose genetic modification of foods, to form a coalition on some issues (Hula, 2005).

## *The Agenda as Defensive Action*

Christian Right leaders argue that the core of their agenda is simply a defensive action against the rapid social change of the past several decades. The successes of other groups—of feminists on abortion and gender equality, gays and lesbians in gaining social and legal acceptance, the environmental movement in protecting endangered species, educational reformers in promoting courses to help children think about values and improve their self-esteem—have sparked a reaction by conservative Christians who preferred the policies of the past. The progress made by liberal groups in these policy areas threatens the worldview of conservative Christians and appears to them to have been possible only because of an almost conspiratorial alliance of liberal forces. For this reason, many Christian Right activists refer to even their policies on abortion, gay rights, and the environment as defensive.

Indeed, many argue that this agenda is necessary to protect their children and families from dangerous temptations. Discussions of gay rights in public schools might lead their children to experiment sexually, and discussions of gender equality might lead their children away from God's chosen gender roles. Yet feminists, environmentalists, gays and lesbians, and educators see these same policies as an attempt to impose an outdated lifestyle on all citizens. One bumper sticker common in the Washington, D.C., suburbs captures this sentiment: "IF YOU OPPOSE ABORTION DON'T HAVE ONE." Gays and lesbians who face discrimination, insults, and even hate crimes see the Christian Right's efforts as an attempt to force them back into the closet. Gay and lesbian couples who wish to marry cannot understand how granting them a day with a wedding cake would endanger marriage for Christian conservatives.

But it is important to understand that most Christian Right activists do not call their agenda defensive solely to make a stronger argument. Christian

Right activists often describe their efforts in ways that resemble someone describing building a wall around a sand castle at the beach. The big tides of liberal change keep coming, and all that is possible is to desperately repair the walls between waves. This belief, and the fear that it entails, helps explain some of the rhetorical exaggerations and seemingly extreme positions of some activists.

For each element of the Christian Right agenda, the policies advocated by movement moderates hold appeal for at least a sizable minority of Americans. Those policies advocated by the more ideological elements of the movement attract support from only a small minority, however, and are passionately opposed by a large number of citizens. Policies advocated by the more ideological fringe of the Christian Right frighten most Americans and provide the evidentiary basis for the most extreme stereotypes of movement activists.

The extreme positions and statements of the fringe elements of the Christian Right movement are not unusual, for all movements attract members who vary in their ideological purity and willingness to compromise. The civil rights movement in the 1960s attracted both pastors who preached nonviolence and Black Panthers who distributed coloring books showing black children killing police officers. The environmental movement includes those who seek to lobby Congress to protect wilderness areas and those who advocate destruction of the equipment used by those who would ravage the earth. Yet anyone evaluating the Christian Right must ultimately choose which of the various factions within the movement is likely to dominate in the future, and much depends on that answer.

## Conclusion

Is the Christian Right a democratic force that is engaging a previously apolitical segment of the public in political action, or is it a dangerous force that will limit civil liberties? This chapter has posed several questions in an effort to address this larger issue.

First, is support for the Christian Right concentrated among individuals with authoritarian personalities? Although the evidence is not definitive, the most parsimonious explanation for membership and support for the Christian Right is that it is a rational choice to support organizations that will advance favored policies. As is the case with other groups, not all Christian Right members and supporters favor all positions taken by their leaders and organizations, and some are more moderate than others. As in all social movements, there are maladjusted citizens in this movement. But compared to other social movements, the Christian Right has more members who believe that their political opponents are dangerous.

Second, has the Christian Right expanded the pluralist system in America by mobilizing previously apolitical groups? After thirty years of mobilization by the Christian Right, white evangelicals do vote as often as other citizens. This is important because evangelicals hold distinctive policy views. Yet it is not certain that this increase is largely due to the efforts of the Christian Right, and the movement takes positions that are far more conservative than those of the majority of white evangelicals.

Third, has the Christian Right mobilized intolerant citizens who would curtail the civil liberties of their opponents? Here there is cause for concern. Many Christian Right activists would extend basic civil liberties to their opponents, but many would not. Many of even the best-educated activists favor arresting known homosexuals, and a majority oppose hiring feminists to teach in public schools. Many others oppose laws that make it easier for women to find employment outside the home or that would bar discrimination against gays and lesbians in the workplace. In each case, movement extremists advocate policies that would result in a severe curtailment of civil liberties, and a majority of activists would limit the lifestyle options of cultural liberals.

Finally, is the agenda of the Christian Right a mainstream agenda, as movement leaders claim, or a radical one, as the movement's opponents charge? Here again the answer is complex, for in each policy area movement pragmatists propose policies that have at least some broad appeal, and movement ideologues propose policies that frighten and repel many Americans.

Thus, the answer to the question of whether the Christian Right is good or bad for America depends on what role the movement plays in the future and which faction within the movement comes to dominate. The next chapter considers the future of the Christian Right.

# 5

## The Future of the Christian Right

"Religious Right R.I.P."

**Columnist Cal Thomas,** November 5, 2008

"The Evangelical Crack-up"

**David Kirkpatrick,** *New York Times Magazine* cover story, October 28, 2007

The media's been telling everybody for months and months that the pro-family movement and the pro-life movement are dying. Well, to the media here, may I say, "Welcome to the morgue. We ain't dead yet."

**James Dobson,** speaking to roughly 2,000 activists at the Values Voter Summit in Washington, D.C., October 20, 2007

AFTER CLARENCE DARROW embarrassed William Jennings Bryan in the Scopes trial, many observers thought fundamentalism was finished. H. L. Mencken, writing in the *Baltimore Sun* in 1925, described fundamentalists variously as "yokels," "half-wits," "gaping primates," "anthropoid rabble," "morons," and "inquisitors" and predicted their eventual extinction. After the trial, it was accepted wisdom that the fundamentalists had lost their battle with modernism and would be forever vanquished by progress and science.

This prediction proved to be far from the mark. In 1981 journalists declared that the fundamentalist Moral Majority was one of the most important forces in American politics, and that its agenda was soon to be realized by the newly elected Republican president and Senate. When Pat Robertson launched his presidential bid in 1987, some sociologists argued that he might win the presidency because of the vast numbers of evangelicals, fundamentalists, and charismatics who would rally to his campaign.

These predictions were also in error, for the Moral Majority accomplished little, and Robertson lost badly. In 1989 it appeared that the third wave of the Christian Right had spent its energies and that evangelicals would again retreat to privatized religious faith. Moral Majority's founder, Jerry Falwell, was immensely unpopular, and his organization was bankrupt. Pat Robertson had been embarrassed during his campaign and was trying to salvage his television empire from its dire financial straits. Many predicted that the Christian Right was defeated, and that evangelicals would again retreat into their private religious world.

In the early 1990s many predicted that the Christian Right would soon take over the Republican Party entirely and begin to influence national politics in a major way. By 1999 some were proclaiming the death of the movement that just a few years earlier they had described as a juggernaut.

After the 2004 election many journalists credited "values" voters with providing George W. Bush's victory margin, and some strategists advised Democratic candidates to moderate their positions on abortion and gay rights. Democrats began to reframe their issues with morality language. But by the final years of the Bush presidency, evangelicals seemed disillusioned with the Republican Party, and moral issues took a backseat to an economic crisis and two wars. A *New York Times Magazine* cover story in October 2007 proclaimed an "evangelical crack-up." Yet Christian Right activists claimed their fund-raising had been "revived" when abortion took center stage in the health-care reform debate in 2009 (Salmon, 2009).

Obituaries of the Christian Right have always proved to be premature, but so have predictions of its inevitable triumph. Clearly, predictions about the future of the Christian Right have great potential to embarrass those bold enough to venture them. Some of the predictions of Christian Right leaders have also been off the mark, such as when Pat Robertson modestly predicted that Christ would come again on April 29, 2007—Robertson's seventy-seventh birthday.

As we begin the second decade of the new millennium, the future of the movement is as cloudy as it has ever been. One observer noted, "The extraordinary evangelical love affair with Bush has ended, for many, in heartbreak. . . . That disappointment, in turn, has sharpened latent divisions within the evangelical world—over the evangelical alliance with the Republican Party, among approaches to ministry and theology, and between the generations" (Kirkpatrick, 2007). Activists had great hope for the efficacy of partisan politics when Republicans won control of Congress in 1995, and especially once they gained unified control of government in 2001.

Some now argue that the time has come to put faith back into religion instead of politics, while others argue that the nomination of Palin and the threat of an Obama presidency justified continued political action. Most (but not all) GOP strategists hope that the Christian Right continues to mobilize voters behind party candidates, and it is likely that activists who are middle aged or older will continue to focus on elections; politics can be habit forming. But younger evangelicals seem less interested in partisan politics and more interested in mission work. Some say that the United States is not a battleground, but a mission field. Christian Right leaders have told us confidentially that they can often attract younger evangelicals to projects that will affect people's lives directly, but that they have much less enthusiasm for partisan mobilization.

Most Christian Right organizations are weaker in 2010 than they were in 2000, with fewer members, state chapters, and activists. Yet paradoxically evangelical churches remain vibrant, and some are attracting hordes of new members. But younger evangelicals are less likely to believe that the Bible is literally true and more moderate on most issues in the Christian Right agenda.

Political scientists differ considerably in their views of the future of the movement. Credible scholars predict the "inevitable failure" of the Christian Right, but others foresee considerable growth and institutionalization for the movement. These disparate evaluations reflect different assessments of the strengths and weaknesses of the movement and, in some cases, wishful thinking by its opponents and supporters.

This chapter considers two specific questions about the future of the Christian Right and then risks some tentative predictions about the movement in the twenty-first century.

## Can the Christian Right Expand?

In the 1970s and 1980s pentecostals and neoevangelicals did not rally to the Moral Majority because of the religious prejudice of its state and local leadership, and it made few inroads among white mainline Protestants, Catholics, and black evangelicals. But since then the Christian Right has succeeded in broadening its religious coalition and may be poised to extend its gains with conservative Catholics. Among movement activists there is strong evidence that the Christian Right has begun to bridge the religious chasms that so severely limited the potential of the Moral Majority. For example, state efforts to ban same-sex marriage attract a religiously ecumenical and racially diverse coalition (Campbell and Robinson, 2007). Conservative Protestants and Catholics achieved such a high level of camaraderie on issues such as abortion and marriage that two historians asked, "Is the Reformation over?" (Noll and Nystrom, 2005).

Surveys indicate that the Christian Right today is far more ecumenical than it was in the past. Among Christian Right presidential donors, for example, nearly half were evangelical Protestants, but a quarter were mainline Protestants, and another quarter were Catholic.[1] A more recent survey of conservative Christian activists showed that more than half were Catholics. Surveys of delegates to state Republican conventions in the 1990s showed that the religious coalitions of the Christian Right varied by state. Only a third of Christian Right activists in Florida were evangelical, compared to half of those in Texas and Virginia. Pentecostals made up 5 percent of Christian Right activists in Minnesota and 20 percent of those in Washington. A third of Christian Right activists in Minnesota were Catholic, compared with only 7 percent in Texas.[2]

This suggests that the Christian Right is reasonably popular among white evangelicals and has attracted activists among white Catholics and mainline Protestants as well. What are the real limits to its potential expansion? Could the movement capture the support of a majority of Americans? Could it rally black evangelicals to its cause?

In part the answers to these questions depend on the moderation of the Christian Right agenda. There is considerable support in the United States for abortion restrictions such as parental consent, informed consent, waiting periods, and bans on late term abortions; for a ban on same-sex marriage; and for greater accommodation for religious displays. A movement built around that moderate agenda could appeal to a very large constituency. On the other hand, there is little support for banning all abortions, recriminalizing homosexual relations among consenting adults, and exclusive displays of Christian religious symbols.

The problem is that a moderate agenda would not appeal to the most ardent movement activists. Consider the issue of abortion. We saw in Chapter 2 that only a minority of even fundamentalist Protestants favor a ban on all abortions, but majorities of all religious traditions favored some limitations on abortion. The Christian Right can attract its largest constituency with continued incremental restrictions on abortion, but this would be unsatisfying to activists who consider abortion to be murder and want a ban on all abortions.

Of course not all potential members of social movements pay close attention to the nuances of the issue positions of such movements. Scholars have shown that many citizens evaluate social groups based on their relations with other groups and not on the details of their agenda (Sniderman, Brody, and Tetlock, 1991). Thus, white evangelicals and others may evaluate the Family Research Council as a group that represents conservative Christians and is opposed by feminist, gay rights, secular, and other liberal groups. They may know little about the specific positions of the organization beyond the impression that it takes conservative stands on social and moral issues.

No social movement reaches its entire potential audience. There are barriers to mobilizing conservative Catholics, different barriers to enlisting white mainline Protestants, and very different barriers to mobilizing black evangelicals. Different strategies might be needed for each target audience.

The Christian Right faces internal dilemmas in choosing its strategies. And Christian conservatives face a dilemma as well in deciding whether to participate in the Christian Right.

### Dilemma 1: Moderation in the Defense of Virtue?

We have shown above that the movement can attract its largest possible constituency by staking moderate positions on most issues. The Christian Right has done this in recent years on abortion, seeking not to amend the Constitution to bar all abortions but to enact restrictions on abortions at the national and state levels. Although most activists would prefer to ban most if not all abortions, the movement has instead sought to pass laws requiring that teenaged girls get their parents' consent before having an abortion, that women wait for a certain period to think over the abortion decision, that doctors tell women various things about abortions (some of which are not consistent with the best medical research), and that fetuses be anesthetized before an abortion, as well as defining the murder of a pregnant woman as a double homicide. By focusing on restrictions to abortion rights rather than on an outright ban on abortions, the Christian Right has won the support of a broader segment of the population for its policies. Similarly, instead of seeking to ban the teaching of evolution, some Christian Right activists have sought to teach that evolution is simply a controversial theory and that intelligent design is a competing theory, a position that commands considerable support among the American public (Berkman and Plutzer, 2010). Focus on the Family and the FRC took a more moderate approach in seeking to ban only same-sex marriage, and not civil unions as well, in a national constitutional amendment.

Moderation might also mean adopting a more diverse set of policies instead of focusing narrowly on policies relating to sexuality. Younger evangelicals are interested in a far broader range of issues than most Christian Right organizations are. The National Association of Evangelicals 2005 document on civic responsibility is a good example of an expanded issue agenda. It calls for bans on same-sex marriage and embryonic stem-cell research, but it also calls upon evangelicals to seek justice for the poor and to protect the environment, issues not normally considered to be extreme or even conservative.[3]

Although the moderate approach has the advantage of broad appeal, moderation does not inspire activists to devote their evenings to the cause. When

Pat Robertson called for moderation on abortion, many activists left the Christian Coalition. The loud applause at the 2008 Values Voters Summit for speakers who took strong positions on abortion and defense suggests that the activists of the movement are not entirely happy with moderation. And there is also less support for a broader agenda among many activists. Armstrong Williams, the only African American to speak at a 2004 Christian Coalition conference, received only weak applause when he asserted, "We should be just as strong against racism as we are against abortion and gay adoption."

The danger of the moderate strategy is that the movement may win a larger audience but lose one of its key assets—the enthusiasm of its volunteers. Activism is not common in America, and most citizens can find more enjoyable things to do after a hard day at work or with their children than stuffing envelopes or working fax machines. Moderation is seldom a rallying cry for social movements, and this is especially true for the Christian Right. Many Christian Right activists see themselves battling for the soul of America, but they may be less willing to engage in combat for goals that they perceive as involving too much compromise.

Many activists argue that it is better to "fight a good fight" than to compromise with the world.[4] They support the ban on late-term abortions but think that this is only a tiny victory and prefer that the movement work publicly to ban all abortions. They seek a spoken school prayer rather than a moment of silence when students might pass notes or plan their after-school activities. They want to enforce laws against homosexuality rather than merely keep gays and lesbians from adopting children. In Massachusetts in 2005, conservative Christian activists in the state legislature voted against an amendment that would have banned same-sex marriage but allowed civil unions, preferring instead the stronger amendment that banned both, but which had no chance of passing.

An examination of Christian Right direct-mail appeals shows that the financial constituency of the movement prefers the strategy of ideological purity. One fund-raising professional who has mailed to Christian Right lists on behalf of conservative presidential candidates told one of us that any hint of moderation in a letter lowers the financial returns significantly.

The solution to this dilemma for the Christian Right may be specialization. Several smaller groups that specialize in particular issues (such as Citizens for Excellence in Education) can make extreme rhetorical appeals and take highly ideological positions—and thereby maintain morale among the activists. With the collapse of the Christian Coalition, however, there is now a major void in the movement. Most other social movements have spawned large, moderate organizations in addition to smaller, more narrowly focused, and extremely ideological groups.

## Dilemma 2: The Republican Big Tent

The second dilemma for the Christian Right is whether to concentrate its efforts solely within the Republican Party, pursue a more nonpartisan stance, or form a third party. Currently the movement is concentrated almost solely in the Republican Party, as noted in Chapter 3. The parade of presidential hopefuls at the Values Voter Summit in 2008 demonstrated that many expected the Christian Right to play an important role in the elections, and that they needed at least the tacit approval of the movement to win.

But the marriage between the Christian Right and the Republican Party has not always been a happy one. Dobson's threat to support a third-party presidential candidate in 2008 if Republicans did not nominate a pro-life candidate is just one example. Many party moderates resent the influence of the Christian Right in candidate selection and party platforms, and many Christian conservatives resent the history of party moderates who have refused to endorse Christian conservative candidates who win intraparty struggles. The passionate struggle over the 1996 presidential nomination platform suggests that these two party factions do not always get along. George W. Bush managed to bring together the factions, as Ronald Reagan did before him. McCain struggled to appeal to both sides in 2008.

In general, abortion has been a litmus-test issue in presidential politics in both parties. In 1998 Jesse Jackson and Richard Gephardt became pro-choice to run for the presidency as Democrats, and George W. Bush became pro-life as a Republican. In 2000 John McCain was angered by attacks on his record on abortion, for he had an almost perfect pro-life record, with one exception: He had voted for the use of fetal tissue in research into cures for Parkinson's disease, which killed his friend Morris Udall. This one defection from pro-life orthodoxy was enough to unleash anti-McCain mailings in the South Carolina primary, which pictured a fetus urging voters to support Bush over McCain. Pro-life activists remained skeptical of McCain through the 2008 election, in part because of this single vote.

More recently, many Republicans have argued that the party is a "big tent" with room for both pro-choice and pro-life candidates and activists, for both moderates and Christian conservatives. The Christian Coalition was willing to set up a booth under that big tent and worked on behalf of moderately pro-choice Republicans against more strongly pro-choice Democrats. But others in the movement point out that the tent has exits, and they have vowed to leave the party rather than support pro-choice candidates. In 1999 Patrick Buchanan deserted the GOP for the Reform Party, arguing that the Republicans were indistinguishable from Democrats on most issues. Christian conservative former senator Bob Smith from New Hampshire also briefly left the GOP. Others remain in the party but refuse to support compromise policies; Republican Tom Coburn from Oklahoma, elected to the Senate in 2004, is considered a "maverick" who ignores the party line when voting on issues related to his Christian faith.

Uneasy relations between parties and social movements are common; a mutually satisfactory relationship must be negotiated, for they have different goals and resources. Social movements have voters, activists, money, and means of mobilization. Parties have easy access to the electoral ballot, an even larger set of supporters, and experience in running and winning campaigns. Social movements would like to use the party machinery to elect their candidates and the party platform to advance their policy goals. Parties would like to use the activists, money, and communication channels of social movements to support their regular candidates.

By pursuing its policies within a single party, the Christian Right has also risked losing its prophetic voice on policy. After supporting Bush strongly in the 2004 election campaign and in many cases implying that he was called by God to be president, the movement had little room to criticize the administration's policies with respect to the torture of prisoners or to demand more forcefully that Bush speak out on abortion or same-sex marriage. By embracing the Republican majority in the House and the efforts by Tom DeLay to create the majority, Christian Right leaders had little ability to condemn his flouting of campaign finance law. This problem exists for all social movements that work within a single political party; for example, feminists found it difficult to criticize Bill Clinton's affair with Monica Lewinsky, although the power imbalance in their relationship would have troubled most feminist theorists.

Indeed, in the early 1990s feminists and African Americans also threatened to launch independent candidates or start third parties if the Democrats did not accede to their policy demands. In neither case was the threat taken especially seriously, and few expect the Christian Right to bolt from the Republican Party.

Although unlikely, it is possible that this troubled marriage might end in divorce. Christian Right activists are justifiably disappointed with the policies that came from six years of unified Republican government. The Republican Congress passed frequent tax cuts for businesses and wealthy Americans and repeatedly voted to appease corporate interests by rolling back regulations that protect workers, public health, and the environment. But its efforts on behalf of the core Christian Right agenda were limited and symbolic. Significant numbers of the movement may become disenchanted with working hard for Republican candidates every two years and then settling for symbolic reassurances when they are in power.

If the Christian Right did leave the Republican Party, it could choose to work within both parties to influence candidate nominations, or it could pursue a more nonpartisan strategy. Such a course would have the potential to attract a wider audience, including more conservative Catholics and especially African Americans. The success of the Christian Right in assembling a large coalition in the fight against same-sex marriage beginning in 2004 shows the potential of a nonpartisan strategy. Indeed, a bipartisan Christian Right might well have a greater policy impact than the current incarnation entrenched within the GOP. A bipartisan strategy seems unlikely for most older activists, who are strong partisans with deep ties to Republicans. But it could be a possible route for a new set of conservative Christian organizations.

### Dilemma 3: Do I Stay or Do I Go?

Christian conservatives face a larger dilemma—whether to continue building a social movement that is primarily political or to concentrate instead on building infrastructure and alternative institutions within their own religious community. In 1999 Paul Weyrich announced that the culture war was lost. "If there really were a moral majority out there, Bill Clinton would have been driven out of office months ago," he said. "It is not only the lack of political will of the Republicans, although that is part of the problem. More powerful is the fact that what Americans found absolutely intolerable only a few years ago, a majority not only tolerates but celebrates."[5] Weyrich argues that the Christian Right's cultural agenda cannot be accomplished through politics. He argues instead that Christian conservatives should withdraw from the culture and build alternative institutions to promote and protect their values.

Former Moral Majority activists Cal Thomas and Ed Dobson produced a book in 1999 titled *Blinded by Might*, which argues that Christian conservatives became obsessed with political victory and in the process abandoned some of their core principles. They suggest that conservative Christians should not withdraw entirely from politics, but should focus on their primary goals of winning souls for Christ and changing the culture through persuasion. Thomas echoed these concerns in a column written in November 2008, just a few days after Obama won the presidential election.

If Christian conservatives abandon the Christian Right early in the new millennium, it might appear to signal the end of the latest wave of the movement. If past experience is any guide, however, evangelicals would continue to build alternative institutions and infrastructure. Moreover, Christian conservatives might emerge with even greater leverage on politics if they engage the culture more broadly without ties to a single party.

Thomas and Weyrich suggest that evangelicals begin to persuade the public on issues they find central, using reason and not political power. Thus conservative Christians could attempt to persuade citizens that abortion is harmful to women, that the homosexual lifestyle is sinful but can be abandoned, or that families are more stable if the mother stays home with the children.

Many Christian Right activists strongly object to Weyrich and Thomas's call to withdraw from partisan politics, however. They continue to hope that with the help of the Republican Party they will be able to enact important elements of their agenda. This suggests a broader question: Could the Christian Right win?

## Can the Christian Right Come to Power?

Those who most fear the Christian Right wonder if its elites could ever seize power and control American politics, perhaps someday ruling by force, as the Nazis did in Germany. Such fears are almost certainly unfounded. Most leaders of the Christian Right are committed to the democratic process and strongly supportive of the American political system (Lienesch, 1994; Reed, 1994a; Shields, 2009). Although some Christian Right activists would like to restrict the civil liberties of their political opponents, only a few isolated extremists would abolish elections and seek to rule by force.[6]

Others worry that Christian Right activists might win control of the Republican Party, perhaps gain control of the political system through democratic means, and enact their entire policy agenda. This is also unlikely. The American political system was designed specifically to prevent any single faction from dominating politics. The shared powers of the presidency, the Congress, and the U.S. Supreme Court provide many avenues to thwart the policy program of any one political group. Even during the Bush administration, with a sympathetic president and sympathetic majorities in the House and Senate, the Christian Right made little progress on its core agenda. The Republican Party is internally divided on most of the issues on the Christian Right agenda. Moreover, the Supreme Court can overturn laws, and state and local governments would retain the authority to legislate policy on education, gay rights, and abortion. The American system would prevent any organized group from imposing its will on a majority opposed to its agenda.

This means that liberals' worst nightmares of an American theocracy are probably just nightmares. But it does not mean that the Christian Right cannot affect public policy in the United States. Social movements can profoundly affect social and political life without ever "taking over" the political system.

Consider the profound changes to policy and government brought about by the civil rights and feminist movements in a relatively short period. In the early 1960s, blacks could not vote in many Southern counties, eat in many restaurants, swim in many swimming pools, or stay in many hotels. There were separate drinking fountains for blacks and whites and a black section in the back of the bus. Today racism persists, but the magnitude of change is astonishing. Andrew Young, a former civil rights activists appointed by Jimmy Carter as ambassador to the United Nations, told a crowd that "my mother told me I could be anything I wanted to be. But she told me today that she never really thought that any black man could rise this high." Since Young spoke, African Americans have held the office of secretary of state (twice), attorney general, and president of the United States.

Similarly, the feminist movement of the 1960s and 1970s radically altered social relations in the United States. Although women remain disadvantaged in many aspects of society, they now constitute more than half of the graduating classes in major law schools and have achieved positions of power in politics, business, and other areas of society. Retiring justice Sandra Day O'Connor was arguably the most influential justice on the Supreme Court during her tenure, and Democratic congresswoman Nancy Pelosi became the Speaker of the House in 2006. Hillary Clinton almost won the Democratic nomination for president, and Sarah Palin was the first woman from her party nominated for a job one heartbeat away from the presidency. Sexism, like racism, still persists, but women have many more life choices today than they had in the 1950s.

To evaluate the impact of the civil rights, feminist, and Christian Right movements, imagine that Rip Van Winkle had fallen asleep in 1960, in the early days of national attention to the civil rights movement and more than a decade before the formation of National Organization for Women, and then awoke on Election Day, 2008. He would have been shocked to see Obama elected president, endorsed by Colin Powell, who had been both chairman of the Joint Chiefs and secretary of state. He would have been startled to learn that the Democratic nomination had almost been won by a woman, to see a mother of five children running for vice president on the GOP ticket, and to see a woman occupy the most powerful leadership position in Congress. He would have been surprised to have heard in the vice presidential debate considerable agreement on a core of equal rights for gays and lesbians, and that the country was seriously debating same-sex marriage. These surprises are signals of the success of the civil rights, feminist, and gay rights movements in changing the way we live and think.

There are no policy areas in which Rip would be surprised at Christian Right victories, despite thirty years of activism. To determine whether the Christian Right could possibly have such a great impact on American society, it is first necessary to consider just what the movement has accomplished to date, and why.

On some of its core issues, the Christian Right has experienced significant defeats. Its efforts to reinforce traditional gender roles have failed, as tens of millions of Americans voted for a woman for vice president in 2008. The enthusiastic endorsement of Palin is perhaps a reluctant acceptance that Americans now support equal political, social, and economic roles for women.

The losses have been almost as great on gay and lesbian rights. In 1978 when the Moral Majority was founded, twenty-nine states had bans on homosexual relations between consenting adults, and in many states sodomy was a felony. Discrimination against gays and lesbians in housing, employment, and other aspects of public life were widespread (Rimmerman, 2007). Gays and lesbians are now also more integrated into American public life and protected from discrimination. Many large companies now offer benefits to the partners of gay employees, and many television shows and

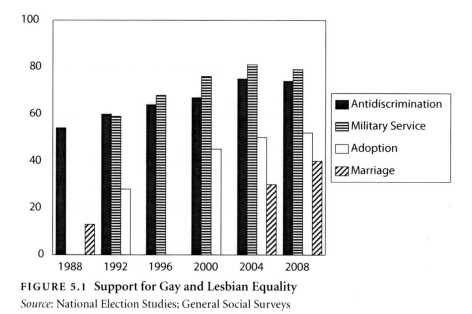

**FIGURE 5.1  Support for Gay and Lesbian Equality**
*Source*: National Election Studies; General Social Surveys

movies have depicted gay and lesbian characters in a positive or sympathetic light. In 2010 same-sex marriage is legal in Massachusetts, Connecticut, Iowa, Vermont, Maine, New Hampshire, and the District of Columbia, and many other states offer same-sex couples most of the legal protections of marriage through civil unions or domestic partnerships. The Christian Right has had great success in passing state constitutional amendments banning same-sex marriage, but in 1978 there were few if any gay rights activists who believed that marriage would be possible anywhere in the country in their lifetimes.

What these two issues have in common is the underlying issue of equality. As women and gays and lesbians have demanded equal rights, men and heterosexuals have (in some cases grudgingly) come to acknowledge the justice of that claim. The Christian Right arguments of damage to family institutions do not in the end trump equality claims in contemporary American politics. The magnitude of changes in public support for gay rights is shown in Figure 5.1. There are few if any other sets of attitudes that have moved this quickly in the United States.

Moreover, this change has occurred not because the public has become libertine in their sexual mores. Figure 5.2 shows the percentage of the public who says that homosexual relations are always wrong, compared with the percentage who say that extramarital sex is always wrong. These two trends

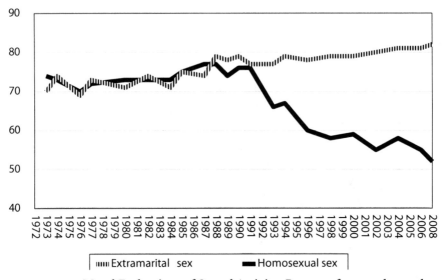

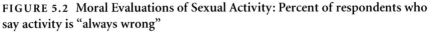

FIGURE 5.2  **Moral Evaluations of Sexual Activity: Percent of respondents who say activity is "always wrong"**
*Source*: General Social Survey, 1972–2008

are in opposite directions, suggesting that attitudes have not changed as a result of more liberal sexual mores, but rather because of a fundamental re-thinking of sexual orientation. The data show that in 2008 a majority of Americans believed that homosexual activity was always wrong, but among those thirty or younger more said that it is never wrong than declared that it was always wrong.

The public has become only slightly more liberal on pornography since the Christian Right mobilization in the late 1970s, but the Internet has made the regulation of explicit sexual materials more difficult. In the early days of the Moral Majority, Christian Right activists would protest outside of bookstores that sold *Playboy* or other erotic publications. Today Internet porn sites make specialized video formats to download to iPhones, so that it is difficult to know precisely where to picket. The public is strongly in favor of filters to prevent those under eighteen from accessing pornography on public computers, and the movement has had success in requiring these filters at all levels of government. Still, sexually explicit material is far more available today than it was in 1978.

The Christian Right has made some gains in the accommodation of re-ligion to public life. The public today is somewhat more supportive of public displays of Christianity than a decade ago, although they are also more supportive of displays of non-Christian faiths. In the language of Chapter 1, they are both more accommodationist and more libertarian (Campbell and Green, 2009). The Christian Right has had some real success on church-state issues in which the free exercise of evangelicals has been limited. In 1994 President Clinton spoke of the need to allow religious expression in the public schools and directed the Department of Education to clarify this position for local schools. As a result of lobbying by the Christian Right and the threat of lawsuits from the movement's legal arm, many communities and school districts have become more accommodating to religious expression by conservative Christians. The Supreme Court has ruled that student religious groups deserve equal access to the use of school property. In other areas where the Christian Right has made claims that rules restricted freedom of religion, society has generally been supportive. At the same time, public opinion has grown more supportive of homosexuals and feminists expressing their beliefs as well.

It is on abortion that the Christian Right has demonstrated some momentum. On the surface the public is only slightly less pro-choice than two decades ago. When asked a four-choice abortion question about whether abortion should be legal never; should be legal for rape, fetal defect, and health of the mother; should be legal for other reasons but not all reasons; or should always be legal, there is little change in the distribution of public attitudes. Between 1980 and 2008 there is a slight increase in the portion of the population who would ban all abortions—from 11 to 14 percent—and a similar increase in the portion that would always allow abortion—from 36 to 40 percent.

But beneath this stable surface, American attitudes on abortion are changing, and this is especially evident when different survey questions are asked. Gallup asks a series of abortion questions that show somewhat different results. One question asks if abortion should be legal under any conditions, under some conditions, or always illegal. There is little change on this question since 1975. But another question asks whether "with respect to the abortion issue, would you consider yourself pro-choice or pro-life?" On this question, there has been a profound shift since 1995, when the question was first asked. In that year 56 percent of the public indicated that they were pro-choice, and 33 percent were pro-life. In the middle of 2009 the pro-choice number had dropped to 42 percent, and the pro-life number increased to 51 percent.

Moreover, there is evidence that the youngest cohort of Americans is much less pro-choice than its older counterparts. The General Social Survey asks six questions about concrete circumstances in which abortion might be allowed: when a woman's health is in danger, when her pregnancy is a result of rape, when the fetus is severely defective, when the family is too poor for another child, when the mother does not want to marry the man who impregnated her, and when a married couple wants no more children. Survey respondents answer each question separately, and if we count the number of "yes" answers, we get a scale that runs from 0 if the person opposed abortion for all reasons to 6 if he or she believed abortion should be legal for all six reasons.

Figure 5.3 shows the average abortion support score for different age groups in the 1970s, 1980s, 1990s, and 2000s through 2008. Because each age group encompasses ten years, we can compare a cohort over time by examining the attitudes of the next oldest group in the next decade. In other words, those who were eighteen to twenty-eight in the 1970s are represented by a dark bar in that decade, by a white bar in the second decade, by the horizontally striped bar in the third decade, and by the polka dot bar in the 2000s. By comparing them across time we can see that theirs is among the most liberal generation in each period, but that they are less pro-choice in the 2000s than they were in the 1970s.

The most important thing to notice in this figure is that in the first three decades, the youngest group (dark bar, far left) is always more pro-choice than the oldest group (diagonally striped bar, far right). That means that for thirty years, generational replacement has increased support for legal abortion, while other factors have decreased support. But in the 2000s the younger group is actually the *least* pro-choice cohort, and if this persists over the next couple of decades, generational replacement will result in decreased support for abortion.

These data are good news for pro-life groups and the Christian Right, but they do not result primarily from Christian Right actions. The youngest cohort is less pro-choice across the board; this is true among fundamentalists, Catholics, and those who never attend church; among Republicans and Democrats; and among those who favor same-sex marriage and those who oppose protecting gays from job discrimination. The cohort is distinctive both in states where the Christian Right has been very active and in states where it has been virtually nonexistent; in states that have adopted abortion restrictions and in states that have rejected them.

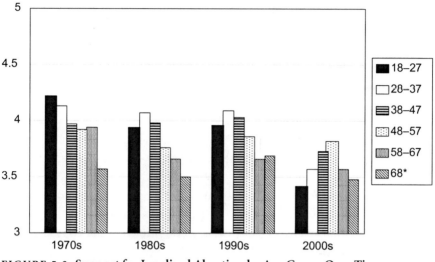

**FIGURE 5.3  Support for Legalized Abortion by Age Group Over Time**
*Source*: General Social Survey, 1973–2008

The "Juno generation" is not much more likely than those who are older to oppose abortion for all reasons, but they are far less likely to *support* abortion for all reasons.[7] They appear to balance fetal and women's rights as most Americans do, while giving neither set of rights absolute influence. But they appear to value fetal rights somewhat more strongly than earlier generations did, which leads them to oppose abortion for some reasons on surveys (Wilcox and Carr, 2009).

At the state and local levels, Christian Right activity has had a greater impact on public policy. This is perhaps most apparent in the field of education; various curricula and programs have been revised or eliminated because of organized protests by parents, including the teaching of modern scientific thinking in biology, geology, and astronomy. In some cities gay rights laws have been overturned, and abortion is more difficult to obtain today in many states than it was in 1978. In 2004 the Virginia state legislature made it a double felony to kill a pregnant woman. After much lobbying by Christian Right groups, they also removed language from a bill that would have instructed school health officials to inform students who have been raped about the availability of legal emergency contraception. Thus a school guidance counselor who learns that a student has been raped can suggest that she consult a doctor but cannot tell her about a legal drug that could terminate her pregnancy. States have adopted a wide variety of restrictions on abortion, including most recently requirements in some states that abortion patients be shown an ultrasound image of the fetus before the procedure begins.

Perhaps more important is the impact the Christian Right has had in framing the policy agenda, as noted by political scientist Kenneth Wald:

> It is difficult to identify any substantive public policy that has been implemented primarily because of the Christian Right. Rather, the mobilization of conservative Christians has affected the agenda of American politics, promoting some issues from obscurity to a central place on the national agenda. We would probably not be arguing about school prayer, tuition vouchers, and other proposals had the Christian Right failed to materialize.[8]

Paradoxically, the movement that seeks to restore America to Christian values may well have had the opposite effect, at least among the young. In the past decade younger Americas have become far more likely than earlier cohorts to tell pollsters that they have no religious affiliation (Wuthnow, 2007). Many appear to believe in God, to pray privately, and to consider religion to be important to them, but they have turned off to organized religion. Several studies suggest that this has happened because young people associate Christianity with the Christian Right, and especially with intolerance toward gays and lesbians (Hout and Fiser, 2002; Putnam and Campbell, 2010). Some Christian Right leaders have acknowledged the problem, calling for a new vocabulary to discuss gay rights issues with the young. At this point, however, it appears that the Christian Right's efforts to protect young Americans from secularism may instead have pushed them to greater secularism.

## The Future of the Christian Right Agenda

Of course, Christian Right activists seek to do more than affect the policy debate—they wish to alter public policy, change the direction of America, and redeem it from what they see as its sinful path. Where are they likely to have success in the future?

In the short term, the future of the Christian Right may be determined by the Supreme Court. With the appointment of John Roberts as chief justice and Samuel Alito as associate justice, Christian conservatives hope for a series of rulings that will reverse their losses in many areas. They hope the

Court will allow for the teaching of intelligent design or religious objections to the theory of evolution. They hope the Court will be more supportive of Christian displays such as the Ten Commandments outside courtrooms and of prayers at high school graduations. Some hope the Court will overturn its earlier ruling barring states from enforcing sodomy laws. Others merely hope the Court upholds the Defense of Marriage Act.

But their biggest hopes lie with abortion, where activists fervently pray that the Court will overturn *Roe* and return abortion to the states. The Court would not rule that abortion is legal, but merely that states can ban or strictly regulate it. At that point the movement would immediately be almost entirely preoccupied with state legislative battles over abortion regulations—fought in states like Texas and California that have professional legislatures, and in Wyoming and Virginia where legislative service is a part-time job.

Some states have laws in place to immediately ban or severely restrict abortion if the Court reverses past rulings. Some of these states might find such laws are more difficult to sustain once they matter than they were to pass while women assumed that abortion rights are safely protected by the Court. But in a large number of states, a majority of voters would support sharp limits on abortion rights, limiting the procedure to confirmed dangers to the life and physical health of the mother, rape, and severe fetal defect. Local governments might also become involved in the debate, which would energize the pro-life side of the Christian Right but also pro-choice activists and the moderate abortion middle, for whom the actual laws will suddenly matter.

The proposed constitutional amendment to ban same-sex marriage faces the hurdles designed by the Founding Fathers to favor the status quo. The failure of popular proposed amendments such as the Equal Rights Amendment and the amendment to ban the burning of the American flag is clear evidence that momentary passions are not enough to change the Constitution. But more states might bar such marriages in referenda and state constitutional amendments, and the Supreme Court might uphold the Defense of Marriage Act, which would allow such states to refuse to recognize gay marriage. In this event, a lesbian couple married in Massachusetts would not be considered married in Texas if they moved there or even took a vacation there.

Longer term, the question is whether the Christian Right can replenish its aging membership with younger members. Throughout history, some organizations have failed to do this and have either disbanded or exist only as pale ghosts of their former selves. Although Christian Right leaders do not state openly the average age of their membership, they admit privately that donors are a very old group.

Here it seems possible that the older Christian Right organizations will either fade away or transform themselves into something different, and that new organizations representing conservative Christians may form. How might these transformed or new organizations differ from the contemporary Christian Right, and should we call them "Christian Right" organizations?

Wary of the potential for predictions about the movement to embarrass those who make them, we think it is possible that a new type of conservative Christian movement might be more visible in ten years, in some ways similar to but in other ways different from the current Christian Right. The Moral Majority, Concerned Women for America, and many other organizations in the movement's recent history were molded by two factors: the theology of fundamentalist and pentecostal Christians and the electoral needs of the Republican party.

The eschatology of American fundamentalism focuses on the battle between the forces of God and those of Satan, with the belief that the latter must win the early battle. Satan is seen as a real, sentient being who walks and talks on the earth, tempting the faithful with lies and deceit. Nearly all of the leaders of the Christian Right in the 1980s, and many of them in the 1990s and 2000s, subscribe to this theological position. This view leads activists to overestimate the danger of their opponents and overstate the magnitude of social change that is occurring. Many Christian Right leaders with whom we have spoken believe that the United States is a single vote away from being to the left of Amsterdam and appear to believe statements like those we have shown in previous chapters: that Hillary Clinton wants the Bible declared "hate speech," and that national health insurance will result in death panels and forced abortions. They truly perceive that all issues are part of a larger war and thus are usually unwilling to consider any common ground.

Younger evangelicals believe in the inspiration and truth of the Bible, but they also believe that not all of it is meant to be interpreted literally (Putnam and Campbell, 2010). Among the smaller group who are literalist, they are more modest in their claims to understand the meaning of the text. This leaves them more open to consider other theological sources such as natural law and less willing to see their opponents as evil. Younger white evangelicals have engaged in dialogue with Catholics and Jews, with African American and Latino Christians, and in some cases even with Muslims. Many have gone on missions, and still others are one or two degrees of separation from someone who has done so. This makes them more likely to engage the broader issues of the world. Without the necessity to respond to every liberal policy as if it were a military advance, younger evangelicals are freer to look at the political and social landscape and think about what they might do to strengthen families, help children, and protect life and God's creation.

The contemporary Christian Right is also a product of Republican political mobilization. Most of the largest Christian Right groups were founded with at least some resources from Republican activists, and in some cases even party committees. The Republican Party has provided resources selectively to help advance their electoral fortunes, as the Democrats do with their allied groups. But this means that the Christian Right evolved in tandem with the Republican party (Wilcox, 2009).

It is likely that ten years from now there will continue to be groups focused primarily on electing Republican officials. But it may well be that there will be other groups seeking to work in politics but more often in society to affect the way that people live and the choices that they make, organizations that see the country as a mission field and not a battle field. Such organizations are certain to be pro-life, perhaps even more ardently so than the contemporary movement, but they may be more likely to consider whether health care might make it easier for a young woman to choose to be a mother. They might oppose same-sex marriage, but might also focus on the health of marriages in their own community—instead of ignoring the infidelities of their political friends. They will more carefully consider their agenda and likely concentrate on projects in their communities, as mainline Protestants have done in the past few decades.

Some of these groups might truly be called Christian conservative but not Christian Right, and they would have the potential to draw widespread support from some mainline Protestants, some Catholics, ethnic minorities, Muslims, and even secular Americans. To do this, the movement would have to accept gender equality and a core of civil liberties for gay and lesbian couples. They would need to consider a broader array of issues, including the environment and economic issues.

## The Christian Right as a Social Movement

The Christian Right has paradoxically been the most successful social movement in influencing elections and party politics over the past century and the least successful in influencing policy and culture. The labor movement, the civil rights movement, the women's movement, and even the gay and lesbian rights movement have created far greater change in politics and society than the Christian Right, for all its political mobilization.

Each of these more successful movements had as its primary goal the amelioration of real social and economic discrimination against its constituency. Blacks and women, for example, were denied jobs, promotions, housing, credit, and access to political office. Such discrimination clearly ran against American notions of fairness and equal opportunity, and the movements ultimately have helped reduce this discrimination. When these groups complained to society that they were treated unfairly, ultimately whites and men agreed with the charge.

Although the Christian Right claims that evangelicals face real discrimination, at best they face cultural, not economic, bias. Christians are not being denied jobs, promotions, housing, credit, or the chance to run for higher office—indeed, numerous leaders in Congress are evangelical. Moreover, despite the heated rhetoric of Christian Right direct mail and e-mails, conservative Christians are free to worship in America as they choose and are in no danger of losing that right. In a country that is overwhelmingly Christian, many Americans regard claims that Christians face serious bias as unbelievable.

The Christian Right has been successful when it has pointed to real discrimination in America. Some misguided school principals have interfered with student religious freedom because they misinterpreted Supreme Court rulings, and the movement has made great strides in protecting student rights. The U.S. Supreme Court ruling that the University of Virginia should provide funds to student religious publications if it funds other kinds of student publications is a case in point. The Christian Right has also been somewhat successful in its advocacy for a greater public acknowledgment of religion in America.

The Christian Right has also succeeded in playing the role of the "Christian Anti-Defamation League," responding quickly and forcefully to real and perceived slights in the media and public life. For example, in December 1995 a poet who regularly contributed to National Public Radio was forced to apologize for his comments after Ralph Reed quickly denounced them. Just as the civil rights movement succeeded in making racist jokes unacceptable in polite company and the feminist movement banished sexist and off-color jokes, so the Christian Right seeks to bar demeaning humor aimed at conservative Christians.

At some point evangelicals may succeed in making the point that popular culture has few positive depictions of the lifestyles of a quarter of the American public. In 1999 black Americans justifiably protested the heavily white fall lineup on the major television networks, but evangelical Christians were far more underrepresented. Television in recent years has featured a few angels and some characters who took religion seriously, but sympathetic portraits of born-again Christians are nonexistent. They are more likely to be ridiculed, as they were in various episodes of *Seinfeld* and *The Simpsons* in the 1990s and in the 2004 movie *Saved*. Thus far, however, conservative Christians have been more interested in creating their own parallel cultural outlets—their own television shows, movies, music, and even comic books (Bates, 2002).

In all of these areas, the Christian Right has had some success and will probably continue to do so in the future. But the core of the Christian Right agenda is not just about allowing conservative Christians to practice their religion and avoid public ridicule; it is about legislating morality. The Christian Right seeks to legislate policies that affect the behavior of others—their sexual relationships, their access to abortion, their ability to read what they choose. Because these behaviors lie in what some have called the "sphere of privacy," social change is much more difficult to achieve. Blacks and women were able to achieve much by calling on Americans to confront their own discriminatory behavior. The Christian Right asks people not just to stop discriminating against Christians but to live their lives according to its version of morality and religion. This is a much harder sell.

## Premillennialists in the New Millennium

In 2010 the Christian Right stands at a crossroads. Its future is far murkier than when the first edition of this book appeared almost fifteen years ago. It is possible that the Christian Right will be revitalized to oppose Obama's health care programs, to oppose same-sex marriage, or to fight for state regulations on abortion if *Roe* is overturned—that it will manage to recruit young, talented leaders committed to the long haul who will not go gently into that good night in response to temporary setbacks. It is also possible that the movement will fragment, with some retreating from politics to build alternative institutions, and others remaining as activists in the Republican Party.

And it is possible that the contemporary Christian Right will fade away, replaced by new, less reactionary organizations that draw on the vibrant evangelical churches to engage society and politics. With younger and more moderate leaders, the new movement might build bridges to other religious groups and seek to work in society while making political work less central.

Ted Jelen (1990) has argued that support for the Christian Right waxes and wanes in a cyclical fashion. As cultural minorities become visible and make demands for social justice, Christian Right movements arise to enforce conventional morality. Yet the movements inevitably fail because of the religious prejudice of the various elements of the movement, and religion again becomes a private matter. Jelen's account seems to fit nicely the rise and fall of the fundamentalist movements of the 1920s, 1950s, and 1980s, but if the movement collapses again it will not be from religious particularism but from the failure of the electoral strategy to lead to the movement's policy goals and its inability to convince a better educated and more theologically moderate generation to share its fears and dreams. Christian conservatives will remain an important constituency for Republican politics, but they may increasingly be mobilized by microtargeting campaigns themselves, rather than by Christian Right organizations.

## Conclusion

In this book we have explored two radically divergent visions of the Christian Right. In the first it is an intolerant, uncompromising movement that would deprive women, gays and lesbians, and others of their rights; in the second it is a defensive movement that would protect conservative Christians from a hostile society and government. As in most heated political debates, the truth appears to lie somewhere between these two positions. Ultimately the Christian Right probably poses only a limited threat to basic American civil liberties, because it is unlikely to gain access to sufficient political power to enact legislation, and because many activists hold conflicting values about intolerance and democratic government. And although the agenda of the Christian Right is in some ways defensive, the movement also asks Americans to adopt policies that would affect the lives and liberties of many citizens.

Is the movement good or bad for America? The answer for each person depends partially on the individual's reactions to the agenda of the Christian Right. For someone who supports restrictions on abortion and civil rights protections for gays and lesbians and supports school prayer and the teaching of creationism, the Christian Right appears to be a very good thing.

For someone who opposes those policies, the movement appears to be a threatening, hostile force.

It is important to go beyond these political calculations, however, and assess the positive and negative things the movement has accomplished. Because these judgments are ultimately normative, we conclude on a personal note. With one of us holding some sympathy for Christian Right policy and one opposed to most of the movement's agenda, we both support the free exercise of religion for conservative Christians and all other Americans and believe that Christian conservatives deserve a place in the political process. And we both believe that Christian Right activists must respect the rights of other groups, including those they fear.

There are several positive aspects to the involvement of the Christian Right in American politics. The mobilization of previously apolitical evangelicals and fundamentalists into politics constitutes a useful broadening of the electorate and the politically engaged public. America's pluralist system works best when all important groups are represented in policy negotiations, and the Christian Right's constituency has a unique set of policy concerns that should be part of the policy debate. The careful monitoring of the rights of religious expression in public schools has also been a positive result, for in a few communities Christian children have been prohibited from engaging in religious activities that do not disrupt the school curriculum. Moreover, the efforts by the Christian Right to counter negative stereotypes in news and popular media have been generally helpful, although claims that anyone who opposes the movement exhibits anti-Christian bias are disingenuous and distort the image of cultural liberals as badly as the media may distort the lives and values of Christian conservatives.

Probably the most important benefit of the Christian Right has been its insistence that America consider basic moral and religious values as it crafts public policy. Often policy debates in America are devoid of any discussion of values, and the Christian Right deserves some credit for the rediscovery of their importance in the 1990s. Moreover, because many Americans are deeply religious, it is odd to deny the role of religious values in policy debates, and the Christian Right has gone far toward legitimizing the inclusion of these values in the larger discussion of America's agenda. If the Christian Right forces America to consider its core values and connect those values to public policy, it will have been a positive force.

The values the Christian Right brings to the debate are but one set of religious values, of course, and we hope that others will engage movement participants in a discussion of competing values, such as social justice, equality, and personal liberation. A political scientist, Clarke Cochran, responded to a paper by Ralph Reed at a conference in the 1990s by noting: "A lot of issues that Christians should be supporting, such things as gun control, justice in health care, protecting the vulnerable widows and orphans (to use Biblical language), dignified work for people, and property for the common good (from the Catholic natural law tradition) never appear because . . . the Christian Coalition . . . has been captured by the conservative ideological position."[9] Cochran's analysis is just one example of the useful debate that could be undertaken on the religious values that underlie public policy.

Yet we also see some negative aspects to Christian Right involvement in American politics. The harsh, uncompromising moral certitude of many Christian Right activists often does not further the policy debate but rather precludes it. For many activists, there is no room for debate because they see their policy preferences as the will of God. One activist in Virginia told one of us in no uncertain terms that a flat tax was biblical policy, and therefore there was no room for discussion. Such certitude actually discourages the inclusion of religious values in the policy debate, because it brands alternative values as illegitimate and encourages others to steer clear of religious argument.

The heated rhetoric of Christian Right direct mail exacerbates this problem by telling contributors that an alliance of liberal groups may take over America, strip them of their basic religious rights, teach their children Satan worship and witchcraft, and implement other almost unspeakably evil policies. It is small wonder that many Christian Right activists fear their political enemies and consider them a danger to the republic. Liberal groups also contribute to this climate of cultural conflict by portraying conservative Christians as jack-booted thugs who would overturn American democracy. The tone of political discourse would be improved if both sides would calm down a bit.

Moreover, the failure of many Christian Right activists to support basic civil liberties is troubling. When movement leaders write that gays and lesbians, feminists, liberals, and secular citizens should not be permitted to teach in schools, they invite their followers to take action against teachers in school districts across the country. We know teachers who have been confronted by movement activists in harsh and unfair ways. At the fringe of the movement, some write that America has no room for anyone but Christian conservatives.

The lasting legacy of the Christian Right will depend critically on whether pragmatists or ideologues come to dominate the movement, how those new leaders choose to mold the movement, and the willingness of their followers to be so molded. If pragmatic leaders dominate, counsel the virtues of bargaining and compromise, and encourage their activists to think of their political antagonists as reasonable citizens with basic rights, the movement may ultimately prove to be a constructive voice in the policy debate. If ideological leaders warn darkly of the dangers of the forces of liberalism and stir up hatred toward gays and lesbians, feminists, secularists, and others with whom they do not agree, the movement will constitute a divisive force in America that threatens the lifestyles and civil liberties of many citizens.

If Christian conservatives choose to follow the suggestion of Cal Thomas and Ed Dobson to pull back from partisan political action and instead engage the culture in a debate and discussion of the religious and moral underpinnings of public policy, it is possible that the movement will have its greatest, and most positive, impact. Because of the partisan nature of the current incarnation of the movement, there has been more shouting than discussion, and both sides have ended up adopting more extreme positions in an effort to mobilize voters. Between the shouting voices there is room for a quieter discussion, where both sides might be surprised to find that they have some common ground.

# Discussion Questions

## Chapter 1

1. How do terms such as "Christian Right," "religious right," "pro-family movement," and "Christian conservative" differ in their meaning? What are the advantages and disadvantages of each term?

2. What is a social movement? How does this label fit the Christian Right? What are examples of other social movements?

3. Why is the Christian Right controversial?

4. How do American religious diversity, civil religion, and constitutional context affect your assessment of the Christian Right?

## Chapter 2

1. What have been the common themes of the various waves of Christian Right activity? How have these manifestations of the Christian Right differed?

2. Why do fundamentalists object to teaching evolution in public schools? Do parents have a right to see that their children are exposed only to ideas of which they approve, or does society have the right to expose children to different ideas as part of the educational process? Would it be fair to teach both evolution and creationism in science classes, or would that constitute teaching religion as though it were science?

3. How do fundamentalists, evangelicals, pentecostals, and charismatics differ? Why are these differences important to individuals within these traditions?

4. Will the Christian Right be able to expand its base among white evangelicals? What are its prospects for attracting Catholics, mainline Protestants, African Americans, and Latinos?

## Chapter 3

1. Consider two theses: (a) The various groups of the contemporary Christian Right compete with one another for members, confuse their constituency by taking different policy positions, and foster rivalries. They constitute a weakness for the movement. (b) The various groups of the contemporary Christian Right are an advantage to the movement because they allow activists to choose among several groups based on their issue positions and thereby attract a wider audience. Which thesis do you think is true, and why?

2. Some writers classify the pro-life movement as part of the Christian Right, but this book does not. What are the arguments for each point of view?

3. How does the Christian Right seek to influence government? How do these strategies and tactics differ from those of the civil rights movement or the feminist movement?

4. What are the advantages and disadvantages to the Republican Party of its alliance with the Christian Right? What are the advantages and disadvantages to the Christian Right of this alliance?

## Chapter 4

1. Explain how mobilizing evangelicals and other conservative Christians into politics might provide a more balanced policy debate.

2. Why do you think Christian Right activists are less supportive of basic civil liberties than other activists? Does this lack of support pose a danger to democracy? How might Christian Right leaders help to increase support for civil liberties among their activist core?

3. Consider the policy agenda of the Christian Right. Why do Christian Right supporters believe that theirs is a defensive agenda, and why do the movement's opponents believe that it is an offensive agenda?

4. Opposition to gay marriage has broadened the Christian Right's constituency. Do you think cooperation among white and black evangelicals, Catholics, and conservative Jews is likely to carry over into other policy issues?

5. Is the Christian Right good or bad for America? Does the movement enhance democracy by mobilizing a new group into the policy debate, or does it threaten democracy and civil liberties?

## Chapter 5

1. What are your predictions for the Christian Right's relationship with the Republican Party in future presidential elections?

2. What are the advantages and disadvantages of a strategy of moderation by the Christian Right? What would the movement gain, and what would it lose, by adopting this strategy?

3. In what ways has the Christian Right affected public policy in America? In what ways has it changed the terms of the debate?

4. Why have attitudes toward abortion changed? Is the Christian Right responsible for decreasing public support for legalized abortion?

5. What does the Christian Right need to do to attract young evangelicals? On what issues do young evangelicals differ from the Christian Right?

# Glossary

**accommodationist** Person who believes that the First Amendment permits the government to support all religions so long as it does not discriminate among religions. Accommodationists welcome public displays of religious symbols and practice.

**Alliance Defense Fund** Christian Right organization committed to working through the courts to ensure religious freedom and defend the traditional family structure.

**Alliance for Marriage** A research and educational organization that seeks to promote traditional marriage more broadly.

**American Center for Law and Justice** Legal organization of the contemporary Christian Right, associated with Pat Robertson and spearheaded by Jay Sekulow. The ACLJ files lawsuits on behalf of Christians who believe they have faced discrimination.

**American Civil Liberties Union** Organization devoted to protecting civil liberties for all Americans, usually through legal action. The group has defended religious liberties of unpopular groups and sought to maintain a strong separation between church and state.

**American Council of Christian Churches** Militant fundamentalist organization, formed in 1941 by Carl McIntyre. The ACCC denounced communist infiltration in society and in mainline Protestant churches and provided resources to the anticommunist groups of the 1950s.

**American Family Association** Organization of the contemporary Christian Right, originally known as the National Federation for Decency, once headed by Donald Wildmon. The AFA focuses primarily on monitoring sex and violence on television and on countering anti-Christian stereotypes on television. It organizes consumer boycotts of the sponsors of offending programs.

**Arlington Group** Coalition of Christian Right leaders that seeks to identify goals and coordinate strategy across movement organizations.

**Bible Crusaders of America** Antievolution organization of the 1920s. The BCA was well funded, linked to Baptist churches, and active primarily in the South.

**Bible League of North America** Organization formed in 1902 that, through arguments and publications, fought the teaching of evolution.

**born-again experience** Experience common in evangelical churches in which an individual repents of his or her sin, accepts Christ as his or her personal savior, and is redeemed by grace. Often an emotional experience, accompanied by a sense of release.

**charismatic** Term used to refer to a religious movement and to certain religious doctrines. Charismatics worship with ecstatic spiritual gifts, including speaking in tongues, faith healing, and being slain in the Spirit. The charismatic movement transcends denominational boundaries, with charismatic caucuses in most denominations and interfaith charismatic gatherings in most major cities.

**Christian Anti-Communism Crusade** Anticommunist organization of the 1950s, which used radio and traveling schools of anticommunism to spread its message. The organization continued into the late 1990s.

**Christian Coalition** Most prominent Christian Right organization in the 1990s, at that time headed by Pat Robertson. In 2010 the organization was largely defunct at the national level, though state affiliates were still active.

**Christian Crusade** Anticommunist organization of the 1950s.

**Christian Defense Coalition** Christian Right organization that encourages direct activism in the form of demonstrations and protests. Founded by Operation Rescue leader Randall Terry, along with Dr. George Grant, Jay Sekulow, and the Rev. Patrick Mahoney.

**Christian preferentialist** Individual who takes an accommodationist position on the establishment clause of the First Amendment and a communitarian position on the free exercise clause. A Christian preferentialist seeks a more open display of Christian symbols and faith but is less willing to allow displays of other American religions.

**Christian reconstructionism** Also known as dominion theology and theonomy, this doctrine teaches that American law and politics should be structured along the lines of Old Testament law.

**Christian Voice** Christian Right organization founded in the late 1970s by Robert Grant with the help of Pat Robertson. The Christian Voice was known for its lobbying and ridiculed for its voters guides, which nonetheless served as the precursors for more sophisticated contemporary efforts.

**Church League of America** Anticommunist organization of the 1950s.

**Citizens for Excellence in Education** Organization of the contemporary Christian Right, headed by Robert Simonds. CEE opposes the teaching of secular humanism and witchcraft in schools and opposes programs to establish national education standards, such as outcomes-based education.

**civil religion** Set of beliefs about the relationship between God and country, generally centering on a special relationship. In America, civil religion is evident in the frequent references to religious images in public life.

**communitarian** (First Amendment) View that religious liberties can be limited by community norms. Communitarians generally disapprove of religious exemptions from otherwise valid laws and hold that the free exercise clause bars government from directly prohibiting religious observance but not from limiting such observance if the law has a secular purpose.

**Concerned Women for America** Organization of the contemporary Christian Right, headed by Wendy Wright. CWA is composed primarily of women and takes a special interest in women's issues.

**Contract with the American Family** Political document of the Christian Coalition that includes ten policy goals.

**Creation Care** Term used by the National Association of Evangelicals to explain its commitment to the environment.

**creationism** Belief that the world, its flora, and its fauna were created by God and that he made humans at that time. Creationists explicitly reject the theory of evolution. Most believe that the world was created in six days in the relatively recent past.

**Defenders of the Christian Faith** Antievolution organization of the 1920s, active primarily in the Midwest.

**Discovery Institute** Conservative think-tank in Seattle, Washington, that is one of the most prominent advocates of intelligent design.

**dispensationalism** Doctrine that God has dealt with humans under different covenants or dispensations at different times in history. Although accounts vary, many dispensationalists believe that the first covenant was the period of innocence in the Garden of Eden, which ended with Eve and the apple; the second was mankind on its own, which ended with the flood of Noah; the third was chastened humanity, which ended with the Tower of Babel; the fourth was God's promise to Abraham, which ended with the captivity in Egypt; the fifth was the covenant with Moses; the sixth was the period of grace ushered in by Jesus; and the seventh will be the millennium, a thousand-year period of perfect peace.

**Eagle Forum** Antifeminist organization headed by Phyllis Schlafly. Eagle Forum was organized to fight the Equal Rights Amendment in the 1970s and now focuses on opposition to feminism, the teaching of secular humanism, and legal abortion.

**establishment clause** Phrase in the First Amendment that is the source of controversy regarding separation of church and state: "Congress shall make no law respecting an establishment of religion."

**evangelical** Term used to refer to a religious movement, specific denominations, and religious doctrine. Evangelicals believe in the importance of personal salvation through Jesus Christ, usually through a born-again experience; the inerrancy of the Bible; and the importance of spreading the gospel.

**Family Research Council** Organization of the contemporary Christian Right, headed by Tony Perkins. The FRC was once the political arm of Focus on the Family, although the two groups are now separate for tax reasons. The FRC specializes in providing detailed research on policy issues.

**Fellowship Foundation** Secretive organization that sponsors the annual National Prayer Breakfast and hosts Bible studies and social events for political elites. The group is not directly part of the Christian Right social movement.

**Flying Fundamentalists** Arm of the Defenders of the Christian Faith that dispatched squadrons of speakers to antievolution rallies in the Midwest. In 1926 the Flying Fundamentalists appeared in more than 200 cities in Minnesota alone.

**Focus on the Family** Primarily a Christian media ministry and organization of the contemporary Christian Right, founded by James Dobson. The organization's political arm is named Focus on the Family Action.

**free exercise clause**  Phrase in First Amendment that is the source of controversy regarding religious liberty: "Congress shall make no law . . . prohibiting the free exercise [of religion]."

**fundamentalist**  Term used to describe a religious movement, specific denominations and churches, and religious doctrine. Fundamentalists believe in the importance of remaining separate from the world, the literal truth of the Bible, and the importance of personal salvation.

**glossolalia**  Commonly known as "speaking in tongues." Religious practice in which individual speaks in no known human language. Some individuals believe they speak in the language of angels; others think they are worshiping in their own private language with God.

**Home School Legal Defense Association**  Organization that defends rights of homeschooling parents, most of whom are Christian conservatives. The HSLDA was founded by Michael Farris.

**intelligent design**  The belief that the earth was created by an intelligent being, not necessarily the God spoken of in Genesis.

**libertarian** (First Amendment)  Individual who believes that free exercise of religion should not be limited. Libertarians generally hold that religious liberty should supersede secular law and that laws that have the effect of limiting the religious practice of one or more groups should have religious exemptions.

**menorah**  Jewish candelabrum displayed during Hanukkah.

**Moral Majority**  Premier Christian Right group of the 1980s, headed by Jerry Falwell. The Moral Majority established paper organizations in all states but was primarily a direct-mail organization that received substantial media attention.

**National Association of Evangelicals**  Organization of evangelical denominations, formed by neoevangelicals in 1942 and still active today.

**National Organization for Marriage** (NOM)  Organization created to defend traditional marriage. Includes a political action committee and an education fund.

**neoevangelicalism**  Term used to describe a religious movement and religious doctrine. Neoevangelicals rejected the militant separatism of the fundamentalists and encouraged an engagement with the modern world.

**Ohio Campaign to Protect Marriage**  State organization led by Phil Burress that coordinated efforts to bar same-sex marriage in Ohio in 2004.

*Old Time Gospel Hour*  Jerry Falwell's televised sermons from the Liberty Baptist Church in Lynchburg, Virginia.

**Operation Rescue**  Antiabortion group that specializes in blockading abortion clinics. Members try to prevent women from entering the clinics by physically blocking their path and harassing them verbally. The organization attracts members of Christian Right groups but also a few pro-life liberals.

**party faction**  Identifiable group within a political party that fields its own candidates for intraparty nomination contests and usually has an identifiable ideology as well.

**pentecostal (pentacostalism)**  Term used to describe a religious movement, specific denominations, and religious doctrine. Pentecostals believe in the second blessing of the Holy Spirit and in worship that includes ecstatic practices such as speaking in tongues. Unlike charismatics, pentecostals are found in specific denominations.

**People for the American Way** Organization founded by Norman Lear to oppose the Christian Right.

**postmillennialism** Doctrinal belief that the millennial kingdom will occur before Christ comes again. The implication of the doctrine is that political action may improve the world and hasten the millennium.

**premillennialism** Doctrinal belief that the millennial kingdom will occur after Christ comes again. Premillennialists believe that the condition of the world must worsen until Christ comes again. The implication of the doctrine is that political action is somewhat futile.

**pro-family** Term preferred by some Christian Right groups to describe their movement.

**religious nonpreferentialist** Individual who takes an accommodationist position on the establishment clause of the First Amendment and a libertarian position on the free exercise clause. A religious nonpreferentialist seeks a more open display of Christian and other religious symbols and practices.

**Religious Roundtable** Christian Right group from the 1980s.

**Scopes trial** Also known as the "Great Monkey Trial," the trial of John Scopes for teaching evolution in Dayton, Tennessee, embarrassed fundamentalists and led them to retreat from politics, but it also led textbook publishers to retreat from including evolution in biology texts.

**secular humanism** Philosophy that centers on human values and denies the influence of supernatural forces such as gods. Although the American Humanist Association has a membership of only around 5,000, Christian Right activists depict secular humanism as a militant religious system that wants to destroy Christianity. In fundamentalist circles, secular humanism is a very broad, vague concept.

**separationist** Person who believes that the First Amendment establishment clause mandates that government not become entangled in religion in any way and must remain neutral between religion and secularism.

**separatism** Doctrinal belief of fundamentalists that Christians should remain apart from the world.

***700 Club*** Pat Robertson's television program, which features interviews with guests of varied religious backgrounds, an African American cohost, and political commentary by Robertson. The *700 Club* provided the financial nucleus of Robertson's 1988 presidential campaign.

**social conservatives** Americans who take conservative positions on issues such as abortion, gay rights, and school prayer.

**social gospel** Doctrine in the early twentieth century that the church should focus its efforts on helping alleviate social problems.

**Traditional Values Coalition** Organization of the contemporary Christian Right, headed by Louis Sheldon. TVC focuses primarily on opposing laws that protect gays and lesbians from job discrimination.

**Vision America** Christian Right organization designed to mobilize pastors. Rick Scarborough is its founder and president.

**voter guides** Materials distributed by Christian Right and other groups providing information on the policy positions of candidates. If voter guides are produced by tax-exempt groups, they must be nonpartisan.

**World's Christian Fundamentals Association** Religious group formed in 1919 to provide structure to the fundamentalist religious movement. The WCFA provided resources for the formation of the antievolution groups of the 1920s.

# Notes

## Chapter 1

1. "McCain Courting Christian Conservatives," February 14, 2007, http://www.msnbc.msn.com/id/17146257/. Accessed March 2, 2009.

2. "Public Support Falls for Religion's Role in Politics Some Social Conservative Disillusionment," August 21, 2008, http://pewresearch.org/pubs/930/religion-politics.

3. Dan Cox, "Young White Evangelicals: Less Republican, Still Conservative," September 28, 2007, http://pewresearch.org/pubs/605/young-white-evangelicals-less-republican-still-conservative. Accessed January 20, 2010.

4. Cal Thomas, "Religious Right R.I.P.," November 5, 2008, http://www.calthomas.com/index.php?news=2419.

5. Whether "family values night" at the GOP convention hurt the Republicans is the subject of some debate. See Cromartie, 1994 and Abramowitz, 1995.

6. Statement made on *The 700 Club*, September 13, 2001.

7. John Green, e-mail message to author, September 1994.

8. Although most movement leaders explicitly include Jews in their discussion of the American religious tradition, others do not. Mississippi governor Kirk Fordice attracted praise and rebuke when he refused to change his statement that the United States was a Christian nation to a claim that it was a Judeo-Christian nation. The statement was made to GOP governors in November 1992.

9. Churches are free to endorse candidates, but if they do so they are no longer considered tax-exempt charities and are then subject to taxes. Religious leaders frequently make it very clear whom they support without explicitly endorsing a candidate.

10. One of the authors attended the event and recorded this statement on September 24, 2004.

11. Letter to members of Focus on the Family Action, March 2009.

12. See the case studies in Green, Rozell, and Wilcox, 2006; see also Wilcox, Green, and Rozell, 1995.

13. Quoted in "GOP Ally's Threat Seen Cause for Party Concern; Dobson Vows to Pull out 2.1 Million Members," *Washington Times*, February 17, 1998.

14. For an overview of public attitudes on these issues, see Jelen and Wilcox, 1995.

15. "Equal Rights Initiative in Iowa Attacked," *Washington Post*, August 23, 1995, A15.

16. Interview with author, November 2004. The analogy was a reference to the national movement's decision to initially forego the ban on civil unions at the federal level to focus on a ban against same-sex marriage.

17. Sandy Banks, "Religious Rhetoric and Gay Marriage," October 21, 2008, http://articles.latimes.com/2008/oct/21/local/me-banks22. Accessed March 2, 2009.

18. Christian Right direct-mail solicitations appear to demonize their opponents at a deeper level than those of liberal groups do, because they frequently associate opposition with evil.

19. Vision America, http://www.visionamerica.us/cwofreg.asp. Accessed September 7, 2005.

20. Statement by William J. Bennett, press conference on religious bigotry in Virginia politics, October 25, 1993.

21. See especially *The Freedom Writer*, published by the Institute for First Amendment Studies, Great Barrington, Massachusetts.

22. Quoted in *Atlanta Journal and Constitution*, December 14, 1994.

23. Christian Anti-Defamation Commission, "Hollywood's Ongoing War on God," February 25, 2009, http://www.christianadc.org/news-and-articles/265-hollywoods-ongoing-war-on-god. Accessed March 2, 2009.

24. A prominent exception is A. James Reichley (1985), who argued that theistic-humanist religions provide the proper values to mold a good society.

25. The Pew Research Center for the People and the Press, "Among Wealthy Nations . . . U.S. Stands Alone in Its Embrace of Religion," December 19, 2002, http://people-press.org/reports/display.php3?ReportID=167. Accessed September 7, 2005.

26. The Williamsburg Charter survey, conducted in 1988, indicated that more than 85 percent would vote for candidates from all religious traditions, but only a third would support an atheist, even if the person were from their party and shared their political views.

27. Pew Research Center and the Pew Forum on Religion & Public Life, "GOP the Religion-Friendly Party, But Stem Cell Issue May Help Democrats," August 24, 2004, http://pewforum.org/docs/index.php?DocID=51. Accessed October 14, 2005.

28. Data are from National Election Study (NES), 2004. The NES includes a separate question to filter out those who do not attend church at all, and this results in lower estimates than single-question measures. Gallup reported that 32 percent attended church weekly in 2005, with 44 percent attending in the last seven days. http://poll.gallup.com/content/default.aspx?ci=1690&pg=2. Accessed October 15, 2005.

## Chapter 2

1. These doctrinal differences have important implications for the policy positions of evangelicals. Guth et al. (1995) have shown that premillennialists are less likely to support environmental protection. If Christ will soon come again, why worry about a little pollution? On the other hand, postmillennialists may support environmental legislation, arguing that God created the snail darter, and it therefore should be present during the millennium that ushers in the kingdom of heaven.

2. See Acts 2:1–23.

3. There is some dispute among pentecostals as to just how many blessings exist. For many, speaking in tongues is part of a third blessing, but for the Assemblies of God it is part of a second blessing.

4. Speaking in tongues generally involves one or more members of a congregation speaking in what the nonbeliever would deem nonsense syllables. Two somewhat dif-

ferent explanations are usually offered by those within the tradition: They are speaking the "language of the angels," or they are speaking different private languages that exist between God and his believers. Being "slain in the Spirit" generally involves falling to the floor, often after the loss of consciousness. In charismatic and pentecostal services, strong men identify those who are likely to be slain and move to catch them as they fall.

5. The biblical account of the Pentecost in the second chapter of Acts describes the apostles speaking in tongues, so that members of the polynational audience all heard the sermon in their native languages. For fundamentalists, this gift was given in the early days of the church to further its evangelical mission. The "tongues" were real, earthly languages.

6. For a detailed discussion, see Furniss, 1963.

7. For an excellent discussion of the movement, see Lienesch, 2007.

8. See Kazin, 2006.

9. For a detailed account of the bills, see Furniss, 1963. See also Hunter, 1987.

10. Some continued to exist, however. The Christian Anti-Communism Crusade was still mailing literature as recently as 1990.

11. The church now has 24,000 members. For more information, see http://www.trbc.org/.

12. Quoted in Harrell, 1988, 140.

13. The Michigan process was a complex, multistage affair, and there was no real counting of delegates after the first stage. But journalists and political professionals polled delegates for the second stage who claimed Robertson was comfortably ahead of Bush. Eventually, however, the Bush forces joined with those who backed Jack Kemp and managed to seize control.

14. For an interesting account of the Robertson campaign, see Hertzke, 1993.

15. For a well-argued example, see Bruce, 1988.

16. Anticommunism played its least important role in the Robertson campaign, although Robertson's claim of secret missiles in Cuba hearkened to the earlier, more conspiratorial accounts of communism.

17. Quoted in Rozell and Wilcox, 1996.

18. Furthermore, today's young people are more likely to "tinker" with their religion, a process that not only involves church hopping and church shopping, but also searching for spiritual answers through such things as music and art outside the confines of orthodox religious institutions, which makes them more difficult to mobilize (Wuthnow, 2007).

19. For the biblical referents to the term "born again," see John 3:5–8; 1 Peter 1:23. For many evangelicals, the born-again experience is a sudden one, marked by an emotional release. Evangelicals in this tradition can usually recite the date and circumstances when they were reborn. For others, it is a gradual process.

20. For example, surveys show that a relatively high portion of churchgoers call themselves fundamentalists, yet many do not support any fundamentalist doctrine.

21. Specifically, literalists are Protestants who are born again and believe the Bible is literally true, and other evangelicals are those who attend evangelical denominations, are born again, and say that the Bible is the word of God but not all of it should be taken literally.

22. The relationship between knowing someone who is gay or lesbian and attitudes toward equality for GLBT citizens is complex. There is little doubt that when someone comes out to friends or family members, it puts a human face on gay rights issues. But part of this correlation is also because GLBT people come out more frequently to those they believe will be tolerant.

## Chapter 3

1. Michael Gerson, "A Righteous Indignation," *U.S. News and World Report,* May 4, 1998, cited in Apostolidis, 2000.

2. National Public Radio, Election 2008 "Secret Money Project," http://www.npr.org/blogs/secretmoney/outside_groups/focus_on_the_family_action/. Accessed April 6, 2009.

3. http://www.citizenlink.org/pdfs/10–22–08_2012letter.pdf. Accessed January 20, 2010

4. "Super Bowl Ad Research: New Barna Study Examines Tebow/Focus Commercial." http://www.barna.org/barna-update/article/14-media/343-super-bowl-ad-research-new-barna-study-examines-tebowfocus-commercial. Accessed March 4, 2010.

5. As in many political organizations, the definition of a "member" of CWA is rather fluid, and the organization relies on a private firm to raise money through direct mail. At any given time CWA, like many other groups, has no idea of the exact number of people who have contributed in the previous year.

6. http://www.nace-cee.org/ceestrategy.htm/. Accessed May 1, 2009.

7. Ibid.

8. There is some disagreement among scholars as to whether the Eagle Forum is a Christian Right organization. Schlafly is Catholic, as are many women in the organization, and the group did base much of its opposition to the ERA on antistatist appeals that the government should not interfere in the relationship between men and women. But much of the organization's literature links its antifeminism to biblical and other religious arguments.

9. Groups that have taken such positions include the now-defunct Just Life political action committee (Bendyna, 1993) and Common Concern (Maxwell, 1994).

10. There is obviously no biblical warrant for opposition to gun control, but in the South many Christian conservatives speak of the "God-given right to carry a gun." Bates (1993) reported that Christian conservative parents who objected to what they perceived to be antibiblical passages in a school text listed among the objectionable passages one that endorsed gun control.

11. For a detailed account, see Lunch, 1995.

12. Virginia's sodomy laws at the time prohibited homosexual relations and some kinds of sexual relations among heterosexuals as well. Although the U.S. Supreme Court overturned state sodomy laws in 2003, Virginia's legislature passed another sodomy statute at the urging of Christian Right groups. The new state law cannot be enforced, however.

13. Robert O'Harrow Jr., "Christian Group's Push Felt in Move Against Gay Paper," *Washington Post,* October 1, 1993, D2.

14. John Green, e-mail message to author, January 2009.

15. Burl Gilyard, "Fake Wobegon," *New Republic,* September 12, 1994, 20.

16. Data and map provided by Kimberley H. Conger. In order to systematically measure the influence of the Christian Right in state-level Republican politics, Conger surveyed state Republican and Democratic party leaders, leaders of religiously conservative political groups, members of both the political and religious media, political consultants of various partisan loyalties, and academic observers. Influence is operationalized as the percentage of each state's Republican party committee who are members or supporters of the Christian Right as perceived by the respondents in the surveys used to construct these measures. Each state is ranked in each of the years as "high," "moderate," or "low" influence. High influence means that more than 50 percent of the state's Republican Party committee was perceived to be supporters of the Christian Right; moderate influence means 25–49 percent of the committee was Christian Right supporters; and low influence means that less than 25 percent of the committee was supporters.

17. Cited in Hertzke, 1993, 149.

18. Surveys show that although most Americans want their president to have strong religious beliefs, many are quite leery of voting for a minister. See Jelen and Wilcox, 1995.

19. Ultimately, however, Robertson lost because voters did not like him or his message.

20. This is not always true; in 1986, when a moderate Republican, Ed Zchau, ran against the incumbent, Alan Cranston, for one of California's U.S. Senate seats, an independent Christian Right candidate pulled enough votes to deny Zchau the victory.

21. For example, the guides listed Robb as favoring taxpayer funding of obscene art and North as opposing it. Yet Robb had voted for the controversial Helms amendment to cut the budget of the National Endowment for the Arts and restrict federal funding for offensive art. The guides said that Robb opposed voluntary school prayer, when he clearly was on record as favoring it.

22. For an account of the earlier PACs, see Wilcox, 1988a.

23. See Ann E. Marimow, "Conservatives Ascendent in Charles Schools," *Washington Post,* September 16, 2005, A1.

24. Moen, 1990. But Moen correctly noted that Christian Right issues were not highlighted in Reagan's State of the Union addresses and that his endorsement of the agenda was not especially ringing.

25. David Kirkpatrick, "In Secretly Taped Conversations, a Portrait of a Future President," February 20, 2005, http://www.nytimes.com/2005/02/20/politics/20talk.html?pagewanted=1&oref=login. Accessed March 6, 2005.

26. "Partial birth" is the term used by pro-life and Christian Right groups to refer to the medical procedure "intact dilation and extraction." Pro-choice groups refer to the procedure as "D & X" or "DNX." Most media accounts of the political debate adopted the term "partial birth"—a clear victory of issue framing by Christian Right groups. We use the term consistently throughout the book for this reason.

27. Dan Gilgoff, "James Dobson's Political Surrender." *U.S. News & World Report Blog,* May 14, 2009, http://www.usnews.com/blogs/god-and-country/2009/05/14/james-dobsons-political-surrender.html. Accessed January 20, 2010.

28. Andy Birkey, "Religious Right Watch: Health Care Reform Is against God's Design," August 7, 2009, http://minnesotaindependent.com/41364/religious-right-watch-obamacare-is-against-gods-design. Accessed January 20, 2010.

29. Religious groups have also become far more active in filing amicus briefs. For an overview of legal activity by religious groups, see Ivers, 1990; 1992.

30. McDonnell's Web page provided substantial details about his proposed economic policies, but only a couple of vague sentences on abortion. When asked about this, McDonnell replied that he had "never made social policy a huge part of his agenda." Yet as a state legislator, McDonnell had introduced thirty-five bills that sought to restrict access to abortion, more than any other state legislator had done, and also more than he had introduced on most other topics. McDonnell's opposition to allowing abortions for rape and incest would have proven unpopular in Virginia, and his vague stance allowed him to win the votes of many moderates; meanwhile pro-life activists were well aware of his record (Pippenger, 2009).

## Chapter 4

1. See, for example, the essays in Schoenberger, 1969.

2. Recent studies have shown that Americans choose their churches based on their preferences for both theology and politics, so it is possible that those who prefer to view the world in dichotomous terms are more likely to join or stay in fundamentalist churches (Putnam and Campbell, 2010).

3. In fact, some researchers have argued that membership in any group that seeks to alter public policy to benefit all citizens is in one sense irrational. From an economic perspective, it is far more logical for individuals to be "free riders," in the hope that the group succeeds without investing their own time and money. It is highly unlikely that ten hours a week or $25 a year will make any difference in the success of the group, and citizens will benefit from the policies enacted whether or not they have contributed to the group's efforts. Yet many citizens are active in political organizations and give their time and money even when they believe that theirs is a lost cause. Many enjoy interacting with others who share their views, and others feel motivated to help pursue their policy goals because of a sense of obligation or because they derive great pleasure from their occasional political victories.

4. See, for example, "The Two Faces of the Christian Coalition," a pamphlet published by People for the American Way.

5. Exodus 22:18.

6. Thanks to John Green for providing these data.

7. Though there is some evidence that exposure to Catholic views in particular makes evangelicals less intolerant of out-groups by making them consider the merits of rationales for opposing views (Robinson, 2008).

8. The Catholic church does not permit abortions to save the life of the mother, but most Protestants in the movement would allow this exception while setting strict limits on doctors to certify that there is a real and present danger.

9. Coburn's comments were made during a debate on *Meet the Press*, October 3, 2004.

10. Transcript of ABC *Nightline* episode, "God and the Grassroots," November 4, 1993.

11. "People and Events," *Church and State*, April 1988, 14.

12. For an account of a Christian school associated with a fundamentalist church, see Ammerman, 1987.

13. "Homosexual Behavior & Pedophilia," http://us2000.org/cfmc/Pedophilia.pdf.

14. Interestingly, this was the position of the first wave of gay rights activists, although many now believe that sexual orientation is fixed by genes or socialization.

15. Interestingly, many Christian Right activists favor repealing the earned income tax credit for poor families, which would lower the incomes of poor families and by the same logic force more women into the labor force.

16. This does not mean, of course, that Christian conservatives advocate spousal abuse. Indeed, Christian conservatives counsel men to offer great respect and support for their wives and advise wives to obey their husbands. Some Christian Right leaders object to spousal abuse laws because they believe they could be misused or provide a wedge for greater government interference in the privacy of families.

17. Sources for these data are the General Social Survey (GSS) and the American National Election Studies (NES).

18. Indeed, one Christian Right activist told one of us that when the character Ned Flanders died on *The Simpsons*, the number of evangelicals on TV was cut in half.

19. Cited in Shupe, 1989, 25.

20. Cited in Neuhaus, 1991.

21. Matthew 19:23–24. Many scholars and activists argue that the Christian Right support for tax policies that benefit affluent families and for cuts in spending on programs that benefit poor families is inconsistent with biblical teachings. See, for example, Wallis, 2005.

22. Liberal Christians argue in response that if Christ returns and finds that we have exterminated a species created by God in pursuit of greater corporate profits, he will not be happy.

## Chapter 5

1. Survey of 2000 presidential nomination contributors, by Alexandra Cooper, John C. Green, Mark J. Rozell, and Clyde Wilcox.

2. Survey conducted of Virginia GOP delegates to 1993 and 1994 nominating conventions and of delegates to other state conventions in 1995 and 1996. Data collected by John C. Green, Mark J. Rozell, and Clyde Wilcox.

3. "For the Health of the Nation: An Evangelical Call to Civic Responsibility," http://www.nae.net/images/civic_responsibility2.pdf.

4. Many activists quote with approval 2 Timothy 4:7, "I have fought a good fight, I have finished my course, I have kept the faith."

5. "Letter to Conservatives by Paul M. Weyrich," http://www.nationalcenter.org/Weyrich299.html. Accessed March 9, 2010.

6. There are some Christian reconstructionists who are willing to dominate society by force, but they constitute the fringe of the movement.

7. *Juno* was a popular movie released in 2007, which sympathetically featured a pregnant teenager who decided to give her child up for adoption rather than have an abortion.

8. Kenneth Wald, e-mail message to author, October 10, 1995.

9. Cited in Cromartie, 1994, 36.

# References

Abramowitz, Alan. 1995. "It's Abortion, Stupid: Policy Voting in the 1992 Presidential Election." *Journal of Politics* 57:176–186.

Adorno, T. W., Else Frenkel-Brunswik, Daniel J. Levinson, and R. Nevitt Sanford. 1950. *The Authoritarian Personality.* New York: Harper & Row.

Ammerman, Nancy Tatom. 1987. *Bible Believers: Fundamentalists in the Modern World.* New Brunswick, NJ: Rutgers University Press.

Anderson-Morshead, Louis. 2009. "Same-Sex Adoption and the Christian Right." Unpublished paper, Georgetown University, December.

Andolina, Molly W., and Clyde Wilcox (with Molly Sonner). 2000. "The Paradoxes of Popularity: Public Support for Bill Clinton During the Lewinsky Scandal." In Mark J. Rozell and Clyde Wilcox (eds.), *The Clinton Scandal and the Future of American Government.* Washington, DC: Georgetown University Press.

Apostolidis, Paul. 2000. *Stations of the Cross: Adorno and Christian Right Radio.* Durham, NC: Duke University Press.

Baker, Peter, and Dan Balz. 2005. "Conservatives Confront Bush Aides." *Washington Post,* October 6, A1.

Barber, Benjamin R. 1984. *Strong Democracy: Participatory Politics for a New Age.* Berkeley: University of California Press.

Barkun, Michael. 1994. *Religion and the Racist Right.* Chapel Hill: University of North Carolina Press.

Barna, Mark. 2010. "Dobson Forced to Sign Off Early, Says Rev. Kenneth Hutcherson." *Colorado Springs Gazette.* March 11. http://www.gazette.com/articles/dobson-95539 -forced-family.html. Accessed March 15, 2010.

Barrett, Greg. 1999. "Why James Dobson's $120 Million Ministry Is a Household Name." *Detroit News,* May 3, A12.

Bartels, Lynn. 2004. "GOP Assailed for Defeat; Jeffco Republican: Party 'Prostituted' Itself on Vouchers." *Rocky Mountain News,* November 16, http://rockymountainnews .com/drmn/election/article/0,1299,DRMN_36_3331828,00.html. Accessed March 30, 2005.

Bates, Stephen. 1993. *Battleground.* New York: Henry Holt.

———. 1995. "The Christian Coalition Nobody Knows." *Weekly Standard,* September 25.

———. 2002. "The Jesus Market: Christianity May Be Struggling in the Public Square, but It's Prospering in the Public Bazaar." *Weekly Standard,* December 16, http:// www.weeklystandard.com/Content/Public/Articles/000/000/001/988ovwyu.asp?pg=1. Accessed October 18, 2005.

Bauer, Gary. 1999. "The New Republican Landscape." *New York Times,* August 17, A12.

Bendyna, Mary. 1993. "Just Life Action." In R. Biersack, P. Herrnson, and C. Wilcox (eds.), *Risky Business: PAC Decisionmaking in Congressional Elections,* Armonk, NY: M. E. Sharpe.

————. 1995. "Catholics and the Christian Coalition." Presented at the annual meeting of the Association for the Sociology of Religion, Washington, DC.

Bendyna, Mary, John C. Green, Mark J. Rozell, and Clyde Wilcox. 2000. "Catholics and the Christian Right: A View from Four States." *Journal for the Scientific Study of Religion* 39:321–332.

Berkman, Michael B. and Eric Plutzer. 2010. *Evolution, Creationism and the Battle to Control America's Classrooms.* Cambridge: Cambridge University Press.

Berry, Jeffrey M., Kent E. Portney, and Ken Thomson. 1993. *The Rebirth of Urban Democracy.* Washington, DC: Brookings.

Berry, Jeffrey M., and Clyde Wilcox. 2007. *Interest Group Society.* New York: Longman.

Blakeman, Bruce W. 1996. "Report of Survey of Concerned Women of America Members and of Randomly Selected Women." Concerned Women of America.

Blaker, Kimberly. 2003. *The Fundamentals of Extremism: The Christian Right in America.* Plymouth, MI: New Boston Books.

Blumenthal, Sidney. 1994. "Christian Soldiers." *New Yorker,* July 18, 31–37.

Brin, David. 1994. *Otherness.* New York: Bantam Books.

Broder, David S. 1995. "Christian Group Flexes Newfound Muscles." *Washington Post,* September 10, A1, A24.

Brown, Clifford W., Jr., Lynda W. Powell, and Clyde Wilcox. 1994. Presidential Contributor Study. Computer data file.

————. 1995. *Serious Money: Fundraising and Contributing in Presidential Nomination Campaigns.* New York: Cambridge University Press.

Brown, Steven. 2004. *Trumping Religion: The New Christian Right, the Free Speech Clause, and the Courts.* Tuscaloosa: University of Alabama Press.

Bruce, Steve. 1988. *The Rise and Fall of the New Christian Right: Conservative Protestant Politics in America, 1978–1988.* Oxford: Oxford University Press.

Bruce, Steve, Peter Kivisto, and William Swatos Jr. 1994. *The Rapture of Politics: The Christian Right as the United States Approaches the Year 2000.* New Brunswick, NJ: Transaction Press.

Bush, George W. 1999. *A Charge to Keep: My Journey to the White House.* New York: William Morrow.

Buss, Doris, and Didi Herman. 2003. *Globalizing Family Values: The Christian Right in International Politics.* Minneapolis: University of Minnesota Press.

Campbell, David, and Carin Robinson. 2008. "Religious Coalitions For and Against Gay Marriage: The Culture War Rages On." In Craig Rimmerman and Clyde Wilcox (eds.), *The Politics of Same-Sex Marriage.* Chicago: University of Chicago Press.

Campbell, David E., and John C. Green. 2009."Where Do Americans Draw the Line Between Church and State? An Update on American Public Opinion Toward Religious Establishment and Free Exercise." Paper presented at the annual meeting of the American Political Science Association, Toronto, September.

Campbell, David E., John C. Green, and J. Quin Monson 2009. "Tolerance? We Have a Ways To Go." *USA Today,* November 30.

Claasen, Ryan L., and Andrew Povtak, "The Christian Right Thesis: Explaining Longitudinal Change in Participation Among Evangelicals." *Journal of Politics* 72 (1):2–15.

Cleary, Edward, and Allen Hertzke, eds. 2006. *Representing God at the Statehouse: Religion and Politics in the American States.* Lanham, MD: Rowman & Littlefield.

Cole, Stewart. 1931. *The History of Fundamentalism.* Westport, CT: Greenwood Press.

Conger, Kimberly H., and John C. Green. 2002. "Spreading Out and Digging In: Christian Conservatives and State Republican Parties." *Campaigns and Elections* 23 (1):59.

Conger, Kimberly H., and Donald Ratcheter. 2006. "Iowa: In the Heart of Bush Country." In John C. Green, Mark J. Rozell, and Clyde Wilcox (eds.), *The Values Campaign? The Christian Right in the 2004 Election.* Washington, DC: Georgetown University Press.

Conover, Pamela, and Virginia Gray. 1981. "Political Activists and Conflict over Abortion and ERA: Pro-Family vs. Pro-Woman." Paper presented at the annual meeting of the Midwest Political Science Association, Chicago.

Cook, Elizabeth Adell, Ted G. Jelen, and Clyde Wilcox. 1992. *Between Two Absolutes: Public Opinion and the Politics of Abortion.* Boulder, CO: Westview.

———. 1993. "Generational Differences in Attitudes Toward Abortion." In M. Goggin (ed.), *Understanding the New Politics of Abortion.* Beverly Hills, CA: Sage.

———. 1994. "Issue Voting in Gubernatorial Elections: Abortion and Post-Webster Politics." *Journal of Politics* 56:187–199.

Cooperman, Alan, and Thomas B. Edsall. 2004. "Evangelicals Say They Led Charge for the GOP." *Washington Post,* November 8, A1.

———. 2006. "Christian Coalition Shrinks as Debt Grows." *Washington Post,* April 10. http://www.washingtonpost.com/wp-dyn/content/article/2006/04/09/AR2006040 901063.html. Accessed March 5, 2010.

Cox, Harvey Gallagher. 1995. *Fire from Heaven: The Rise of Pentecostal Spirituality and the Reshaping of Religion in the Twenty-first Century.* New York: Da Capo Press.

Cromartie, Michael, ed. 1994. *Disciples and Democracy: Religious Conservatives and the Future of American Politics.* Washington, DC: Ethics and Public Policy Center.

Dao, James. 2004. "Flush with Victory, Grass-Roots Crusader Against Same-Sex Marriage Thinks Big." *New York Times,* November 23, A28.

Davis, James Allan, and Tom W. Smith. 2004. General Social Surveys, 1972–1994. National Opinion Research Center, University of Chicago. Computer data file.

Deckman, Melissa M. 2004. *School Board Battles: The Christian Right in Local Politics.* Washington, DC: Georgetown University Press.

Dillon, S. 1993a. "Catholics Join Bid by Conservatives for School Boards." *New York Times,* April 16.

———. 1993b. "Fundamentalists and Catholics." *New York Times,* November 14, 6.

Dodson, Debra L. 1990. "Socialization of Party Activists: National Convention Delegates, 1972–1981." *American Journal of Political Science* 34:1119–1141.

Duin, Julia. 2005. "Christian Coalition Falls on Lean Days." *Washington Times,* October 13, http://www.washingtontimes.com/national/20051013–121940–9083r.htm. Accessed October 17, 2005.

Edsall, Thomas B. 1995. "Robertson Urges Christian Activists to Take Over GOP." *Washington Post,* September 10, A24.

Ellison, Christopher G., Samuel Echevarría, and Brad Smith. 2005. "Religion and Abortion Attitudes Among U.S. Hispanics: Findings from the 1990 Latino National Political Survey." *Social Science Quarterly* 86 (1):192–208.

Emerson, Michael O., and Christian Smith. 2000. *Divided by Faith: Evangelical Religion and the Problem of Race in America.* Oxford: Oxford University Press.

Erzen, Tanya. 2006. *Straight to Jesus: Sexual and Christian Conversions in the Ex-Gay Movement.* Berkeley: University of California Press.

Falwell, Jerry. 1981. *The Fundamentalist Phenomenon.* Garden City, NJ: Doubleday.

Farrell, John Aloysius, and Anne C. Mulkern. 2005. "Dobson Seen as Driven, Divisive—As Respect Rises, Worries Surface: The Evangelical Leader's Resounding Plunge into Politics Has Stirred Both Democrats and the GOP." *Denver Post*, April 27, A1.

Farris, Michael P. 1992. *Where Do I Draw the Line?* Minneapolis, MN: Bethany House.

Finke, Roger, and Rodney Stark. 1992. *The Churching of America, 1776–1992.* New Brunswick, NJ: Rutgers University Press.

Furniss, Norman. 1963. *The Fundamentalist Controversy, 1918–1931.* Hamden, CT: Archdon Books.

Gamble, Barbara S. 1995. "Putting Civil Rights to a Popular Vote." Unpublished manuscript.

Georgianna, Sharon Linzey. 1988. Moral Majority Survey. Computer data file. Collected at Indiana University.

———. 1989. *The Moral Majority and Fundamentalism: Plausibility and Dissonance.* Lewiston, NY: Edwin Mellon Press.

Gimpel, James G. 1994. *Risky Business? PAC Decisionmaking in Congressional Elections.* Armonk, NY: M. E. Sharpe.

Goodstein, Laurie. 1999. "Coalitions's Woes May Hinder Goals of Christian Right." *New York Times*, August 2, www.nytimes.com.

Goodstein, Laura. 2010. "Radio Show for Focus on the Family Founder." *New York Times*, January 16, http://www.nytimes.com/2010/01/17/business/media/17dobson.html. Accessed January 19, 2010.

Green, John, Kimberly Conger, and James Guth. 2006. "Agents of Value: Christian Right Activists in 2004." In John C. Green, Mark J. Rozell, and Clyde Wilcox (eds.), *The Values Campaign? The Christian Right in the 2004 Election.* Washington, DC: Georgetown University Press.

Green, John C. 1995. "The Christian Right and the 1994 Elections: An Overview." In M. Rozell and C. Wilcox (eds.), *God at the Grassroots: The Christian Right in the 1994 Elections.* Lanham, MD: Rowman & Littlefield.

———. 2000. "The Christian Right and the 1998 Elections: An Overview." In John C. Green, Mark J. Rozell, and Clyde Wilcox (eds.), *Prayers in the Precincts.* Washington, DC: Georgetown University Press.

Green, John C., and James L. Guth. 1988. "The Christian Right in the Republican Party: The Case of Pat Robertson's Contributors." *Journal of Politics* 50:150–165.

Green, John C., James L. Guth, Lyman A. Kellstedt, and Corwin E. Smidt. 1990–1991. Survey of Religious Activists, 1990–1991. Computer data file. Collected at the University of Akron.

———. 1992. National Survey of Religion and Politics, 1992. Computer data file. Collected at the University of Akron.

———. 1994. "Uncivil Challengers? Support for Civil Liberties Among Religious Activists." *Journal of Political Science* 24:25–49.

Green, John C., James L. Guth, and Clyde Wilcox. 1995. "The Christian Right in State Republican Parties." Paper presented at the annual meeting of the Midwest Political Science Association, Chicago.

———. 1998. "The Social Movement Meets the Party: The Christian Right in the GOP." In Anne Costain and Andrew S. McFarland (eds.), *Social Movements and American Political Institutions.* Lanham, MD: Rowman & Littlefield.

Green, John C., Robert P. Jones, and Daniel Cox. 2009. *Conservative and Progressive Religious Activists Surveys.* Akron, OH, and Washington, DC: Bliss Institute for Applied Politics at the University of Akron and Public Religion Research.

Green, John C., Lyman Kellstedt, Corwin Smidt, and James L. Guth. 1992. "National Survey of American Evangelicals." Ray C. Bliss Institute of Applied Politics and Survey Research, University of Akron.

Green, John C., Mark J. Rozell, and Clyde Wilcox, eds. 2006. *The Values Campaign? The Christian Right in the 2004 Election.* Washington, DC: Georgetown University Press.

Green, John C., and Mark Silk. 2009. "No Saints Need Apply," http://www.trincoll.edu/depts/csrpl/RINVol11No3/No%20Saints%20Need%20Apply.htm.

Griffith, R. Marie. 2000. *God's Daughters: Evangelical Women and the Power of Submission.* Berkeley: University of California Press.

Grove, Steve. 2004. "Reading, Writing & Right-Wing Politics." *Boston Globe,* August 15, D1.

Grupp, Fred. 1969. "The Political Perspectives of the John Birch Society Members." In R. Schoenberger (ed.), *The American Right Wing.* New York: Holt, Rinehart & Winston.

Guth, James L. 1983. "The Politics of the Christian Right." In A. Cigler and B. Loomis (eds.), *Interest Group Politics.* Washington, DC: CQ Press.

Guth, James L., John C. Green, Lyman A. Kellstedt, and Corwin E. Smidt. 1995. "Faith and the Environment: Religious Beliefs and Attitudes on Environmental Policy." *American Journal of Political Science* 39:364–382.

Guth, James L., and Lyman A. Kellstedt. 1999. "Religion on Capitol Hill: The Case of the House of Representatives in the 105th Congress." Paper presented at the Biennial Meeting of Christians in Political Science, Calvin College, Grand Rapids, MI.

Hacker, Hans J. 2005. *The Culture of Conservative Christian Litigation.* Lanham, MD: Rowman & Littlefield.

Hackett, Conrad, and D. Michael Lindsay. 2008. "Measuring Evangelicalism: Consequences of Different Operational Strategies." *Journal for the Scientific Study of Religion* 47:499–514.

Hadden, Jeffery K., Anson Shupe, James Hawdon, and Kenneth Martin. 1987. "Why Jerry Falwell Killed the Moral Majority." In M. Fishwick and R. Browne (eds.), *The God Pumpers: Religion in the Electronic Age.* Bowling Green, OH: Popular Press.

Haider-Markel, Donald P., and Kenneth J. Meier. 1996. "The Politics of Gay and Lesbian Rights: Expanding the Scope of the Conflict." *Journal of Politics* 150:47–62.

Hale, John. 1995. "Mainers Face Off on Gays." *Bangor Daily News,* October 28, 14.

Harden, Blaine. 2005. "The Greening of Evangelicals; Christian Right Turns, Sometimes Warily, to Environmentalism." *Washington Post,* February 6, A1.

Harrell, David E. 1988. *Pat Robertson: A Personal, Religious, and Political Portrait.* San Francisco: Harper & Row.

Hedges, Chris. 2005. "Soldiers of Christ II: Feeling the Hate with the National Religious Broadcasters." *Harper's Magazine,* May.

Hertzke, Allen. 1988. *Representing God in Washington: The Role of Religious Lobbies in the American Polity.* Knoxville: University of Tennessee Press.

———. 1993. *Echoes of Discontent: Jesse Jackson, Pat Robertson, and the Resurgence of Populism.* Washington, DC: CQ Press.

Hout, Michael, and Claude S. Fiser. 2002. "Why More Americans Have No Religious Preference: Politics and Generations." *American Sociological Review* 67:165–190.

Hula, Kevin W. 2005. "Dolly Goes to Washington: Coalitions, Cloning, and the Role of Inter-Group Trust." In Paul S. Herrnson, Ronald G. Shaiko, and Clyde Wilcox (eds.), *The Interest Group Connection: Electioneering, Lobbying, and Policymaking in Washington.* 2nd ed. Washington, DC: CQ Press.

Hunter, James Davison. 1987. "The Evangelical Worldview Since 1890." In R. Neuhaus and M. Cromartie (eds.), *Piety and Politics.* Washington, DC: Ethics and Public Policy Center.

———. 1991. *Culture Wars: The Struggle to Define America.* New York: Basic Books.

Ivers, Gregg. 1990. "Organized Religion and the Supreme Court." *Journal of Church and State* 32:775–793.

———. 1992. "Religious Organizations as Constitutional Litigants." *Polity* 25:243–266.

Jacobs, Mike. 1995. "A Tale of Two Cities: Christian Right Activism in the New York City and Vista, California, School Districts." Unpublished manuscript.

Jacoby, Mary. 1999. "What Has She Done to the Christian Coalition?" *St. Petersburg Times,* October 3, A1.

Jelen, Ted G. 1990. *The Political Mobilization of Religious Belief.* New York: Greenwood.

———. 1991a. "Religion and Democratic Citizenship: A Review Essay." *Polity* 23:471–481.

———. 1991b. *The Political World of the Clergy.* New York: Praeger.

———. 2004. *Sacred Markets, Sacred Canopies: Essays on Religious Markets and Religious Pluralism.* Lanham, MD: Rowman & Littlefield.

Jelen, Ted G., and Clyde Wilcox. 1995. *Public Attitudes Toward Church and State.* Armonk, NY: M. E. Sharpe.

Jorstad, Erling. 1970. *The Politics of Doomsday.* Nashville, TN: Abingdon Press.

Kazin, Michael. 2006. *A Godly Hero: The Life of William Jennings Bryan.* New York: Knopf.

Kellstedt, Lyman. 1989. "The Meaning and Measurement of Evangelicalism: Problems and Prospects." In T. Jelen (ed.), *Religion and Political Behavior in the United States.* New York: Praeger.

Kirkpatrick, David. 2005. "In Secretly Taped Conversations, a Portrait of a Future President." *New York Times,* February 20, 1.

———. 2007. "The Evangelical Crack-Up." *New York Times,* October 28, http://www.nytimes.com/2007/10/28/magazine/28Evangelicals-t.html?_r=1&pagewanted=all. Accessed January 20, 2010.

Kirkpatrick, David D., and Albert Salvato. 2005. "In Telecast, Frist Defends His Effort to Stop Filibusters." *New York Times,* April 25, A14.

Koeppen, Sheilah. 1969. "The Radical Right and the Politics of Consensus." In R. Schoenberger (ed.), *The American Right Wing.* New York: Holt, Rinehart & Winston.

Larson, Carin. 2006. "An Uphill Climb: The Christian Right and the 2004 Election in Colorado." In John C. Green, Mark J. Rozell, and Clyde Wilcox (eds.), *The Values Campaign? The Christian Right in the 2004 Election.* Washington, DC: Georgetown University Press.

Larson, Carin, David Madland, and Clyde Wilcox. 2006. "Religious Lobbying in Virginia: How Institutions Can Quiet Prophetic Voices." In Edward Cleary and Allen Hertzke (eds.), *Representing God at the Statehouse: Religion and Politics in the American States.* Lanham, MD: Rowman & Littlefield.

Larson, Carin, and Clyde Wilcox. 2005. "Sowing on Rocky Soil: The Christian Right on College Campuses." Paper presented at the University of Maryland.

———. 2006. "The Faith of George W. Bush: The Personal, Practical, and Political." In Mark J. Rozell and Gleaves Whitney (eds.), *Religion and American Presidents.* New York: Palmave/McMillan.

LaRue, Jan. 2005. "The Nomination of Harriet Miers to the U.S. Supreme Court." Concerned Women for America, memorandum to constituents, October 10, http://www .cwfa.org/articles/9148/LEGAL/scourt/. Accessed October 15, 2005.

Layman, Geoffrey C. forthcoming." Religion and Party Activists: A 'Perfect Storm' of Polarization or a Recipe for Pragmatism?" In Alan Wolfe and Ira Katznelson (eds.), *Religion and Democracy in The United States: Danger or Opportunity.* Princeton, NJ: Princeton University Press.

Levy, Leonard W. 1986. *The Establishment Clause.* New York: Macmillan.

Lewis, Gregory B., and Jonathan L. Edelson. 2000. "DOMA and ENDA: Congress Votes on Gay Rights." In Craig A. Rimmerman, Kenneth D. Wald, and Clyde Wilcox (eds.), *The Politics of Gay Rights.* Chicago: University of Chicago Press.

Liebman, Robert C. 1983. "Mobilizing the Moral Majority." In R. Liebman and R. Wuthnow (eds.), *The New Christian Right: Mobilization and Legitimation.* New York: Aldine.

———. 1995. "New Perspectives on the New Christian Right." Paper presented at the annual meeting of the American Sociological Association, Washington, DC.

Lienesch, Michael. 1994. *Redeeming America.* Chapel Hill: University of North Carolina Press.

———. 1995. "Mobilizing Against Modernity: The World's Christian Fundamentals Association and the Fundamentalist Movement." Paper presented at the annual meeting of the American Political Science Association, Chicago.

———. 2007. *In the Beginning : Bundamentalism, the Scopes Trial, and the Making of the Antievolution Movement.* Chapel Hill: University of North Carolina Press.

Lindsay, Michael D. 2007. *Faith in the Halls of Power: How Evangelicals Joined the American Elite.* Oxford University Press.

Lunch, William. 1995. "Oregon: Identity and Politics in the Northwest." In M. Rozell and C. Wilcox (eds.), *God at the Grassroots.* Lanham, MD: Rowman & Littlefield.

Malbin, Michael. 1978. *Religion and Politics: The Intentions of the Authors of the First Amendment.* Washington, DC: AEI Press.

Marsden, George. 1980. *Fundamentalism and American Culture.* New York: Oxford University Press.

Martin, William. 1996. *With God on Our Side: The Rise of the Religious Right in America.* New York: Broadway Books.

Maxwell, Carol J. C. 1994. "Meaning and Motivation in Pro-Life Direct Action." Ph.D. diss., Washington University.

Mill, John Stuart. 1862. *Considerations on Representative Government.* New York: Harper and Brothers.

Miller, Lisa. 2008. "A Religious Right Revival." *Newsweek,* September 6. http://www .newsweek.com/id/157570. Accessed February 25, 2010.

Miller, Warren E., Donald Kinder, Stephen Rosenstone, and the National Election Studies. 1952–2004. American National Election Study, 1952–2004. Computer file. Center for Political Studies, University of Michigan.

Millsaps, Rhett. 1999. "Loving the Sinner and Hating the Sin: The Emerging Ex-Gay Movement in Christian Right Politics." Unpublished manuscript.

Moen, Matthew. 1989. *The Christian Right and Congress.* Tuscaloosa: University of Alabama Press.

―――. 1990. "Ronald Reagan and the Social Issues: Rhetorical Support for the Christian Right." *Social Science Journal* 27:199–207.

―――. 1992. *The Transformation of the Christian Right.* Tuscaloosa: University of Alabama Press.

―――. 1994. "From Revolution to Evolution: The Changing Nature of the Christian Right." In S. Bruce, P. Kivisto, and W. Swatos (eds.), *The Rapture of Politics.* New Brunswick, NJ: Transaction Press.

―――. 1995. "The Christian Right in the Twenty-First Century." Paper presented at the annual meeting of the Northeastern Political Science Association, Newark, NJ.

Monson, J. Quinn, and J. Baxter Oliphant. 2007. "Microtargeting and the Instrumental Mobilization of Religious Conservatives." In D. Campbell (ed.), *A Matter of Faith: Religion in the 2004 Presidential Election.* Washington, DC: Brookings.

Morken, Hubert. 1994. "'No Special Rights': The Thinking Strategy Behind Colorado's Amendment #2 Strategy." Paper presented at the annual meeting of the American Political Science Association, New York.

Murphy, Caryle, and Hamil R. Harris. 2004. "Thousands Rally on the Mall to Protest Same-Sex Marriage." *Washington Post,* October 16, B1.

Neuhaus, Richard. 1991. "The Theonomist Temptation." *First Things* 35:151–155.

Noll, Mark, and Carolyn Nystrom. 2005. *Is the Reformation Over? An Evangelical Assessment of Contemporary Roman Catholicism.* Grand Rapids: Baker Academics.

Numbers, Ronald N. 1992. *The Creationists.* New York: Alfred A. Knopf.

Nunn, C., H. Crockett, and J. A. Williams. 1978. *Tolerance for Nonconformity.* San Francisco: Jossey-Bass.

O'Hara, Thomas J. 1989. "The Civil Rights Restoration Act: The Role of Religious Lobbies." Paper presented at the annual meeting of the American Political Science Association, Atlanta.

Owen, Dennis E., Kenneth D. Wald, and Samuel S. Hill. 1991. "Authoritarian or Authority-Minded? The Cognitive Commitments of Fundamentalists and the Christian Right." *Religion and American Culture* 1: 73–100.

Penning, James M., and Corwin E. Smidt. 2006. "A War on the Home Front? The Christian Right in the 2004 Elections." In John C. Green, Mark J. Rozell and Clyde Wilcox (eds.), *The Values Campaign? The Christian Right in the 2004 Election.* Washington, DC: Georgetown University Press.

People for the American Way. 1995. "The Two Faces of the Christian Coalition."

Persinos, John F. 1994. "Has the Christian Right Taken Over the Republican Party?" *Campaigns and Elections* September: 21–24.

Peterson, Kavan, and Mark K. Matthews. 2005. "Evangelical Law Firm at Front of Culture War." *Stateline.org.,* June 18.

Pippenger, Nathan. 2009. "Social Issues and the Future of the Christian Right" Unpublished paper, Georgetown University, Fall.

Putnam, Robert. 2001. *Bowling Alone: The Collapse and Revival of American Community.* New York: Simon & Schuster.

Putnam, Robert, and David E. Campbell. 2010. *American Grace: How Religion Is Reshaping Our Civic and Political Lives.* New York: Simon & Schuster.

Quebedeaux, Richard. 1983. *The New Charismatics II.* New York: Harper & Row.

Randolph, E. 1993. "In NY School Board 'Holy War,' Vote Is Split but Civics Triumph." *Washington Post,* May 22, A5.

Rankowitz, Colin. 2009. "The Ex-Gay Movement on the World Wide Web." Unpublished paper, Georgetown University, December.

Reed, Douglas S. 1998. "I Can Play That: Social Movement Repertoires and State Constitutional Politics." Paper presented at the annual meeting of the American Political Science Association, Boston.

Reed, Ralph. 1994a. *Politically Incorrect: The Emerging Faith Factor in American Politics.* Dallas: Word Publishing.

———. 1994b. "What Do Religious Conservatives Really Want?" In Michael Cromartie (ed.), *Disciples and Democracy.* Washington, DC: Ethics and Public Policy Center.

Reichley, A. James. 1985. *Religion in American Public Life.* Washington, DC: Brookings.

Ribuffo, Leo. 1983. *The Old Christian Right.* Philadelphia: Temple University Press.

Rimmerman, Craig A. 2007. *The Lesbian and Gay Movements: Assimilation or Liberation?* Boulder, CO: Westview Press.

Robertson, Pat. 1992. *The New World Order.* Dallas: Word Publishing.

Robinson, Carin. 2006. "From Every Tribe and Nation? Blacks and the Christian Right." *Social Science Quarterly* 87 (3):591–601.

———. 2008. "Doctrine, Discussion and Disagreement: Evangelicals and Catholics in American Politics." Ph.D. diss., Georgetown University.

Rozell, Mark. 2002. "The Christian Right in the 2000 GOP Presidential Campaign." In Mary C. Seegers (ed.), *Piety, Politics, and Pluralism.* Lanham, MD: Rowman & Littlefield.

Rozell, Mark J., and Clyde Wilcox, eds. 1995a. *God at the Grassroots: The Christian Right in the 1994 Elections.* Lanham, MD: Rowman & Littlefield.

Rozell, Mark J., and Clyde Wilcox. 1995b. Virginia Delegate Survey. Computer data file. Collected at Georgetown University.

———. 1996. *Second Coming: The New Christian Right in Virginia Politics.* Baltimore, MD: Johns Hopkins University Press.

———. 1997. *God at the Grassroots, 1996: The Christian Right in the 1996 Elections.* Lanham, MD: Rowman & Littlefield.

———. 2000. "Virginia: Prophet in Waiting?" In John C. Green, Mark J. Rozell, and Clyde Wilcox (eds.), *Prayers in the Precincts.* Washington, DC: Georgetown University Press.

Sandeen, Ernest. 1970. *The Roots of Fundamentalism.* Chicago: University of Chicago Press.

Salmon, Jacqueline L. 2009. "Faith Groups Increasingly Lose Gay Rights Fights." *Washington Post,* April 10, http://www.washingtonpost.com/wp-dyn/content/article/2009/04/09/AR2009040904063.html. Accessed January 18, 2010.

Schoenberger, Robert. 1969. *The American Right Wing.* New York: Holt, Rinehart & Winston.

Sharlet, Jeff. 2009. *The Family: The Secret Fundamentalism at the Heart of American Power.* New York: HarperPerennial.

Shields, Jon. 2009. *The Democratic Virtues of the Christian Right.* Princeton, NJ: Princeton University Press.

Shields, Jon C. 2007. "Between Passion and Deliberation: The Christian Right and Democratic Ideals." *Political Science Quarterly* 122: 89–113.

Shupe, Anson. 1989. "The Reconstructionist Movement in the New Christian Right." *Christian Century* 106:880–882.

Sigelman, Lee, Clyde Wilcox, and Emmett Buell. 1987. "An Unchanged Minority: Popular Support for the Moral Majority in 1980 and 1984." *Social Science Quarterly* 68:876–884.

Simon, Stephanie. 2005. "Grooming Politicians for Christ; Evangelical programs on Capitol Hill Seek to Mold a New Generation of Leaders Who Will Answer Not to Voters, but to God." *Los Angeles Times,* August 23, A1.

————. 2010. "Evangelical Group Seeks Broader Tent." *Wall Street Journal.* February 16. http://online.wsj.com/article/SB10001424052748703894304575047500910380386.html. Accessed March 15, 2010.

Smidt, Corwin. 1980. "Civil Religious Orientations Among Elementary School Children." *Sociological Analysis* 41:25–40.

Sniderman, Paul M., Richard A. Brody, and Philip E. Tetlock. 1991. *Reasoning and Choice: Explorations in Political Psychology.* New York: Cambridge University Press.

Solon, Emily. 2009. "When Being a Woman Means . . . Navigating Womanhood in the Christian Right." Unpublished paper, Georgetown University.

Sprengelmeyer, M. E. 2005. "Salazar Regrets Antichrist Barb." *Rocky Mountain News,* April 28, http://www.rockymountainnews.com/drmn/state/article/0,1299,DRMN _21_3735539,00.html. Accessed October 17, 2005.

Stouffer, Samuel A. 1955. *Communism, Conformity, and Civil Liberties.* New York: Doubleday.

Suczek, Yohanna M. 1995. "Christ, the Internet, and You." Unpublished manuscript.

Sullivan, Robert. 1993. "An Army of the Faithful." *New York Times Magazine,* April 25, 32–35, 40–44.

Suro, Roberto, Richard Fry, and Jeffrey Passel. 2005. "Hispanics and the 2004 Election: Population, Electorate, and Voters." *Pew Hispanic Center,* June 27, http://pewhispanic .org/files/reports/48.pdf. Accessed October 16, 2005.

Thomas, Cal, and Ed Dobson. 1999. *Blinded by Might: Can the Religious Right Save America?* Grand Rapids, MI: Zondervan.

Tocqueville, Alexis de. 1945. *Democracy in America.* Ed. P. Bradley. 2 vols. New York: Vintage Books.

Vaughan, Joel D. 2009. *The Rise and Fall of the Christian Coalition: The Inside Story.* Searcy, AR: Resources Publications.

Verba, Sidney, and Norman Nie. 1972. *Participation in America: Political Democracy and Social Equality.* Cambridge, MA: Harvard University Press.

Wald, Kenneth J. 1992. *Religion and Politics in the United States.* 2nd ed. Washington, DC: CQ Press.

Wald, Kenneth J., Dennis Owen, and Samuel Hill. 1988. "Churches as Political Communities." *American Political Science Review* 82:531–549.

Wald, Kenneth D., and Richard K. Scher. 2003. "A Necessary Annoyance?': The Christian Right and the Development of Republican Party Politics in Florida." In John Green, Mark J. Rozell, and Clyde Wilcox (eds.), *The Christian Right in American Politics: Marching to the Millennium,* 79–100. Washington, DC: Georgetown University Press.

Wallis, Jim. 2005. *God's Politics: Why the Right Gets It Wrong and the Left Doesn't Get It.* San Francisco: HarperSanFrancisco.

Warren, Mark. 1993. "New Patterns of Politicization: Implications for Participatory Democratic Theory." Paper presented at the annual meeting of the American Political Science Association, Washington, DC.

———. 1996. "Deliberative Democracy and Authority." *American Political Science Review* 139:96–115.

———. 2000. *Democracy and Association.* Princeton, NJ: Princeton University Press.

Waters, David. 2010. "Will Christian Right join the Tea Party?" February 10. http://newsweek.washingtonpost.com/onfaith/undergod/2010/02/will_christian_right_join_the_tea_party.html?hpid=talkbox1. Accessed March 4, 2010.

Wesskopf, Michael. 1993. "'Gospel Grapevine' Displays Strength in Controversy over Gay Ban." *Washington Post,* February 1, A10.

White, Gayle. 2001. "Evangelical Power Couple; Authors Tim and Beverly LaHaye, with Scores of Books Between Them, Rank as Four-star Generals to Many Conservative Christians." *Atlanta Journal-Constitution,* July 7, 1B.

Whitley, Tyler. 1994. "GOP Factions Square Off at Local Level." *Richmond Times-Dispatch,* April 30, A1, A8.

Wilcox, Clyde. 1987. "Popular Support for the Moral Majority in 1980: A Second Look." *Social Science Quarterly* 68:157–167.

———. 1988a. "Political Action Committees of the New Christian Right: A Longitudinal Analysis." *Journal for the Scientific Study of Religion* 27:60–71.

———. 1988b. "American Religion and Politics in Comparative Perspective." Paper presented at the annual meeting of the World Congress on Sociology, Madrid.

———. 1992. *God's Warriors: The Christian Right in 20th Century America.* Baltimore: Johns Hopkins University Press.

———. 1995. *The Latest American Revolution?* New York: St. Martin's.

———. 2002. "Wither the Christian Right: The Elections and Beyond." In Stephen J. Wayne and Clyde Wilcox (eds.), *The Election of the Century and What It Tells Us About the Future of American Politics.* Armonk, NY: M. E. Sharpe.

———. 2005. "Religious Dreams and Political Realities: Religion and Social Movements in the United States." Paper presented at the conference Faith-based Radicalism: Christianity, Islam, and Judaism Between Constructive Activism and Destructive Fanaticism, September 14–25, University of Antwerp, Belgium.

———. 2009. "Of Movements and Metaphors: The Coevolution of the Christian Right and the Republican Party." In Steven Brint and Jean Reith Schroedel (eds.), *Evangelicals and American Democracy*, Vol. 2: *Religion and Politics.* New York: Russell Sage Foundation Press.

———. 2010. The Christian Right and Civic Virtue. In Alan Wolfe and Ira Katznelson (eds.), *Religion and American Democracy.* Princeton, NJ: Princeton University Press.

Wilcox, Clyde, Paul Brewer, Shauna Shames, and Celinda Lake. 2006. "'If I Bend This Far I Will Break?' Public Opinion on Same Sex Marriage." In Craig Rimmerman and Clyde Wilcox (eds.), *The Politics of Same-Sex Marriage.* Chicago: University of Chicago Press.

Wilcox, Clyde, and Patrick Carr. 2009. "The Puzzling Case of Abortion Attitudes and the Millennium Generation." In B. Norrander and C. Wilcox (eds.), *Understanding Public Opinion.* 3rd ed. Washington, DC: CQ Press.

Wilcox, Clyde, Matthew DeBell, and Lee Sigelman. 1999. "The Second Coming of the New Christian Right: Patterns of Popular Support in 1984 and 1996." *Social Science Quarterly* 80: 181–192.

Wilcox, Clyde, John C. Green, and Mark J. Rozell. 1995. "Faith, Hope, and Conflict: The Christian Right in State Republican Politics." Paper presented at the annual meeting of the American Sociological Association, Washington, DC.

Wilcox, Clyde, and Rentaro Iida. 2010. "Evangelicals, the Christian Right, and Gay/Lesbian Rights in the United States: Simple and Complex Stories." In D. Rayside and C. Wilcox (eds.), *Religion, Sexuality, and Politics in Canada and the United States*. Vancouver: University of British Columbia Press.

Wilcox, Clyde, and Ted G. Jelen. 1990. "Evangelicals and Political Tolerance." *American Politics Quarterly* 18:25–46.

Wilcox, Clyde, Ted G. Jelen, and Sharon Linzey. 1991. "Reluctant Warriors: Premillennialism and Politics in the Moral Majority." *Journal for the Scientific Study of Religion* 30:245–258.

———. 1995. "Rethinking the Reasonableness of the Religious Right." *Review of Religious Research* 36:263–276.

Wilcox, Clyde, Linda Merola, and David Beer. 2006. "The Gay Marriage Issue and Christian Right Mobilization." In John C. Green, Mark J. Rozell, and Clyde Wilcox (eds.), *The Values Campaign? The Christian Right in the 2004 Election*. Washington, DC: Georgetown University Press.

Wilcox, Clyde, Mark J. Rozell, and Roland Gunn. 1996. "Religious Coalitions in the New Christian Right." *Social Science Quarterly* 77:543–559.

Wilcox, Clyde, and Robin Wolpert. 2000. "Gay Rights in the Public Sphere: Public Opinion on Gay and Lesbian Equality." In Craig A. Rimmerman, Kenneth D. Wald, and Clyde Wilcox (eds.), *The Politics of Gay Rights*. Chicago: University of Chicago Press.

Williamsburg Charter. 1988. Surveys of Church-State Attitudes. Computer data file. Williamsburg, Virginia.

Wills, Garry. 1990. *Under God: Religion and American Politics*. New York: Simon & Schuster.

Wimberly, Ronald C. 1976. "Testing the Civil Religion Hypothesis." *Sociological Analysis* 40:59–62.

Wolfinger, Raymond E., Barbara Kaye Wolfinger, Kenneth Prewitt, and Sheilah Rosenhack. 1969. "America's Radical Right: Politics and Ideology." In R. Schoenberger (ed.), *The American Right Wing*. New York: Holt, Rinehart & Winston.

Wuthnow, Robert. 2007. *After the Baby Boomers: How Twenty-and Thirty-Somethings Are Shaping the Future of Religion*. Princeton, NJ: Princeton University Press.

Zwier, Robert. 1984. *Born-Again Politics: The New Christian Right in America*. Downer's Grove, IL: Intervarsity Press.

# Index

CPSIA information can be obtained at www.ICGtesting.com
Printed in the USA
BVOW02s1629160615

404545BV00001BA/49/P

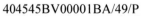